Kazakhstan and the Soviet Legacy

Jean-François Caron
Editor

Kazakhstan and the Soviet Legacy

Between Continuity and Rupture

palgrave
macmillan

Editor
Jean-François Caron
Nazarbayev University
Astana, Kazakhstan

ISBN 978-981-13-6692-5 ISBN 978-981-13-6693-2 (eBook)
https://doi.org/10.1007/978-981-13-6693-2

Library of Congress Control Number: 2019933293

This Palgrave Macmillan imprint is published by the registered company Springer Nature Singapore Pte Ltd.
The registered company address is: 152 Beach Road, #21-01/04 Gateway East, Singapore 189721, Singapore

Contents

Notes on Contributors

Aziz Burkhanov is an assistant professor in the Graduate School of Public Policy at Nazarbayev University in Astana, Kazakhstan. His research interests include nationalism and identity theories, and national identity politics, policies, and practices, with a special focus on identity issues and their perceptions in the public narratives in the former Soviet area. He has worked in policy analysis and consulting as a research fellow at the IWEP, a think-tank advising the Kazakhstan government on policies, and as a senior associate at IHS Cambridge Energy Research Associates (CERA). He has authored and co-authored "Kazakhstan's National Identity-Building Policy: Soviet Legacy, State Efforts, and Societal Reactions," *Cornell International Law Journal* (2017); "The Determinants of Civic and Ethnic Nationalisms in Kazakhstan: Evidence from the Grass-Roots Level" *Nationalism and Ethnic Politics* (2017); and "Kazakh Perspective on China, the Chinese, and Chinese Migration," *Ethnic and Racial Studies* (2016), among others.

Jean-François Caron is an associate professor and chair of the Department of Political Science and International Relations at Nazarbayev University. His doctoral dissertation completed at the *Université* Laval (Canada) in 2010 focused on identity politics in multinational states. His articles on this topic have appeared in *National Identities, Nationalism & Ethnic Politics* as well as the *Journal of Intercultural Studies.*

Neil Collins is Professor of Political Science at the School of Humanities and Social Sciences, Nazarbayev University, Kazakhstan. He has held academic posts at universities in Ireland, the UK, and the United States.

Before moving to Kazakhstan, he was a professor and head of the Department of Government at the University College Cork (UCC) in Ireland. Neil Collins has a PhD in Political Sciences from Trinity College Dublin. His research interests include political marketing, Irish politics, public policy and regulation, corruption, the politics of China and of the European Union.

Azamat Junisbai is Associate Professor of Sociology at Pitzer College. He holds a PhD in Sociology from the University of Indiana. His research focuses on social stratification and inequality, political sociology, post-Soviet transitions, and survey research.

Barbara Junisbai is Assistant Professor of Organizational Studies at Pitzer College. She holds a PhD in Political Science from Indiana University. Her research focuses on comparative political organizations and institutions, authoritarianism, democratization, and post-Soviet politics and society.

Beatrice Penati is a historian of Central Asia under Russian and Soviet rule. She specializes in the history of economic policies, taxation, agriculture, and the environment. She is a lecturer in the Department of History at the University of Liverpool.

Dina Sharipova is Assistant Professor of Political Science in the Department of International Relations and Regional Studies at KIMEP University. Since 2016 she is also the research director of College of Social Sciences. Dina serves on the Board of the European Society for Central Asian Studies, an organization established in 1995 to promote research collaboration among scholars of Central Asia and Europe. Dr. Sharipova's research interests include nation and state-building, formal and informal institutions, identity politics, and social capital in Central Asia.

Gavin Slade is Associate Professor in Sociology at Nazarbayev University in Kazakhstan. He researches criminal justice issues in the former Soviet Union with a specific interest in policing, prisons, and organized crime. His book *Reorganizing Crime: Mafia and Anti-Mafia in Post-Soviet Georgia* was published in 2013.

Charles J. Sullivan is Assistant Professor of Political Science and International Relations at Nazarbayev University in Astana, Kazakhstan. Dr. Sullivan specializes in Central Asian and Russian politics and political violence. Dr. Sullivan received his PhD from The George Washington University in Washington, DC, and his articles have appeared in *Canadian Slavonic Papers*, *East European Quarterly*, *REGION*, *The U.S. Army War College Quarterly—Parameters*, *Strategic Analysis*, as well as *Vedomosti*.

Hélène Thibault is an assistant professor in the Department of Political Science and International Relations at Nazarbayev University since 2016. Prior to that, she served as a lecturer at the University of Ottawa and at the Université de Montréal. Her recent publications include a book *Transforming Tajikistan: State-Building and Islam in Post-Soviet Central Asia* with I.B. Tauris and an article in "Labour Migration, Sex, and Polygyny: Negotiating Patriarchy in Tajikistan" in Ethnic and Racial Studies. She specializes in political ethnography, Islam, and gender in Central Asia. Apart from research activities, she also took part in multiple election observation missions with the Organization for Security and Cooperation in Europe (OSCE) in Ukraine and traveled extensively in the former USSR.

Alexei Trochev is Associate Professor of Political Science at Nazarbayev University. He is the author of *Judging Russia: The Constitutional Court in Russian Politics, 1990–2006* (Cambridge University Press, 2008) and many articles and chapters on post-communist law and politics, including pieces in *Journal of Law and Courts*, *American Journal of Comparative Law*, *Communist and Post-Communist Studies*, and *International Political Science Review*, to name a few. Dr. Trochev is editor of the journal *Statutes and Decisions: The Laws of the USSR and Its Successor States*, which has recently covered issues of judicial politics in Ukraine, police reform in Russia, and administrative justice in Kyrgyzstan.

List of Figures

List of Tables

CHAPTER 1

Introduction

Jean-François Caron

Kazakhstan is proud to boast about its independence gained in December 1991 after the unexpected collapse of the Soviet Union. This pride has, for instance, been constantly reiterated by the country's first, and so far only, president, Nursultan Nazarbayev in his various speeches and in his policies. But this desire to affirm its sovereignty and to dissociate itself from its colonial past appears to be mainly a matter of rhetoric. Indeed, and contrary to what has been argued by some authors (Cummings 2005), it is obvious in many regards that the Soviet legacy, as well as the Russian influence on Kazakhstani politics, is still being felt today. This is what the various chapters of this book will explore by explaining that Kazakhstan's governance is showing more continuity with its colonial past and that its willingness to assert its uniqueness is still mainly a symbolic phenomenon than a reality. Indeed, the continuity thesis with the Soviet legacy allows us to explain not only the persistence of the Russian influence on Kazakhstani politics but also its patterns of centralization and bureaucratization, as well as its reliance on autocracy and a lack of transparency and accountability.

It is a truism to say that being able to promote one's independence and to avoid being seen in another country's pay is fundamental for any nation. From a symbolic perspective, this capacity to show and promote one's uniqueness on the world stage is a central tool for any nation-building

J.-F. Caron (✉)
Nazarbayev University, Astana, Kazakhstan
e-mail: jean-francois.caron@nu.edu.kz

J.-F. Caron (ed.), *Kazakhstan and the Soviet Legacy*,
https://doi.org/10.1007/978-981-13-6693-2_1

process. This could, however, be very challenging for a nation that is geographically located next to a superpower, since the latter will very often tend to see the former as a necessary satellite that should dance to the sound of its tune. It is therefore very difficult for such a country to appear unique in the eyes of its people and not be seen as simply 'bandwagoning' with their nearby giant.[1] History shows us that consequences can be serious when smaller or weaker countries have tried to severe ties with such a powerful state. This has been the case with Ukraine when it has tried to leave Moscow's sphere of influence in favour of building closer connections with the West or when the Estonian government moved the Bronze Soldier of Tallinn, which led to great anger on the part of Moscow.[2]

Of course, as it is shown by Aziz Burkhanov and Neil Collins, Kazakhstan's political culture is not homogeneous and solely associated with a willingness to replicate the Soviet legacy. This dominant political narrative is challenged by alternative views resulting from the appearance of an educated middle class as well as from individuals promoting a Kazakh nationalist agenda.

So far, the country's president has been able to juggle with these competing narratives by the use of a skilful rhetoric that tends to affirm the specificity of the 'Kazakhstani way' in a manner that is not actually threatening for its powerful Russian neighbour. This is especially the case with Kazakhstan foreign policy commonly referred to as 'multivectorism'. As Charles Sullivan is showing in his chapter, this policy that emphasizes the importance of maintaining cordial relations with all other states (especially, the great powers) is usually seen, and presented to Kazakhstani citizens, as a tool to affirm the country's independence and to prevent it from becoming Moscow's puppet by diversifying its political and economic ties with other powerful nations. As long as this policy was not impairing Russia's international prestige and economic development, the Kremlin has shown a form of indifference with its biggest Central Asian ally. However, it is often said that war and conflict usually reveal a country's true interests, and when asked to make a choice between its former colonial power and the West, the Kazakhstani government's decision was clearly in favour of

[1] This has been, for instance, a long-time concern of Canadian nationalists who have tried to affirm Canada's independence via a unique foreign policy while still remaining a close ally of the United States (Caron 2014; Grant 1965)

[2] Indeed, following this incident, Estonia was targeted by numerous cyberattacks, which has led many to believe that they were guided by Russia as a retaliation for Tallinn's decision (Landler and Markoff 2007).

Moscow's interests. Indeed, recent events that have exacerbated the tensions between Russia and the West tend to make this policy untenable and have led Kazakhstan to make decisions that clearly show that the country's friendly relations with Russia (and China as another giant neighbour) supersede those with the West.

Moreover, as Beatrice Penati shows in her chapter, the way the Kazakhstani government has been dealing with the protection of environment over the last 25 years also shows a lot of similarities with the old Soviet way. Even though the government has emphasized its willingness to correct the environmental tragedies of the past, namely, the drying up of the Aral Sea and the long-term nuclear contamination in eastern Kazakhstan, it has not challenged the former logic. Indeed, the economic development of the country is still not prioritizing the externalities of projects on people and communities, but is rather focusing almost exclusively on the economics outputs that will result from them.

The judicial system is also another field where we can observe the persistence of the Soviet legacy. As shown by Alexei Trochev and Gavin Slade, the Kazakhstani penal culture, the emphasis on getting low numbers of acquittals, the pro-accusation bias in the criminal proceedings, as well as the lack of autonomy of the judicial system because of improper government influence are all signs of the remnants of the Soviet era. This is why, just as it was the case in the Soviet Union, Kazakhstani citizens continue to show a lack of trust towards criminal justice institutions and an unwillingness to cooperate with police forces.

The persistence of the Soviet legacy can also be seen from the angle of the civil society, namely, from those known as members of the 'Nazarbayev generation' (individuals aged between 18 and 29). As it has been regularly affirmed by the country's president, it is obvious that these young individuals are privileged, compared with their elders. Indeed, they can benefit from a modern educational system, a world-class university in Astana and a possibility to pursue graduate studies abroad thanks to the *Bolashak* programme. For President Nazarbayev the development of their independent thinking will be a factor in the further development of their country. However, as data from Azamat Junisbai and Barbara Junisbai's chapter show, these individuals are not advocating for political changes. On the contrary, their way of thinking about politics has a lot of similarities with the traditional Soviet attitude that emphasized a strong vertical and distant relationship between those in power and the citizens who remained disengaged, thereby reinforcing Kazakhstan's authoritarianism and the power of its ageing nomenklatura that has been ruling the country since 1991.

In the same vein, Dina Sharipova also emphasizes the impact of the Soviet legacy when it comes to the structure, symbols and the administration of the state-created youth organizations. Despite the fact that the Soviet youth organizations—namely, the Komsomol and the Pioneers—have disappeared with the collapse of the Soviet Union, their model has nonetheless survived. It has indeed inspired the Kazakhstani authorities when they created similar organizations in the 2000s. For Sharipova, this legacy clearly shows how the state-society model of the former Soviet Union remains a central feature of post-independent Kazakhstan.

The persistence of the Soviet legacy among the Kazakhstani people can also be seen when it comes to religious practices. In appearance, it looks like there has been a dramatic shift when it comes to the practice of Islam since independence in light of the more than 2,500 mosques that have been built in Kazakhstan since 1991. But these data are hiding the fact that Kazakhstani people remain globally as atheist as they were before independence. Moreover, as Hélène Thibault shows in her chapter, this trend within the civil society must be coupled with the way the Kazakhstani government is managing religious diversity: a control that bears enormous similarities with the way religion was managed under the USSR.

While it is true that paternalism and a nostalgia for the former USSR are still the main features of the relationship between the Kazakhstani people and their government, there is, however, a growing willingness on the part of some citizens and members of the elite to really dissociate themselves from their past. This Kazakh nationalism is indeed more and more explicit in state's discourses and in official policies that tend to reaffirm its language and culture. What has been labelled by many as the policy of 'Kazakhisation', for example, a form of ethnic conception of the nation, can be observed in many ways, such as the decision to abandon the Cyrillic alphabet in favour of the Latin one by 2025 or the celebration of the historical legacy of the Kazakh Kanate (kingdom) in 2015. However, this rhetoric of rupture with the Soviet legacy is especially seen in the urban development and architecture of the country's planned capital Astana. As Jean-François Caron's chapter argues, this form of Kazakhisation seems to be only the tip of the iceberg of a broader process that has become more and more explicit in the official rhetoric in the last five years, which may lead Kazakhstan onto a path that might create ethnic strife between the more than 100 ethnic and religious groups that can be found in the country.

Many reasons can explain Kazakhstan's incapacity or unwillingness to dissociate itself from its past. The power of the Russian influence is certainly the main factor, as well as the fact that the country has been ruled since its independence by the same man whose political life was strongly influenced by the legacy of the Soviet Union.[3] But, in light of the advanced age of its ruler, it is obvious that Kazakhstan is on the eve of a political transition that will see new faces ruling the country with potentially new ideas about how the country should affirm itself. Will this lead to a real break-up with the country's past and a radical shift in the country's policies? If this is the case, what will be the geopolitical consequences of this discontinuity? Only time will tell what might result from this hypothetical scenario. However, one cannot avoid thinking that the country's smooth political and economic transitions, as well as its stability from the past 25 years, might be the result of this deliberate willingness to pursue a course of action that is basically the same as the one that had been in place for decades prior to the country's independence. Old habits die hard, as it is often said, and Kazakhstan's success story since its independence in 1991 might very well be the quintessential example of such a proverb.

References

Caron, Jean-François. 2014. *Affirmation identitaire du Canada: politique étrangère et nationalisme*. Montréal: Athena.

Cummings, Sally. 2005. *Kazakhstan: Power and Elite*. London: I.B. Tauris.

Grant, George. 1965. *Lament for a Nation: The Defeat of Canadian Nationalism*. Montreal and Kingston: McGill-Queen's University Press.

Landler, Mark, and John Markoff. 2007. Digital Fears Emerge After Data Siege in Estonia. *New York Times*, 29 May.

[3] It is important to note that Nursultan Nazarbayev was foreseen by Mikhail Gorbachev to become Vice-President of the Soviet Union in 1990.

CHAPTER 2

Political Culture in Kazakhstan: Extension and Reflection

Aziz Burkhanov and Neil Collins

The British politician Harold Macmillan is famously misquoted as saying, in response to a journalist's question about what may precipitate the fall of the government, 'events, my dear boy, events' (Knowles 2006: 9). The implication of this assessment was that politics was a matter of happenchance in which it was not possible to see patterns. The idea of political culture, on the other hand, suggests that there are certain attitudes and beliefs that identifiable groups of people bring to bear on politics and that, without an understanding of these, even 'events' cannot be fully understood. The idea that the daily narrative of politics needs to be set in the context of a relatively homogenous system of collectively shared meanings and unifying values is central to the analysis of political culture[1]:

> A strength of the concept of political culture as an analytical tool … is the micro-macro character. Political culture in a macro sense is a complex totality of patterns and subpatterns of political culture operative in a given

[1]For a similar framework in marketing theory, see Arnould and Thompson (2005: 868–882).

A. Burkhanov (✉) • N. Collins
Nazarbayev University, Astana, Kazakhstan
e-mail: aziz.burkhanov@nu.edu.kz; neil.collins@nu.edu.kz

J.-F. Caron (ed.), *Kazakhstan and the Soviet Legacy*,
https://doi.org/10.1007/978-981-13-6693-2_2

society. Its components, the micro elements, are individual patterns or clusters of them. (Tucker 1992: 190)

The popularity of the idea of political culture is in part due to the observation that political systems with very similar legally defined institutions and structures practise politics in clearly distinct ways. The proponents of the idea suggest that politics is shaped by deeply held beliefs and attitudes that are peculiar to different nationalities in the groups or regions. Political cultures are not fixed forever but only change slowly, even in the face of marked discontinuities in the institutional arrangements of the state. An understanding of the political cultures in different states helps to predict the patterns of behaviour observed and why some are more likely than others.

Most of the early work on political culture took the state as the unit of analysis and was written at a time when many new political jurisdictions were being created through decolonisation, even though the antecedents of political culture discussions can be found in the writings of Montesquieu, de Tocqueville, Locke and Herder. Almond's seminal work (1956) considered political culture as a mere pattern connecting and transforming the political system into political action. This interpretation of culture was later developed in the Almond and Verba's classic 1963 text. This work is a comparative study of states, which offered an explanation of stability and identified three types of citizens' political orientations: parochial, subject and participant. It also provided the definition of political culture that has guided most research in the field of political culture since then: 'the particular distribution of patterns of orientation toward political objects among the members of the nation' (13).

These orientations were categorised into cognitive, affective and evaluation orientations—beliefs, feelings and values. Nevertheless, it is recognised that, even within the same state, there may be distinct differences between diverse groups that reflect distinct historical and cultural experiences. Almond and Verba were concerned to analyse democratic states and supposed that such polities worked best when a high level of trust was found between citizens and political elites. Similarly, Elazar (1984) suggested that within American political culture there were three subtypes, to which each American state belonged: individualist, traditionalist and moralist. These subtypes, in Elazar's discourse, were fundamentally rooted in the historical experiences of particular groups of people. In the same vein, Putnam et al. (1993) in his seminal study of Italian regional politics highlighted that ancient and medieval historical and cultural differences between regions deeply affected contemporary politics, the stability of the regional governments and the level of civic involvement across the country.

There is now a large body of work developing the concept and empirical base of political culture, but few studies examine it in non-democratic systems. Much of this new work downplays the element of trust towards the elite but reaffirms the centrality of faith in the political system itself. Interestingly, the newly named 'critical citizens' are found in both autocracies and democracies (Norris 2011). Perhaps more threatening to the legitimacy and efficiency of any kind of state is another post-Almond and Verba category of 'disenchanted citizens' who 'in surveys express only tepid support for democracy' (Diamond 2012: 6).

The early authors of works on political culture seem to have been of the view that there was a normative hierarchy in which the most advanced were states where citizens were both politically knowledgeable and engaged. In these civic cultures, citizens participated in politics with confidence that a democratic outcome would prevail. The observation that there were political systems in which citizens did not display this optimistic outlook led to suggestions that political culture would eventually develop into the 'civic' kind:

> The ideas of democracy—the freedoms and dignity of the individual, the principle of government by consent of the governed—are elevating and inspiring. They capture the imagination of many of the leaders of the new States and of Westernising old ones. (Almond and Verba 1989: 5)

In the meantime, there were democracies that were characterised by 'fragmentation of political culture' with significantly separate 'political subcultures' (Lijphart 1969: 207). In the event, these divided societies have not always followed the predicted path towards democracy and, in some, the demarcation of the state itself did not survive. Given the diversity of contexts in which political culture as a concept is employed, it would be easy to lose sight of its usefulness in comparative political analysis. Similarly, though its exponents frequently use quantitative methodologies, political culture analysis is not the sole preserve of surveys or database modelling. Instead, the study of deeply entrenched political predilections suggests the need for methodological pluralism.

What does generally unite analysis that employs the concept of culture is an assumption that political stability is directly linked to some level of compatibility between political culture and political institutions. As Coakley puts it:

> The way in which a society is governed must not deviate too far from the system of government favoured by the politically conscious public ... [E]ven authoritarian government presupposes a supportive political culture unless it is to rely entirely on rule by force. (2000: 37–38)

In this chapter, we examine the peculiarities of the development of political culture in Kazakhstan, a relatively new state in which it is possible to identify competing sets of attitudes and beliefs that are projected into the domestic political discourse. In doing so, we seek to advance the theory of political culture by asking 'what values really are the most fundamental' (Rogowski 2015: 10) and how rapidly they may be expected to change in the context of new political structures. The chapter also expands the literature on post-communist states, which to date has largely concentrated on the new democracies of Central and Eastern Europe (Denk et al. 2015). In Central Asia, however, the scholarship switched to focus on the notion of 'continuity and break' with the Soviet past. Cummings (2005) advocated that the new policy styles and practices of policy-making contained a great deal of institutional innovation and only minimally corresponds to the preceding Soviet practices. Others, while agreeing on the appearance of new institutions, suggested that on a closer examination these institutions and policy styles represent a much greater degree of continuity with the Soviet past than was expected and that the entire process by which the Central Asian states adopted new political institutions and policy-making practices indicates the enduring strength of the Soviet system. This school of thought highlights the role that elites' perceptions of power shifts during the transition play in shaping both the degree of institutional change versus continuity and the direction of regime change (Luong 2004). Still others took the 'continuity and change' discussion further and focused more on the personalistic factors and the balance of power at the exact moment of transition between the retrogrades, mostly former Communist Party nomenklatura members, and newcomers, mostly coming from former dissidents and academic circles (McFaul 2002). The assumption here is that the newcomers will seek to design new institutions that redistribute goods and benefits accordingly, while the retrogrades will prefer institutions that retain as much of their previous distributional advantage as possible.

In terms of value orientation, political culture can embrace several areas, which we explore below. The World Values Survey (WVS) includes, for instance, support/trust to country's political institutions, leaders or the political system itself. The *WVS* data can also highlight the level of generalised interpersonal trust within a society, a horizontal trust to the fellow citizens, which is essential for overcoming societal cleavages. A sub-discourse here would discuss trust to the fellow ethnic group members rather than to the entire citizenry.

Identity, ethnicity and nationalism remain salient markers of political affiliations in many societies. In Kazakhstan, diverse ethnic composition and complicated language situation juxtaposed to the revengeful Kazakh nationalist discourse and policies further contributed to the alienating of certain groups from the political process. Related to this, the scholarship also discussed factors of national pride and patriotism and their relation to the trust to country's political institutions. Previous exploration of the issue suggests that the level of trust in political institutions is a significant explanatory variable accounting for civic–nationalist sentiments at the individual level. People are more likely to engage in an inclusive civic nationhood when they trust political institutions of the country (Sharipova et al. 2017).

In this study, we focus on the social and cultural factors which are responsible for people's engagement with politics in Kazakhstan. Our particular focus is on the trust in the political system and its institutions as well as the government's discourse and external events, such as the Crimea crisis of 2014, which further highlighted existing cleavages in the society. The argument here will suggest that, in Kazakhstan in particular, different groups of citizens can be categorised using the subdivisions of political culture with reference to their historical experiences and to their attitudes to the main political and societal cleavages and divisions. These cleavages may reflect ethnic, linguistic and cultural lines; however, as we discuss below, they may also overlap and cross these lines.

Following the categories advanced in previous research, we suggest the applicability of the following dichotomies:

- disenchanted or 'critical' citizens;
- civic or 'stealth' citizens; and,
- nostalgic or 'enthusiastic' citizens.

'Disenchanted' or 'Critical' Citizens

The 'critical' citizen concept was developed to summarise the political culture of those in the Western world who expressed negative evaluations of their current political authorities but had positive views about democratic institutions as a whole. They were interested and often engaged in politics. Critical citizens retain the belief that they can influence political decisions. In Hirschman's (1970) terms, the critical citizen believes in 'voice' even through protest or other collective action. 'Disenchanted' citizens, on the other hand, were regarded as displaying low levels of trust in the political institutions as well as very little faith that their views were taken into account by the system as a whole. The notion of disenchantment in this context has frequently been employed to describe the relationship between the institutions of the European Union (EU) and its citizens: 'A lack of political interest is seen as a primary sign of political disenchantment whereas the critical citizen is seen as acutely aware of political matters and willing to take action when need arises' (Christensen 2012).

The political culture of any country reflects values and attitudes that are relatively stable and resistant to change. Nevertheless, marked historical discontinuities can have a profound effect on people's attitudes towards the state. Thus, for example, in many places, the attempts by a new regime to establish what it sees as a historic wrong may have the impact of entrenching social divisions. In the case of Kazakhstan, the newly formed government was keen to undo the damages that it identified as having been inflicted on the Kazakh language. For this reason, public sector employment and high political offices were linked to an ability to speak the 'state language' with a passable level of proficiency, official government paperwork was gradually (though not without problems) shifted to Kazakh and laws requiring an increase in the usage of the Kazakh language in mass media outlets were introduced. Some citizens saw this privileging of one language as righting a historic wrong and others, primarily ethnic Russians, interpreted it as marginalising their status within the new state. This political cleavage does not, however, simply mirror existing ethnic divisions. Kazakhstan, which fell under Russian influence in the eighteenth century, experienced a dramatic demographic shift during the Soviet era with significant immigration of Slavs and other ethnicities as a result of the Soviet industrialisation campaign, labour camps and deportations of

Koreans, Germans, Poles and Chechens under the official accusation of being traitors. In addition:

> Beginning in 1927 the Soviet government pursued a vigorous policy of transforming the Kazakh nomads into a settled population organised into collective farms with communal property. The campaign was launched with the confiscation of livestock and redistribution of land. Kazakhs resisted by selling and slaughtering their animals in great numbers ... More than 1.5 million ... died during this period from starvation, related diseases and violence. (Spehr and Kassenova 2012: 138)

Later, in the 1950s, the country had become a destination for Soviet pioneers under the Virgin Lands Campaign, an ambitious plan initiated by Nikita Khrushchev with the aim of developing vast areas of 'virgin' territories in Northern and Central Kazakhstan for grain production. At the same time, the number of ethnic Kazakhs decreased because of forced settling of the nomadic population and collectivisation campaigns. The resultant mass starvation had disastrous effects on the nomadic population and its descendants, which became a minority in their own land.

When the Soviet Union collapsed in 1991, the diverse population of Kazakhstan presented a great challenge to the new regime in terms of identity-building. Analysts discussed whether Kazakhstan would choose to develop:

- a civic nationhood as a state for all of its citizens, irrespective of their ethnic background;
- a bi-national or multinational state, seen as a state with two or more 'core' nations; or,
- a revengeful nationalist agenda in favour of the main or 'titular' nation.

As discussed in detail in Jean-François Caron's chapter, the regime ended up demonstrating internationalist rhetoric and declaring commitment to the friendship of the peoples living in the country, while unofficially overlooking revengeful moves pushed by Kazakh nationalists. For instance, the country's constitution admits that 'ideological and political diversity is recognised in the Republic of Kazakhstan' and emphasises the commitment of the state to developing 'national cultures and traditions of all ethnic groups living in the country' (Constitution of the Republic of Kazakhstan, Article 5). In this framework, each of the officially recognised minority groups has a so-called national-cultural centre, which is usually granted some state-funding and overseen by an umbrella agency called the Assembly of the People of Kazakhstan (APK), which holds the status of a consultative body to mediate potential conflicts among different ethnic groups.

At the same time, the current national identity policy of the Kazakhstan government clearly demonstrates some of the country's leadership concerns about the complex ethnic situation. Kazakhstani law explicitly prohibits creating political parties on an ethnic basis, and the government is usually very suspicious of any kind of organised political activity by ethnic minorities. However, laws related to ethnic (as well as religious) issues appear tolerant in comparison with other post-Soviet states. In both post-Soviet constitutions of Kazakhstan (adopted in 1993 and 1995 respectively), human rights are declared guaranteed by the state and discrimination is strictly forbidden on the basis of 'origin, social, official and property status, as well as gender, race, nationality, language, religion, creed, [or] place of residence' (Constitution of the Republic of Kazakhstan, Article 14). In the same vein, any actions violating the 'citizen's rights on the basis of ethnic origin, race, language and religious affiliation' are explicitly mentioned in the Criminal Code of the Republic of Kazakhstan (Article 141) and considered a major crime.

As with many nationalist movements, history comes to be interpreted as subjugation by an imperial or colonial power that is periodically resisted through heroic but unsuccessful attempts at revolt. In the Kazakh case, Russian domination dates back to the mid-eighteenth century and involved systematic and regular suppression of the native population. Under Tsarist rule, the Kazakh population declined while Russians and other groups increased in numbers. Anti-Russian revolts and uprisings took place throughout the eighteenth and nineteenth centuries and again in 1916. On this last occasion, the Imperial Russian Army succeeded in putting down the insurrection and forcing many Kazakhs to leave for refuge in China, Afghanistan, Iran and other places. When the Tsarist regime itself fell in 1917, Kazakh nationalist intelligentsia members united under *Alash* Party demanded political autonomy as well as the reinstatement of local culture, in particular the language. Such demands were met neither by the White movement nor by the Red Army or, later, by the new Soviet administration. Indeed, the Red Army was as resolute as its Tsarist predecessors in suppressing Kazakh and other non-Russian bids for political power. As in 1916, during the early Soviet era many Kazakhs fled Soviet rule for neighbouring parts of China, Mongolia, Afghanistan and elsewhere. Many also fell victim to severe famine in the early 1930s and were then subject to further suppression under Stalin. In the 1930s and 1940s, the demographic balance of Kazakhstan changed profoundly as a result of forced relocation of various ethnic groups to the country. By 1959, the percentage of the country's population that was ethnically Kazakh was reduced to 30% and, while this proportion rose in the next three decades, at the time of independence, Kazakhs still made up only about 40%. According to the population census of 2009, the figure is closer to 65% but not spread evenly across the state (Table 2.1).

The place of the Kazakh language within the Soviet Union reflected that of the Kazakhs as an ethnic group—marginalised and underdeveloped. The number of schools with Kazakh as the language of instruction decreased dramatically during the late Soviet era, and proficiency in the Russian language became a necessity for a successful career in Soviet society. Many ethnic Kazakhs started using Russian as a primary communication tool and preferred to send their children to Russian-language schools and universities. The Kazakh language remained the vernacular mostly in rural agricultural areas, while more prosperous and industrial urban areas became primarily Russian-speaking. This added an important socio-economic consideration to the country's linguistic and ethnic divisions: in the eyes of the urban population, the Kazakh language became associated with poverty and backwardness, while ethnic Kazakhs moving from rural areas to cities have developed a sense of being underprivileged in their own state.

Table 2.1 Changes in ethnic composition of Kazakhstan's population in accordance with censuses of 1989, 1999 and 2009

Ethnicity	*1989 (%)*	*1999 (%)*	*2009 (%)*
Kazakhs	39.7	53.4	63.1
Russians	37.8	30.0	23.7
Uzbeks	2.0	2.5	2.8
Ukrainians	5.5	3.6	2.1
Uyghurs	1.1	1.4	1.4
Tatars	2.0	1.7	1.3
Germans	5.8	2.4	1.1
Other ethnic groups	6.1	5.0	4.5

Statistics Agency of the Republic of Kazakhstan

After Kazakhstan gained independence in 1991, the linguistic situation remained complicated. For many, the Kazakh language became a profound symbol of identity after independence even though many ethnic Kazakhs (mostly those living in urban environments) use Russian for day-to-day business and social interaction. As Aksholakova and Ismailova (2013: 1580) state, 'the purposeful displacement of Russian with the Kazakh language is still in progress … from now on career growth issues … directly depend on state language acquisition'.

Similarly, universities in Kazakhstan started to require passing some exams in the Kazakh language, even for those studying in Russian. According to Brubaker, the language policy is largely symbolic:

> There is no serious expectation that Russians would learn the language, indeed the language is widely understood as the exclusive possession of Kazakhs. And while Russified Kazakhs have been pressured to incorporate a bit of Kazakh in their linguistic repertoire, they have encountered no major economic, professional or social pressures to master the language or use it actively. (2014: 25)

The symbolism is vital in terms of political culture because it effectively devalues the political status of an identifiable and significant group. Unlike in Estonia or Latvia, after independence, all residents were permitted Kazakh citizenship; however, 'informal signals and practices … have been strongly nationalising. Kazakhstan is understood—by both Kazakhs and Russophone minorities—as the state of and for Kazakhs, and most Russophones believe they have no long-term future in the country' (Brubaker 2014: 17).

Brubaker may be overstating the case, though many Russophones have chosen exit over voice or loyalty. Nevertheless, the political culture in Kazakhstan does reflect divergent assumptions about the nature of the state. The depth of the rift is hard to measure with the available data, but the breadth of it is routinely underestimated because the non-ethnic Kazakh 'populations are overwhelmingly Russophone, and they are not divided by any significant social boundaries, such as barriers to intermarriage. In this context, counting by ethnic nationality … serves to reduce the perceived size of the minority population' (2014: 20).

Similarly, the issue of citizenship was another important point in the early years after independence. The Citizenship Law adopted on 1 March 1992 granted the right for Kazakhstani citizenship to every individual living in the country at the moment of independence. In contrast to some new post-Soviet states, there were no additional conditions, such as language proficiency or citizenship tests. On the other hand, the Constitution of Kazakhstan prohibits dual citizenship; this provision had more importance for many ethnic Russians as they had to choose between Kazakhstani and Russian citizenship, though many would gladly have kept both. After obtaining citizenship of Kazakhstan, Russians became foreigners in Russia, their 'historical homeland', but the adoption of Russian citizenship would have made them aliens in the country in which they lived and worked. Therefore, the requirement of dual citizenship was mentioned in almost all documents of the Russian political activist groups and organisations and is often named as the main reason for the dissatisfaction of Russians living in Kazakhstan.

Despite these legal and constitutional reassurances, within a relatively short time employment in the public sector came to be dominated by ethnic Kazakhs. Regardless of the fact that most day-to-day business was conducted in Russian, the civil service became a 'cold place' for ethnic Russians. As a result, those Russians who stayed in the new country increasingly sought employment in the private sector. Thus, positions in areas such as retailing and real estate became disproportionately Russian, while the public services, and especially law enforcement agencies, became overwhelmingly occupied by ethnic Kazakhs:

> The neopatrimonial Kazakhstani regime has exercised close control and supervision of all key industries, major business and financial groups are dominated by Kazakhs with close ties to the president... Already in the late Soviet era, Kazakhs had been displacing Russians in key positions. This process accelerated after independence as informal hiring and promotion practices worked in a strongly nationalising direction. (Brubaker 2014: 27)

The number of Russians and other ethnic groups in senior positions in the government institutions and their political representation in independent Kazakhstan are fairly minor, and political offices become more and more monopolised by the ethnic Kazakhs. Some scholars even argue that Russian passivity and underrepresentation in the government might be a special form of protest by Russians to demonstrate their dissatisfaction with the policies of the new state. On the other hand, the increasing dominance of Kazakhs in the government and legislature does not mean less tolerant policies towards minorities; as in Kazakhstan's political context, personal loyalties and informal networks and connections seem to prevail. Russians, as well as other ethnic minorities, have a chance to succeed when working in the government if they belong to the loyal elite close to President Nazarbayev.

In the political culture framework, however, the 'non-Kazakh' element of the cleavage would be fitting to the disenchanted citizenship, a group with negative feelings towards politicians and the whole political system. The critical citizens share the scepticism about the current incumbents but crucially not the propensity for disengagement.

'Stealth' or 'Civic' Citizens

The concept of 'stealth' citizens was generated in studies of liberal democracies and so may need to be rebalanced for use in this case study. It implies that the citizens have a high level of trust in the institutions of the state but little interest or engagement in politics. However, if 'one proposes to the most stealth citizens a concrete opportunity to deliberate, they will accept' (Gourgues and Sainty 2012: 11).

The bar to participation may be higher in autocracies, but expressions of disgruntlement are possible. Furthermore, ironically, less democratic regimes may be more alert to complaints expressed indirectly because their 'customer' feedback mechanisms are less immediate and efficient. In terms of political culture as employed here, 'stealth' citizens are those with generally positive attitudes towards the political system who engage reluctantly and infrequently in the political process.

Although the word 'stealth' needs to be used cautiously so as not to imply any particular moral judgement, it does resonate with some of the explanations of political culture in the former Soviet Union. The use of the concept of political culture presupposes the existence of particularly persistent patterns of political behaviour. It is, thus, not entirely inappropriate in the case of Kazakhstan to investigate what may have been inherited in cultural terms from the Soviet Union.

It is difficult sometimes to disentangle observation about the Soviet Union *per se* and studies of Russia itself. Commentaries on Soviet political culture often identify with the idea that political and historical continuity was more important than the apparent impact of revolutionary change (Hahn 1991).

Thus, Pipes (1997) and others suggest that the political culture exhibited under the Soviet regime was a continuity of the pattern presented under the Tsarist regime. Pipes, writing about post-Soviet Russia, suggests that a 'fledgling democracy contends with ancient authoritarian traditions; private enterprise struggles against a collectivist culture; frustrated nationalist and imperialist ambitions impede the enormous task of internal reconstruction'.

It is not implausible to project similar tensions in independent Kazakhstan. Similarly, Keenan (1986: 117), who subscribes to the cultural continuity thesis, suggests that there was a strong political orientation under Soviet rule that emphasised traditional patterns of centralisation, bureaucratisation and risk avoidance. He goes so far as to trace this trait, in admittedly Russian political culture, to Muscovite rule in the sixteenth century.

Writing in the 1980s, Keenan suggests that Soviet political culture is predominantly autocratic in character. Again writing about Soviet times, White notes the absence of institutions for communicating popular demands, a highly centralised and largely unlimited autocracy and highly personalised relations between the vast majority of the population and their autocrats:

> It will not ... [be to] oversimplify greatly if I suggest that the dominant tendency in the political cultural analysis of the USSR has been to emphasise the autocratic character of pre-revolutionary Russia and the continuing relevance of that tradition to an understanding of contemporary Soviet politics. (1984: 352)

Clearly, it would be misleading to suggest that one could compare commentaries directly on the now-defunct Soviet Union with politics in contemporary Kazakhstan. Nevertheless, it would be equally disingenuous to suggest that independence in the early 1990s eradicated all traces of the Soviet and Tsarist political cultures that had dominated life in Kazakhstan for so long. Many observers point out a strong continuity from the Soviet time and how the Soviet autocratic political culture, in fact, tends to reappear and to reproduce itself, though under different slogans. Equally, many of the current citizens of Kazakhstan have experienced the kinds of social change that are associated with greater political contestation at least at elite level elsewhere, namely an increasing middle class, greater participation in higher education and more urbanisation:

> an important political by-product of economic reform in Kazakhstan is the transformation of the country's elite from a monolithic group with more or less homogenous interests to one of intra elite cleavage … a critical step in creating the necessary underlying conditions for political transition. (Junisbai and Junisbai 2005: 375)

Arguments along these lines tend to suggest that the increased complexity of social structures associated with increased social mobility and urbanisation makes it extremely difficult for an authoritarian state system to survive. This line of reasoning has been applied to China also (Collins and Butler 2015). There the question is asked, how long a population increasingly accustomed to choice in the marketplace would tolerate a lack of similar options in the political system itself? In the Chinese case, however, economic development and other signs of modernity have not resulted in more democracy. If stealth citizens represent a significant proportion of citizens in Kazakhstan, this might be reflected in evidence of low levels of engagement generally but a feeling of potential political influence. As Denk and Christensen (2016: 180) put it, 'Stealth citizens are content leaving the political decision-making to politicians and experts and generally prefer political systems with democratic procedures that are non-visible most of the time'.

In an authoritarian political system, it is reasonable to assume that such potential influence would not be seen as utilising the ballot box but engaging informally with the system via contacts and connections. Isaacs (2011: 163) suggests that 'the reliance on informal politics by political actors depends on their perceived interests during the dynamic period of early post-soviet transition'.

Thus, the origins of this kind of informal politics may share with other aspects of political culture roots in the period after independence as well as representing the continuity of a pre-Soviet *modus operandi*. It is, however, distinct from the informal politics associated with actively pro-regime supporters, such as membership of the ruling party. The stealth citizen uses a clan or clientelist relationship infrequently. They may be open to tactics, such as protest or open dissent, as a short-term pragmatic response but the evidence suggests not. In the World Values Survey (WVS), interviewers asked people in Kazakhstan and elsewhere about their political and other values. Clearly, in surveys of this type carried out in autocracies, some scepticism may be warranted as issues of respondents' accuracy or bias may be accentuated. Nevertheless, in relation to political activism, it is notable that 84% of respondents would never sign a petition, 93% had never joined a boycott and 76% had never attended a peaceful demonstration. As Camacho (2014: 2) states, 'The longer the experience with democracy, the more the political sphere becomes autonomous vis-à-vis the social and economic spheres and the citizens' orientations become more civic'.

The 'civic' citizen is almost the 'hero' of political culture studies. Indeed, in his study drawing on the European Values Survey (EVS), Christensen employs the adjective 'ideal' to characterise them (2012: 2). The iconic Almond and Verba (1989) study attributed to this group both trust in the system and a belief that, as active participants, they could influence political decisions. More recent studies suggest that civic political culture captures the attitudes of a small minority even in functioning liberal democracies. It is clearly questionable whether civic citizens can be found in autocracies.

Nevertheless, if the category has relevance to Kazakhstan, its civic citizens would be identifiable by their trust in the political system and its democratic credentials. Furthermore, this group would be prone to an interest in politics and convinced of their ability to influence it. In a study of 'electoral autocracies' (Ukraine, Russia and Azerbaijan) Haerpfer and Kizilova (2014: 183) suggest, 'In these countries, the contemporary political culture exhibits modest support for democracy but high levels of national pride. At the same time, citizens … show rather strong confidence in their political institutions'.

There are some grounds for suggesting that there are more civic citizens in Kazakhstan than in other former Soviet political states. Sapsford et al. (2015) conclude from two large-scale surveys of levels of trust in 2001 and 2010/2011 that Kazakhstan has the highest level. Further, they report that, in relation to whether the majority of their fellow citizens can be trusted, 'those who trust still outweigh those who distrust' (528). Though the levels are generally low:

> Kazakhstan is the one country to appear consistently at the top of the rankings by economic variables in 2001, and it appears there for six of the variables in 2010—level of GDP, GDP growth, rating of household income, rating of the national economy, hope for the future of the economy and satisfaction with social welfare institutions. (534)

Similarly, Kazakhstan respondents displayed the highest satisfaction with 'how democracy is developing' and on 'satisfaction with what the

Government is doing'. A major factor in regenerating political culture is socialisation, the way one generation passes its worldview to the next. Clearly, political socialisation can change the political culture of a country and the way in which its citizens, or at least some of them, experience politics. In the case of a new nation, such as Kazakhstan, it is possible that this process may be accelerated. The impact of official propaganda, school textbooks and the media may help build an entirely new political culture for some citizens. Thus, it is not altogether fanciful to suggest that civic citizens may be increasing in number.

'Nostalgic' or 'Enthusiastic' Citizens

The notions of nostalgic or enthusiastic citizens are introduced here to capture dichotomous orientations to the newly formed political structure and are not drawn from the wider literature. 'Nostalgic citizens' have as a guiding touchstone their positive perception of life under the previous regime while their enthusiastic counterparts focus on an underlying sense of progress. Nikolova reflects some of the differences with the idea of the 'happiness gap':

> people in post-socialist economies paid for these tectonic transformations with their subjective well-being. While income is certainly part of the explanation… it does not account for the entire puzzle. Other causes … could include the depreciation of education acquired under socialism, deteriorating public goods, income inequality, worsening social protection and stagnating employment conditions, and changing norms and volatility. (2015: 4)

Different reactions to the increasing uncertainty of the economic situation, the instability of international context, internal socio-economic problems and the psychological shock after Kazakhstan gained its independence created a significant socio-political cleavage. In Kazakhstan, instability and uncertainty after the collapse of the Soviet Union divided society into two parts based on their reaction and reflection towards the future. Because independence was achieved so rapidly, reactions to it reflect conflicting core narratives. Here they are characterised as 'nostalgic' and 'enthusiastic'.

Amongst the citizens, the one group experiences a nostalgic mood connected with 'the golden days' of Soviet times. As a rule, this group refers to such positive features of life before independence as 'free access to medicine and education', 'stability and predictable future', 'awareness of tomorrow', 'the guarantee that you will be employed after graduating college/university', 'stable salary' and 'bright future'. Some people emphasise not only communal and economic advantages of being beneath the umbrella of the USSR but also social values, characterising Soviet society as friendly, hospitable and responsive. The research of Flynn et al. finds similar patterns across Central Asia: 'Reflections upon and positive perceptions of life under late socialism by residents of the former Soviet Union … have been an increasingly widespread phenomenon … despite warning messages from above (from the state), [citizens] remember this period in positive terms' (2014: 1501). Interestingly, this nostalgia is not confined to ethnic Russians.

With these ideas in mind, this is why, like it is shown in Dina Sharipova's chapter, that many former Soviet organisations were revived in Kazakhstan after its independence under different names. In some rural areas in southern Kazakhstan, citizens preserved and re-established a monument to Stalin (later, however, it was taken down by the local authorities). These instances demonstrate that creating 'linking objects' and 'linking phenomenon' make a reference to the idealised version of what the people had in the past and now in the present have lost. These external items, such as Soviet movies and songs, memorials and organisations 'unconsciously connect the lost representation [of the past] with [the people's] self-image and representation' (Volkan 1999). Nostalgia for the Soviet past is not an unusual reaction. Haerpfer and Kizilova, using the political culture analytical framework and WVS and EVS data to look at post-communist European and post-Soviet Eurasian nations, found that in the latter support for democracy was relatively low while criticism of authoritarianism was muted:

> Between 1989 and 1999, there was a rapid triple transformation … in some 30 communist countries. One might quickly conclude that the general direction of the transition [to democracy] is predestined … Yet, the more eastward we look, the more thwarted … these transitions appear to be. (2014: 159)

The political culture model suggests that such nostalgia may remain influential for some time. It is not that nostalgic citizens are unaware of the past but, as Fimyar and Kurakbayev (2016: 90) put it when reviewing the attitudes of some school teachers, 'there was a silent acknowledgement of the darker side of Soviet history'. The second category suggested here, the enthusiastic citizens, may embrace and support various political agendas. The common denominator bringing these different groups together is a more active political stance and a deeper involvement.

The first subgroup here sees the future of Kazakhstan as bright and promising, thus affirming the rise of a national consciousness. As a rule, these people, when discussing the Soviet past, recall the widespread famine in the 1930s, mass repression and deportation, the policy of Russification and cultural genocide. For this group, the current political elite is to be trusted and the institutions of the state supported. They mirror the Asian political culture's emphasis on hierarchical authority and deference to authority (Pye and Pye 2009), often praising the paternalistic strongman leadership–based modernising practices of Singapore, Taiwan, South Korea and Malaysia.

The other subgroup is 'nostalgic', yet taking their *nostalgy* to a level of a more active involvement in current affairs rather than just praising the glorious Soviet past. This kind of group has existed in Kazakhstan and many other post-Soviet societies throughout the post-independence period. However, this cleavage obtained a whole new meaning after the Ukraine revolution of 2014 and the Russian annexation of Crimea. Putin's efforts to promote and protect the so-called Russian world made visible a new cleavage in relation to the Russian world: the 'pro-Russians' (also pejoratively referred as *vatniki*) and the pro-Western/pro-independence group.

The *vatniki* group includes advocates and supporters of the so-called Russian world. The policy of the Russian Federation towards ethnic Russians who ended up living in the former USSR countries after 1991 has been fluctuating, ranging from a total indifference to occasional manifestations of support. Things changed quite a bit after Vladimir Putin's coming to power and especially so after the Ukrainian events of 2014. The annexation of Crimea and the hybrid war in eastern Ukraine demonstrated Russia's willingness to take violent measures in order to protect their sphere of influence, as understood in *realpolitik* terms. The Ukraine events were a total surprise for most other former USSR countries, even those with the closest ties to Russia, such as Kazakhstan and Belarus. On the one hand, Kazakhstan's leadership was projecting Ukrainian events to the mostly ethnic Russian-populated northern Kazakhstan; on the other, they wanted to preserve an alliance with Russia.

The Ukraine events also inspired a significant portion of the population loyal to Russia and gave ethnic Russians living in Kazakhstan (and other post-Soviet countries) a sense of pride for their homeland. All of a sudden, they felt support from their motherland and had hopes for enhanced political roles. This pride was transmitted, for example, via visual symbols such as the St George ribbon—an orange-black ribbon associated with St George's order—one of the main military decorations of the Russian Empire, later reincarnated in the Order of Glory in the Soviet Union. The colours were often used in thematic decorations for the Victory Day (9 May) celebrations in the Soviet Union, though were mostly abandoned afterwards. Since 2005, however, through a Kremlin-sponsored initiative, they have become largely used again and their appearance on cars, houses and clothing has, since the events in Ukraine in 2014, become a visual manifestation of support for the 'Russian world'. The Kazakhstani government tried to counter the St George ribbon by introducing and encouraging the wearing of its own 'patriotic' band of blue and yellow colours with traditional Kazakh ornamentation while wearing St George's band was unofficially but persistently discouraged.

Another important factor was the anti-Ukraine and anti-Western TV propaganda campaign launched on Russian television channels, which are widely available and watched in the media space of Kazakhstan. The Ukrainian revolution and Yanukovych's overthrow were labelled continuously as 'illegal' and the new regime of Kiev referred to as a 'fascist junta'. With most Russian media available in Kazakhstan and very few alternatives (Western media has, in general, a much smaller level of penetration), a significant part of the Kazakhstani public started to express support for Putin's actions in Ukraine.

This group, however, does not include only ethnic Russians. A substantial number of ethnic Kazakhs, mostly born and raised in the cities, who have little or no fluency in the Kazakh language and attended schools and universities in Russian, endorsed stronger Russian policies in the former Soviet area. The same can be said about many other ethnic minorities, which operate in the Russian language and also follow Russian media discourse. The Russian-language discourse of Kazakhstan (primarily in the private media outlets) advocates a 'civilising' mission of Russian/Soviet modernisation, arguing that most of modern Kazakhstan's infrastructure was developed during Soviet times. This discourse also produced a certain stereotypical depiction of Kazakh-speaking Kazakhs as coming from remote rural areas, unfamiliar with modern technologies, lacking knowledge about global culture and history, and only concerned with praising glorious Kazakh heroes of the past.

The third subgroup is very critical of the latest political developments in Russia and denounces Russia's claims for a 'sphere of influence' over the former Soviet countries. This subgroup brings together two elements which would otherwise have very little in common in their political agendas: a cosmopolitan urban and often Western-educated youth, and conservative Kazakh nationalists calling for 'traditional values' who possess an idealised version of Kazakh history. As stated above, in other conditions, these two constituencies would have very little in common as they would be appealing to very different segments of modern Kazakhstani society; yet, when juxtaposed with the 'Russian world' and pro-Russian rhetoric, these groups present a unified front.

The conservative Kazakh nationalist discourse appeals to the (re)establishment of the Kazakh state (*Qazaq Eli* is an often-used term), built on the historical legacy of the Kazakh Khanate (kingdom), its *khans* (rulers), *batyrs* (military heroes) and *bis* (legists); or, in some instances, the Alash-Orda government, as these existed, or are thought to have existed, prior to Russian colonisation and Soviet rule. Denunciation of the Russian/Soviet colonisation and appeals for revenge; references to the 'dreams about independence'; sacrifices of the Kazakh intelligentsia, who suffered in Stalin's purges; mentions of the damage inflicted upon the Kazakh language and culture, especially traditional culture; and, lately, protection of the country's land resources from foreign ownership are all themes that the Kazakh nationalist agenda put forward. Although this narrative does admit modernising results of the Russian/Soviet rule, it also emphasises the damage that has been done to the language, culture and environment by Russian and Soviet policies. Within this narrative, Kazakh culture is often depicted as rural, traditional, patriarchal, self-sufficient and built on the idealised version of nomadic pastoralism.

The other subsegment, the urban cosmopolitan and pro-Western youth, has a different agenda—they advocate following Western modernisation patterns which would touch upon fundamentals of the economic and political structure of Kazakhstan. Mostly (but not exclusively) coming from urban areas, this group also primarily operates in Russian and their fluency in Kazakh remains rather limited. They are heavily criticised by Kazakh nationalists for their limited fluency in Kazakh, as well as for their views being too 'cosmopolitan' and putting Kazakh culture at risk of disappearance. Yet, this pro-Western group was very critical towards Russia's efforts to spread their influence over former Soviet space and in general tends to question the choice of Russia as a model for Kazakhstan; in this regard, their rhetoric overlaps with the Kazakh traditionalist discourse.

Conclusion

The notion of political culture, especially in the new states, has relatively rarely been the focus of the existing scholarship. In this chapter, we aim to fulfil this gap by examining the peculiarities of the political culture of Kazakhstan with its competing attitudes and beliefs that are projected into the domestic political discourse. In doing so, we explore the competing values and narratives in Kazakhstan and their positioning vis-à-vis the continuity and break approach from Soviet times.

The chapter suggests that, in Kazakhstan in particular, different groups of citizens can be categorised using the subdivisions of political culture with reference to their historical experiences and their attitudes to the main political and social cleavages and divisions. These categories can also be divided across their attitudes and involvement in the political dynamics rather than specific political agendas—as they can combine citizens with rather competing views on various domestic or international political developments who take an active stance in the matter versus sceptical and 'disenchanted' citizens. Political culture in Kazakhstan is, hence, a remarkable combination of continuity of the Soviet 'passive majority' political legacy and a new, emerging group of pro-active citizens, who are able to act even in a politically restrictive environment.

References

Aksholakova, A., and N. Ismailova. 2013. The Language Policy of Kazakhstan and the State Language in Government Service. *Procedia—Social and Behavioral Sciences* 93: 1580–1586.

Almond, G.A. 1956. Comparative Political Systems. *Journal of Politics* 18 (3): 391–409.

Almond, G.A., and S. Verba. 1989. *The Civic Culture: Political Attitudes and Democracy in Five Nations.* Newbury Park, CA: Sage.

Arnould, E.J., and C.J. Thompson. 2005. Consumer Culture Theory: Twenty Years of Research. *Journal of Consumer Research* 31 (4): 868–882.

Brubaker, R. 2014. Nationalizing States Revisited: Projects and Processes of Nationalization in Post-Soviet States. In *New Nation-States and National*

Minorities, ed. J.D. Iglesias, N. Stojanovic, and S. Weinblum. Colchester: ECPR Press.
Camacho, L.A. 2014. *Understanding Regime Support in New and Old Democracies.* Bonn: Deutsches Institut für Entwicklungspolitik.
Christensen, Henrik Serup. 2012. Political Disenchantment and Citizen Involvement in Representative Democracies. Paper prepared for the IPSA's 22nd World Congress of Political Science.
Coakley, J. 2000. Society and Political Culture. In *Politics in the Republic of Ireland*, ed. John Coakley and Michael Gallagher. London: Routledge.
Collins, N., and P. Butler. 2015. A Marketing Perspective on the Rise of China: Monopoly, Politics and Value. *Journal of Marketing Management* 31 (3/4): 269–288.
Constitution of the Republic of Kazakhstan. Accessed 14 August 2016. http://www.akorda.kz/ru/official_documents/constitution.
Criminal Code of the Republic of Kazakhstan. Accessed 14 August 2016. http://online.zakon.kz/Document/?doc_id=31575252.
Cummings, Sally. 2005. *Kazakhstan: Power and Elite.* I.B. Tauris.
Denk, T., and H.S. Christensen. 2016. How to Classify Political Cultures? A Comparison of Three Methods of Classification. *Quality & Quantity* 50 (1): 177–191.
Denk, T., H.S. Christensen, and D. Bergh. 2015. The Composition of Political Culture—A Study of 25 European Democracies. *Studies in Comparative International Development* 50 (3): 358–377.
Diamond, L. 2012. The Coming Wave. *Journal of Democracy* 23 (1, Jan.): 5–13.
Elazar, D. 1984. *American Federalism: The View from the States.* New York: Harper & Row.
Fimyar, O., and K. Kurakbayev. 2016. 'Soviet' in Teachers' Memories and Professional Beliefs in Kazakhstan: Points for Reflection for Reformers, International Consultants and Practitioners. *International Journal of Qualitative Studies in Education* 29 (1): 86–103.
Flynn, M., N. Kosmarskaya, and G. Sabirova. 2014. The Place of Memory in Understanding Urban Change in Central Asia: The Cities of Bishkek and Ferghana. *Europe-Asia Studies* 66 (9): 1501–1524.
Gourgues, G., and J. Sainty. 2012. Does Public Participation Only Concern Upper Classes? The 'Social Oligarchisation' of New Types of Democracy. *CIRES Working Paper.* Florence: University of Florence.
Haerpfer, C., and K. Kizilova. 2014. Support for Democracy in Postcommunist Europe and Post-Soviet Eurasia. In *The Civic Culture Transformed*, ed. R.J. Dalton and C. Welzel, 158–190. Cambridge: Cambridge University Press.
Hahn, J.W. 1991. Continuity and Change in Russian Political Culture. *British Journal of Political Science* 21 (4): 393–421.

Hirschman, A.O. 1970. *Exit, Voice, and Loyalty: Responses to Decline in Firms, Organizations, and States*. Cambridge, MA: Harvard University Press.

Isaacs, R. 2011. *Party System Formation in Kazakhstan: Between Formal and Informal Politics*. London: Routledge.

Junisbai, B., and A. Junisbai. 2005. The Democratic Choice of Kazakhstan: A Case Study in Economic Liberalization, Intra Elite Cleavage, and Political Opposition. *Demokratizatsiya* 13 (3): 373–392.

Keenan, E.L. 1986. Muscovite Political Folkways. *The Russian Review* 45 (2): 115–181.

Knowles, E. 2006. *What They Didn't Say: A Book of Misquotations*. Oxford: Oxford University Press.

Lijphart, A. 1969. Consociational Democracy. *World Politics* 21 (2): 207–225.

Luong, P.J. 2004. *Institutional Change and Political Continuity in Post-Soviet Central Asia: Power, Perceptions, and Pacts*. Cambridge: Cambridge University Press.

McFaul, M. 2002. The Fourth Wave of Democracy and Dictatorship: Noncooperative Transitions in the Postcommunist World. *World Politics* 54: 212–244.

Nikolova, M. 2015. Minding the Happiness Gap: Political Institutions and Perceived Quality of Life in Transition. *Discussion Paper No. 9484*. Bonn: IZA.

Norris, P. 2011. *Democratic Deficit: Critical Citizens Revisited*. Cambridge: Cambridge University Press.

Pipes, R. 1997. Is Russia Still an Enemy? *Foreign Affairs*, September/October 1997 Issue. Accessed 17 January 2016. https://www.foreignaffairs.com/articles/russia-fsu/1997-09-01/russia-still-enemy.

Putnam, R., R. Leonardi, and R. Nanetti. 1993. *Making Democracy Work: Civic Traditions in Modern Italy*. Princeton, NJ: Princeton University Press.

Pye, L.W., and M.W. Pye. 2009. *Asian Power and Politics: The Cultural Dimensions of Authority*. Cambridge, MA: Harvard University Press.

Rogowski, R. 2015. *Rational Legitimacy: A Theory of Political Support*. Princeton, NJ: Princeton University Press.

Sapsford, R., P. Abbott, C. Haerpfer, and C. Wallace. 2015. Trust in Post-Soviet Countries, Ten Years On. *European Politics and Society* 16 (4): 523–539.

Sharipova, D., A. Burkhanov, and A. Alpeissova. 2017. The Determinants of Civic and Ethnic Nationalisms in Kazakhstan: Evidence from the Grass-Roots Level. *Nationalism and Ethnic Politics* 23 (2): 203–226.

Spehr, S., and N. Kassenova. 2012. Kazakhstan: Constructing Identity in a Post-Soviet Society. *Asian Ethnicity* 13 (2, Mar.): 135–151.

Tucker, R.C. 1992. Sovietology and Russian History. *Post-Soviet Affairs* 8 (3): 175–196.

Volkan, V. 1999. Nostalgia as a Linking Phenomenon. *Journal of Applied Psychoanalytic Studies* 1: 169–179.

White, S. 1984. Political Culture in Communist States: Some Problems of Theory and Method. *Comparative Politics* 16 (3): 351–365.
World Values Survey. Field-Work Dates: Nov.–Dec. 2011. Wave 6 (2010–2014). Accessed 19 January 2016. http://www.worldvaluessurvey.org/WVSDocumentationWV6.jsp.

CHAPTER 3

End of an Era? Kazakhstan and the Fate of Multivectorism

Charles J. Sullivan

Introduction

Since the early days of its independence from Soviet rule, the Republic of Kazakhstan has adhered to a foreign policy commonly referred to as "multivectorism", emphasizing the maintenance of "cordial relations" with other states and especially the Great Powers of the international system (Sullivan 2017: 274). For years the Kazakhstani government has adhered to this doctrine on a multidimensional level, with multivectorism enhancing Kazakhstan's stature on the world stage and buttressing its sovereignty. However, the recent downturn in relations between the Russian Federation and the West is jeopardizing Astana's preferred foreign policy, thereby making it exceedingly difficult for Kazakhstan to balance competing Great Power interests. In brief, Kazakhstan's multivectorism is becoming increasingly "reactive" in nature with Astana assuming cautious stances whenever international disputes involving Russia arise (such as the 2008 Russia-Georgia War, Russia's annexation of Crimea in 2014 and ongoing involvement in Ukraine, and Russia's military intervention in Syria). This chapter posits that although Kazakhstan aspires to promote a "proactive" foreign policy, Astana's hesitancy to rebuke Moscow for its military adventurism

C. J. Sullivan (✉)
Nazarbayev University, Astana, Kazakhstan
e-mail: charles.sullivan@nu.edu.kz

J.-F. Caron (ed.), *Kazakhstan and the Soviet Legacy*,
https://doi.org/10.1007/978-981-13-6693-2_3

in Georgia and Ukraine, coupled with the decision to host negotiations concerning the civil war in Syria, saps at the spirit of multivectorism and weakens Kazakhstan's geopolitical position. Kazakhstan is interested in upholding its sovereignty, ensuring its political stability, and sustaining its economic development (Sullivan 2017: 273). In response, this chapter contends that Kazakhstan should strive to reinvent its foreign policy, namely by establishing Western-oriented frameworks for sustained cooperation and adopting a regional agenda emphasizing political and economic reform in Central Asia.

Proactive Multivectorism

As a newly independent, landlocked, multiethnic country bordering Russia and China, it is important for Kazakhstan to adhere to a wise foreign policy. Under the stewardship of President Nursultan Nazarbayev (who rose to power as First Secretary of the Central Committee of the Communist Party of the Kazakh SSR in 1989), Kazakhstan abides by multivectorism, which entails "maintaining cordial relations with virtually every other state (including the Great Powers)" (Sullivan 2017: 274, 281). Kazakhstan's unique foreign policy amounts to "a pragmatic strategy to further its national interests and achieve policy objectives by cultivating good foreign relations in all directions" (Holmquist 2015). At its core, however, multivectorism "is concerned with ensuring Kazakhstan's independence and sovereignty by offsetting traditional Russian hegemony through the diversification of political and economic ties with other major power centers" (Clarke 2015). Kazakhstan is militarily aligned with Russia via its membership in the Collective Security Treaty Organization (CSTO) and embedded within a set of economic and political-military organizations (such as the Eurasian Economic Union [EEU] and the Shanghai Cooperation Organization [SCO]) dominated by neighboring Great Powers. Russia also stands as "Kazakhstan's top partner in defense trade by dominating the supply of military platforms for Kazakhstan's ground forces and navy" (Omelicheva 2016: 6). Nevertheless, Kazakhstan seeks to enhance its stature and loosen Moscow's grip. In doing so, Kazakhstan has adhered to a proactive version of multivectorism. Multivectorism arose as the foreign policy of the Kazakhstani government in response to a "period of elevated tension between Kazakhstan and the Russian Federation in the early 1990s" which, in turn, spurred the Nazarbayev administration to tailor a foreign policy that could serve as "a counterweight to the frequently aggressive, sometimes uncooperative, and from the Kazakh perspective, occasionally menacing stance of Russia toward Kazakhstan's territorial legitimacy" (Hanks 2009: 263). In response, the Kazakhstani government sought "close cooperation" with the United States in particular and the West in general "on the issue of controlling and disposing of Kazakhstan's nuclear arsenal" and courted foreign (primarily Western) investment in the oil and gas industry "to break its dependency on Russian transport infrastructure" (Hanks 2009: 263–264). In addition, the Nazarbayev administration has fashioned a set of institutions and laws to allay the concerns of ethnic Russians in Kazakhstan and suppress any calls for separatism emanating from within the country.

In the early 1990s, the domestic situation in Kazakhstan was uncertain. According to (former) Foreign Minister Kassymzhomart Tokaev, at the time Kazakhstan was contending with "runaway inflation; the total lack of basic necessities; a high level of unemployment; the mass exodus of the Russian-speaking population to Russia; the uncertain legal status of state borders with China, Russia, and the states of Central Asia; and an escalation of tension in interethnic relations". Amid this backdrop, Kazakhstan (with the assistance of the United States) made the bold decision "to renounce its nuclear legacy and to accede to the Nonproliferation Treaty" by signing the Lisbon Protocol (Tokaev 2004: 93). Kazakhstan arguably weakened its own defenses by disarming and agreeing to abide by the Nonproliferation Treaty. Yet in taking into consideration the economic incentives for complying with the disposal of its nuclear weapons (and the particularly high costs involved in maintaining an effective nuclear force on its own), a security assurance offered by Russia, China's stated absence of any territorial interests in Kazakhstan, the formation of the Collective Security Treaty Organization, and the Kazakhstani government's desire to be perceived at the outset of independence as a responsible international partner characterized by internal stability, the decision to denuclearize becomes much more understandable (Potter 1995: 39–42). Interestingly, the Nazarbayev administration spins the abdication of Kazakhstan's nuclear arsenal to the international media by claiming that the tragic experience of the Soviet past (in which the USSR regularly used the Semipalatinsk site for testing its nuclear weapons) primarily shaped President Nazarbayev's calculus on the matter. However, Kazakhstan's decision to relinquish control over its nuclear weapons was the product of a negotiated compromise (Kucera 2013).

Kazakhstan has courted foreign investment to develop its oil and gas industry. For years, the Central Asian states have aspired to serve as a "bridge" connecting Asia, Europe, and the Middle East. Yet infrastructure is largely considered to be "obsolete", thereby hindering the "economic potential" of the region (Baizakova 2010: 108). Kazakhstan's economy was hit hard by the Soviet collapse. In the early 1990s, the country found itself in an unfavorable position vis-à-vis Russia. Kazakhstan depended on Russia and Uzbekistan for oil and gas supplies, and much of Kazakhstan's oil was transported onto Russia for processing. In turn, Kazakhstani refineries mainly served as processing centers for Siberian oil. In response, the Nazarbayev administration set out to "pursue a hydrocarbon-based path to economic development by attracting foreign direct investment in the oil and gas sectors" (İpek 2007: 1180–1181). The fact that Soviet planners had routed all oil and gas pipelines through Russia made it all the more difficult for Kazakhstan to lessen Moscow's influence (İpek 2007: 1186). Fortunately though, in "carefully cultivating its international partners in the extraction, processing, and export of its natural resources" Kazakhstan tapered its dependency on Russia "while maintaining friendly and productive partnerships" (Roberts 2015: 2). As an example, Nazarbayev contracted with American (Chevron and Mobil) and Russian (Lukoil) firms to partake in the development of the Tengiz and Karachaganak fields, and although no Western-oriented pipeline has been constructed to date, Kazakhstani crude is transported today onto Xinjiang via the Kazakhstan-China pipeline (İpek 2007: 1185–1190). The Central Asia-China pipeline (which transports gas onto Xinjiang and transverses Turkmenistan, Uzbekistan, and Kazakhstan) is another achievement in the quest to break free from Russia's supremacy. Of course, there have been some setbacks in trying to diversify. For instance, the Nabucco gas pipeline has not materialized and Moscow opposes the construction of any pipelines that will undercut Russia's primary energy supplier role vis-à-vis Europe. The Turkmenistan-Afghanistan-Pakistani-India gas pipeline also remains stuck in the planning stages due to the instability plaguing Afghanistan. Still, Kazakhstan has come a long way in terms of developing its hydrocarbon industry since the early days of its independence.

It is also important to highlight that Kazakhstan's decisions to denuclearize and court foreign investment in the oil and gas industry were undertaken during a period of tense relations with Russia. In light of the nationalistic jingoism emanating from Russia in the wake of the Soviet collapse, the Kazakhstani government feared that Russia may attempt to seize control over the country's northern regions, which are densely populated by ethnic Russians (Hanks 2009: 261–263). Although Kazakhstan is a unitary state, the Nazarbayev administration understands that the continuation of peace and prosperity depends on the Kazakhstani government's ability to ensure harmonious multiethnic relations. Ethnic Russians account for nearly a quarter of the country's population, and "a Slavic majority" resides "in most administrative districts of the North Kazakhstan, Kostanay, and Akmola regions, as well as along the eastern borders of the East Kazakhstan and Pavlodar regions" (Morozov 2015: 1). In the interest of enhancing the ethnic Russians' sense of belonging within the current system, the Kazakhstani government recognizes Kazakh and Russian as official languages and treats them as equal under the law. The Nazarbayev administration has also established an institution known as the Assembly of the People of Kazakhstan (which assists the government in formulating policies and elects several members to serve in the Majlis) to further solidify Kazakhstan as a peaceful multiethnic state. That said, Kazakhstan adheres to a strict line (especially since 2014) on issues related to calls for separatism. The newly revised Criminal Code of Kazakhstan now stipulates that individuals who foster separatism can receive a prison sentence of up to ten years if found guilty in a court of law (Tashkinbayev 2014). Meanwhile, the Kazakhstani government continues to emphasize to the general public that Russia is a reliable and friendly neighbor.

Kazakhstan has performed quite admirably in promoting a proactive version of multivectorism. By disarming and advocating on behalf of nuclear nonproliferation, inviting foreign corporations to jointly partake in the development of its oil and gas industry, and taking special care to ensure that the interests of ethnic minorities are respected, the Nazarbayev administration has sought to make the best of Kazakhstan's respective position within the international system as a developing country (and balance the competing interests of the prevailing Great Powers). Recently, though, Kazakhstan's proactive foreign policy has been eclipsed by the occurrence of several unfortunate events on the world stage involving Russia's employment of military power, followed by a worsening of Great Power relations.

Reactive Multivectorism

While multivectorism has considerable merits, its success is largely predicated on a spirited degree of Great Power competition. Should one Great Power lose interest in Kazakhstan in particular or Central Asia in general, it then becomes all the more difficult for Astana to effectively balance against the hegemonic aspirations of the other Great Powers. In addition, multivectorism works best when Great Power relations are tolerable. In the event that the Great Powers assume a confrontational stance, multivectorism suffers as a result. This is largely due to geography, with Kazakhstan being sandwiched in between two Great Powers. On this point, since Kazakhstan's "immediate neighborhood is obviously more consequential than those farther afield" it stands to reason that Astana's relations with Moscow and Beijing will supersede those with the West (Ambrosio and Lange 2014: 549) in the event that a major crisis erupts. Unfortunately, relations between Russia and the United States and Europe have deteriorated, largely due to Great Power feuding over Russia's position vis-à-vis other neighboring countries. In response, Kazakhstan has embraced a reactive version of multivectorism. Kazakhstan maintains the image of a stable and prosperous state. But reactive multivectorism is primarily designed to satisfy Russia's international aims when it comes to Great Power disagreements. In the short term, Astana perceives this as a sensible policy. In the long term, however, reactive multivectorism is risky, for repeatedly siding with one Great Power over time can serve to estrange Kazakhstan from the others.

The origins of Kazakhstan's reactive multivectorism can be traced to the summer of 2005, during which member states of the SCO (upon meeting in Astana) requested that the United States set a timetable for vacating all of its military installations in the region (Cooley 2012: 39). The SCO issued this declaration not long after a massacre had ensued in Andijon, Uzbekistan, in which the United States criticized the Uzbekistani government for deploying forces to slaughter civilians in response to an armed prison break and the assembly of protesters within the city's main square (Cooley 2012: 38–39). The United States vacated the Karshi-Khanabad airbase in Uzbekistan in 2005 and the Manas Transit Center in Kyrgyzstan in 2014, but American military forces remain in Afghanistan to this day. Overall, the 2005 SCO declaration was largely a response (put forth by Tashkent) to counter any momentum of the Color Revolutions and US democracy promotion efforts, as well as to ease concerns about regime change (particularly after the 2005 Tulip Revolution and the Andijon crackdown) (Cooley 2012: 82). Furthermore, as Great Powers, Moscow and Beijing view the US presence in Central Asia with mistrust and seek to impose limits on Washington's regional ambitions. Astana thus faces an uphill struggle in promoting a proactive multivectorism due to prevailing suspicions and wariness among the Great Powers, and therefore needs to tread carefully when formulating policies. That said, Kazakhstan (in response to a series of recent events on the world stage) has chosen to embrace a reactive brand of multivectorism as its foreign policy, presumably in the hopes of keeping a belligerent Russia at bay.

Georgia

The brief interstate war fought between Russia and Georgia in August of 2008 further inflamed an already antagonistic relationship that had been seething for years. Since achieving independence from Soviet rule, Georgia has been plagued by state weakness and calls for secession emanating from its regions. Two regions (Abkhazia and South Ossetia) fended off Tbilisi's attempt to reassert control in the early 1990s. In response to these armed conflicts, Russia deployed peacekeeping forces (with Georgia's support) to assist Tbilisi in brokering a cessation of hostilities (King 2008). With the passage of time, however, Georgia began to perceive Russia's assistance as a veiled attempt by Moscow to establish client states in the disputed territories and freeze these conflicts in place. For years this strategy worked quite well, at least until the occurrence of the 2003 Rose Revolution. With the forced resignation of President Eduard Shevardnadze and ensuing rise of Mikheil Saakashvili to political stardom, relations between Moscow and Tbilisi took a turn for the worse. For a considerable time, Russia had arguably been prodding Georgia into a lopsided military conflict by retaining Russian peacekeeping forces in Abkhazia and South Ossetia and even providing Russian passports to ordinary civilians in the disputed territories. When war finally commenced, Georgian soldiers clashed with such forces, triggering a Russian invasion (King 2008). Initially, it seemed as if Russia's soldiers might march all the way to Tbilisi and overthrow the pro-Western Georgian government. But after less than a week of fighting, Russia decided to pull its forces back to the breakaway territories. To this day, Russia retains a military presence in Abkhazia and South Ossetia and recognizes both as independent countries, thereby effectively blocking

Georgia's aspirations of breaking free from its former overlord's grasp with its sovereignty and territorial borders fully intact.

In retrospect, there was not much that Kazakhstan could do to protest against Russia's military invasion of Georgia and capture of Abkhazia and South Ossetia. To its credit, Astana has not recognized Sukhumi and Tskhinvali as sovereign states, thereby taking a quiet stance in defense of the sovereignty principle. Yet it is important to recall that the Russia-Georgia War took place amid the backdrop of the 2008 Summer Olympics in Beijing, followed by the onset of the global financial crisis and a US presidential election. Too many things were happening on the international stage for the free world to come together and stand in defense of Georgia. In assessing this situation, Kazakhstan issued a muted protest. Furthermore, the US government did not impose economic sanctions on Russia. Instead, the Obama administration sought to "reset" relations with the Kremlin, essentially permitting Moscow to get away with biting off two substantial chunks of Georgian territory and preventing Tbilisi from establishing firmer links to the West. The Obama administration committed a strategic blunder by not penalizing Russia. However, this mistake would not become apparent until after another former Soviet republic was forced to pay an exacting price for attempting to exit from Russia's geostrategic orbit several years later.

Ukraine

Similar to Georgia, Ukraine has been victimized by Russian aggression on account of Kiev trying to extricate itself from Moscow's sphere of influence. In response to embattled Ukrainian President Viktor Yanukovych's abdication of office in 2014 and the ensuing power grab by proponents of the Euromaidan revolution, Russia dispatched soldiers to Ukraine and seized Crimea. Russia then proceeded to annex the peninsula after the holding of a referendum in Crimea. In comparison to Moscow's actions in the 2008 war against Georgia, Russia has been more brazen in Ukraine. By annexing Crimea, Moscow has conveyed a message to the international community that it will not respect the sovereignty of neighboring states if doing so does not suit Russia's realpolitik interests. Furthermore, annexation carries with it significant costs. Aside from the West's imposition of economic sanctions on Russia and the ensuing fallout between Moscow and Kiev, annexation cannot be easily rescinded. In this sense, the Russian government has stated to its own citizens that annexing Crimea was the right and proper course, in spite of the economic and international-reputational costs sustained. At this point, Putin cannot walk back the decision to annex Crimea without incurring severe political-reputational damage to his own image. Finally, Russia has taken matters even further by aiding and abetting separatists in eastern Ukraine. Although the Kremlin rejects the claim that it is supporting the separatists, ample evidence indicates that the rebels have received substantial assistance from Russia over time (Robinson 2016: 510–517).

The West's imposition of sanctions on Russia played a contributory role in causing the rapid devaluation of Kazakhstan's currency over the course of 2014–2015. In response, Nazarbayev has stated that Western sanctions are "barbaric" and argued that Kazakhstan's membership in the EEU is not the reason behind the country's current economic troubles (Tengri News 2015). Kazakhstan has also rekindled its (formerly suspended) policy of assisting ethnic Kazakhs living abroad with resettlement, but with a focus on resettling in the northern regions of the country (Schenkkan 2016: 2–3). With regard to Russia's actions, however, Astana has kept quiet. In March of 2014, Kazakhstan abstained from voting on the United Nations resolution concerning the "territorial integrity of Ukraine" (Roberts 2015: 5). Russia also imposed countersanctions on the EU without consulting other EEU member states, and the economic fallout from the depreciation of the ruble (combined with the collapse in the price of oil) has further weakened Kazakhstan's economy (Schenkkan 2016: 3). Upon receiving a back-handed compliment from Putin, who iterated at a Russian youth camp in 2014 that the Kazakhstani leader should be praised for establishing "a state in a territory that never had a state before", Nazarbayev emphasized that Kazakhstan could withdraw from the EEU if Astana sensed a threat to its sovereignty (Najibullah 2014). Aside from this, however, Kazakhstan has voiced a willingness to host formal talks (in the hopes of seeing the controversy resolved) and supports the implementation of the Minsk II Agreement. Minsk II calls for the cessation of hostilities between Ukrainian forces and separatists, the withdrawal of heavy weapons from the front lines on both sides, Kiev's granting of amnesty to combatants who lay down their weapons, the holding of elections in eastern Ukraine and adoption of a constitutional amendment granting this region an unspecified degree of autonomy, and Ukraine's resumption of control over its eastern border. Aside from the lack of any enforcement mechanism, another drawback of Minsk II is that it overlooks Russia's seizure of Crimea (Roth 2015). Overall, it appears as if Russia wishes to utilize Minsk II to create a "frozen conflict" in eastern Ukraine which Moscow can regulate, thereby preserving its influence and restricting Kiev's sovereignty to an extent (MacFarquhar 2015). Therefore, in defense of the sovereignty principle, Kazakhstan should not endorse Minsk II. Ukraine has suffered a military invasion, with the situation amounting to an unprovoked attack by a Great Power against a smaller and peaceful state in blatant violation of international law, followed by Russia's unwarranted meddling in Ukraine's domestic affairs.

In the spirit of multivectorism, it seems wise on behalf of Kazakhstan to adopt a stance vis-à-vis Ukraine which does not antagonize Russia. After all, the Kremlin seeks to prevent any realignment of the former SSRs to Western blocs and has shown a willingness to resort to brute force if necessary. Based upon Russia's actions in Georgia and Ukraine, Moscow is attempting to preserve a sphere of influence. Stating this hard fact aloud may have the adverse effect of undermining Kazakhstan's own security (Ambrosio and Lange 2014: 555). But Astana has already acknowledged that Russia retains political-military supremacy in the post-Soviet space by refraining from criticizing Moscow for its belligerency. From Kazakhstan's unique perspective, the West will not come rushing to its defense in the event that Russian troops decide to march southward. That said, the chances of this happening are slim. Russia has incurred tremendous economic and international-reputational costs (such as being suspended from the G8) for invading Ukraine and meddling in its eastern regions, and thus likely has little appetite for attacking yet another neighbor (particularly a fellow CSTO member). As such, by not reproaching Russia for violating Ukraine's sovereignty and by advocating on behalf of Minsk II's implementation, Astana has forfeited an opportunity to demonstrably distance itself from Russia, lend much needed support to Ukraine, and further buttress its own sovereignty. This last point is especially important over the long term, for if Russia decides for some reason to attack Kazakhstan in the future and lay claim to its northern regions, Astana would then likely be forced to accept some variant of a Minsk II proposed solution.

Syria

Since 2011, Syria has fallen victim to a catastrophic civil war. The origins of this conflict can be traced to the Arab Spring, during which millions of Arabs took to the streets to protest against tyranny. In Tunisia, in the face of mounting popular protests against governmental corruption and the killing of innocent civilians President Zine El Abidine Ben Ali fled the country and sought refuge in Saudi Arabia. In Egypt, President Hosni Mubarak was ousted from power, arrested, and forced to stand trial. In Libya, Muammar Gaddafi's regime crumbled to local militias as a result of NATO's military intervention. Syria though bucked this trend. In this case, President Bashar al-Assad refused to cede power to protesters, opting instead for massacring civilians and instigating a civil war. Today, Syria's civil war appears to be intractable, namely on account of the multiplicity of actors fighting on the ground and a considerable number of foreign powers providing their proxies with various means of support. In addition, the Syrian government retains control over a sizable tract of slowly expanding territory, thanks largely to Russia.

In the fall of 2013, Putin issued a public plea in a *New York Times* op-ed to the United States not to militarily intervene in Syria in response to a chemical weapons attack allegedly carried out by government forces (Putin 2013). Russia would go on to play an instrumental role in averting a US-led attack by convincing the Assad regime to surrender control over its chemical weapons stockpiles. Two years later, however, Russia became a direct participant in the civil war. In deploying a few thousand troops and relying primarily on airpower, Russia reinforced the embattled Syrian government and pummeled various opposition groups into submission. By early 2017, the stage had been set for delegations from Moscow, Ankara, Tehran, Damascus, and Syrian opposition forces (but excluding groups such as the Kurdish YPG, the Islamic State of Iraq and the Levant or ISIL, and Al-Qaeda affiliates) to travel to Astana in the hopes of establishing a permanent ceasefire. This round of talks (held from January 23 to 24 at the Rixos President Hotel) did not yield any significant outcomes, other than Russia, Turkey, and Iran's signed affirmation of their support for the "sovereignty, independence, unity and territorial integrity of the Syrian Arab Republic" and agreement to uphold a "partial cease-fire" (though no mechanism was agreed upon by signatories to enforce it). Incidentally, neither the Syrian government nor the opposition delegation signed the declaration which stipulates such terms (Barnard and Saad 2017). Rounds of talks have been held since early 2017 in Astana with Russia, Turkey, and Iran (serving as the sponsors of the negotiations) agreeing to the creation of "de-escalation zones". But the Syrian opposition has rejected this proposal, and many valid questions remain unanswered with regard to the establishment, maintenance, and securitization of such zones (Barnard and Gladstone 2017).

The Kazakhstani government has hailed the success of the Astana talks. In adopting a critical perspective, however, the talks have arguably sullied Kazakhstan's reputation by making Astana appear as a pawn of a Russian-inspired stratagem. According to such thinking, Russia seemingly sought to have Kazakhstan host the talks at an opportune moment, when the incoming Trump administration was just assuming office and busy with filling cabinet positions. At first, it appeared as if the United States had not even been invited to the talks, but Washington ended up sending its ambassador to Kazakhstan as an observer. In an effort to garner support from other states (namely Turkey) for the Assad regime and pressure Syrian opposition forces into a Melian dialogue (following the destruction of Aleppo), Russia presumably hopes to fortify the position of its client in Damascus (perhaps for the purpose of influencing the course of future rounds of peace talks in Geneva). But the unwillingness of the Syrian opposition forces to succumb to such pressure and the inability of Damascus and the rebels to find common ground continue to overshadow the Astana talks. At this point, there is still no end in sight to the civil war.

On the surface, it is understandable as to why Kazakhstan agrees to serve as host to the talks. By doing so, Kazakhstan can use the negotiations as a platform to further demonstrate to the world that it is a sovereign state which should be taken seriously. In line with multivectorism, Kazakhstan seeks to enhance its image as a responsible actor committed to help bring about an end to a devastating civil war. In light of worsening relations between Moscow and Ankara (as evidenced by Turkey's shooting down of a Russian warplane in 2015 and the assassination of the Russian ambassador to Turkey in 2016), Kazakhstan also likely sees an opportunity to bring these two together, in the hopes of ironing out their respective differences over Syria. Lastly, in hosting a forum where Russia can solicit support for the Assad regime, Kazakhstan implicitly stakes out a position in support of the sovereignty principle. That said, the costs of Kazakhstan becoming involved in Syria (even solely in a diplomatic capacity) far outweigh the potential gains. As a case in point, the Syrian government's (alleged) use of chemical weapons against civilians in the spring of 2017 and ensuing US strike on a Syrian military base highlight the risks Kazakhstan faces in terms of alienating Western states by engaging in any venue with associates of the Assad regime. Furthermore, Kazakhstan stresses that the Astana talks are not intended to undermine the peace process in Geneva, but rather "to create the conditions to resolve the conflict in Syria through the framework of the Geneva negotiations" (Embassy of the Republic of Kazakhstan in USA 2017). This point has to be stated aloud because no Western states sponsor the talks. In summary, it appears as if Russia is searching for a way out of Syria while ensuring that the Assad regime retains control over a portion of the country, and Moscow is arguably using Astana to facilitate the realization of this international aim. As a case in point, Russia is interested in seeing Kazakhstan (along with Kyrgyzstan) send troops to Syria to help secure the aforementioned "de-escalation zones". Astana though denies this claim, arguing instead that it is not involved in negotiations involving the deployment of troops to Syria (Taylor 2017). Shouldering more of a proactive role in Syria could serve to tarnish Kazakhstan's standing in the world. After all, Western states perceive the Syrian government as illegitimate and incapable of reacquiring its sovereignty. Assuming that Astana wishes to remain within the West's graces, it may be most prudent to abstain from any further involvement in Syria. Moreover, the Syrian civil war appears to be intractable on account of a widening of Sunni-Shia sectarianism due to hegemonic competition taking place between Saudi Arabia and Iran across the greater Middle East today. Therefore, any effort to bring about a peaceful resolution to this conflict without the involvement of these adversaries will likely fail.

Reinventing Multivectorism

Over the course of the past several years, Kazakhstan has been parading itself on the world stage. In 2015, Kazakhstan joined the World Trade Organization. The 2016–2017 winter months marked Almaty's hosting of the 28th Universiade Winter Games. Astana also recently hosted Expo 2017 over the summer. Lastly, Kazakhstan assumed a non-permanent seat on the United Nations Security Council for 2017–2018 (Sullivan 2017: 278). Such initiatives arguably have been undertaken in furtherance of proactive multivectorism. But these moves are symbolic, not designed to balance the competing interests of the Great Powers, and Kazakhstan is running out of ways to position itself as a country that is rising in stature. Such maneuvers retain significance, but mainly within a domestic context. In other words, they serve to reinforce (at least in the short term) the legitimacy of the Kazakhstani government as the elites try to navigate the country through an economic crisis and prepare for an impending succession. Meanwhile, a series of regional challenges threaten to further undermine Kazakhstan's multivectorism.

One of the most pressing challenges facing Central Asia concerns the ongoing civil war in Afghanistan. It remains to be seen as to whether the United States can succeed in effectively propping up a dysfunctional and corrupt Afghan government undergirded by a shaky economic foundation (Sullivan 2015: 2, 2016: 63). Based upon the rise of ISIL in the aftermath of the US military withdrawal from Iraq and the terrorist organization's ensuing capture of large swaths of territory, it is unlikely that Washington will completely vacate Afghanistan because the Taliban apparently wish to accomplish in Afghanistan what ISIL was able to achieve in Iraq and Syria (Sullivan 2015: 3–4). That said, if the United States decides to retain only a small military footprint in Afghanistan, certain aspects of the war could carry over into Central Asia. America's military strategy in Iraq and Syria consists of relying on air power, drone strikes, Special Forces, and the provision of assistance to designated local militias to fight against enemy forces. Should the United States choose to replicate this strategy in Afghanistan, deploy more troops to support the Afghan National Army, privatize the war effort, or some combination thereof, the possibility exists that such courses of action could cause enemy forces to scatter. Granted, it is noteworthy that many forces fighting against US troops in Afghanistan have taken up residence in Pakistan. That said, two security issues which merit close attention are the narcotics trade and a possible mass influx of Afghan refugees into Central Asia, should America withdraw and/or leave Kabul to fend for itself.

Central Asia's future seems a bit worrisome because the governments, in general, utilize a mixture of patronage, repression, and exclusionary mechanisms of rule to hold power. As a consequence, the administrative capacity and legitimacy of some of these states are quite tenuous, rendering the region prone to failure. States can succumb to failure over time according to a variety of "pathways" (Goldstone 2008). Yet this danger is somewhat magnified in Central Asia by the narcotics trade. With Afghanistan producing much of the world's opium, the empowerment of criminal organizations and/or terrorist groups coupled with the various social, political, economic, as well as environmental ill-effects of the drug trade could foster instability in Central Asia in the future (Cornell and Swanström 2006), particularly if the Afghan government implodes. Moreover, a return to warlordism would trigger the displacement of the Afghan population and the exodus of some peoples to neighboring countries. The arrival of Afghan refugees in Tajikistan, Turkmenistan, and Uzbekistan could serve to destabilize these already fragile political systems. And if this happens, then Kazakhstan's chances of reviving its proactive multivectorism will dwindle.

Nazarbayev has toyed with the idea of changing Kazakhstan's name to "Kazakh Eli" in the hopes of enhancing the country's global reputation and distancing itself from the other "Stans" (Ford 2014). But Astana needs to realize that if Central Asia grows exceedingly unstable, Russia and China could assume more of an assertive role over security matters while the United States and Europe simply check out. On the flip side, in the event that Central Asia becomes engulfed by instability, Moscow and Beijing may intervene only under certain circumstances, thereby essentially leaving the Central Asian republics to solve their own problems. As a case in point, Moscow rebuffed Bishkek's request in 2010 to deploy CSTO troops to halt the ethnic violence that gripped the south of Kyrgyzstan in the aftermath of President Kurmanbek Bakiyev's overthrow (Cooley 2011: 3). To avoid such undesirable outcomes, Kazakhstan needs to incorporate a regional agenda into its foreign policy. Overall, Kazakhstan will not benefit if the West politically disengages from the region while neighboring "Stans" begin succumbing to state failure.

In the fall of 2015, US Secretary of State John F. Kerry visited Central Asia. During this tour, the United States along with the Central Asian republics participated in the inaugural meeting of the C5+1 in Samarkand to discuss security-related issues pertaining to Washington, Astana, Bishkek, Dushanbe, Ashgabat, and Tashkent. Foreign ministers representing the C5+1 states convened again in the fall of 2016 in Washington DC to discuss "regional security, economic connectivity, humanitarian issues, environmental issues and climate change" while highlighting "the importance of developing the transport, logistics and energy potential of Central Asia" (Orazgaliyeva 2016). From Washington's perspective, the overriding goal of C5+1 is to enhance the interconnectedness of the region so that the C5 states can realize their full potential. But C5+1 is a new and underdeveloped institution. Thus far, the C5 states have agreed to back several US-funded projects to "support small businesses, help enhance the competitiveness of local producers, reduce intra-regional trade barriers, fight international terrorism, develop alternative energy sources, and enhance energy efficiency" (Orazgaliyeva 2016). Yet in order for C5+1 to bear fruit the Central Asian republics must commit to reforming their own political systems. C5+1 should not be perceived solely through the lens of a forum for the C5 states to publicly assert their sovereignty. Instead, Astana, Bishkek, Dushanbe, Ashgabat, and Tashkent need to collectively focus their efforts on keeping the United States engaged in the region's affairs, and Kazakhstan (in the interest of reviving its proactive version of multivectorism) is the best-positioned of all to assume a leading role among the C5 states.

In late 2014, Kazakhstan accepted the US-initiated transfer of several detainees formerly held by the US military in Guantanamo Bay, Cuba (Cooper 2014). In offering to resettle these individuals, the Nazarbayev administration has demonstrated a willingness to maintain friendly relations with Washington. Building on this, C5+1 is an ideal forum for the United States and the Central Asian republics to analyze and discuss the aforementioned potential side effects of the war in Afghanistan and possible responses to prevent seepage across the wider region. Equally as important, C5+1 can be used by the Central Asian republics to try to convince the United States to support China's Belt and Road Initiative. Also known as the "Silk Road Economic Belt", China seeks to promote "greater economic interconnectivity through the improvement of critical infrastructure such as oil and gas pipelines, highways, railways, and telecommunications networks" through the BRI (Clarke 2015). In addition, some of the Central Asian republics may wish to use C5+1 to solicit advice from the United States on how to avoid EEU free trade pitfalls. Astana stands in a favorable position to steer the United States in this direction because Kazakhstan (according to the "Kazakhstan 2050" strategy) has committed to implementing a domestic reform package known as the "100 Concrete Steps" and aspires to be one of the world's "top 30 economies" by 2050 (Sullivan 2017: 274). Overall, Kazakhstan can blaze a trail in the interest of reviving its preferred version of multivectorism, but the pathway entails interweaving the aspirations of the Russian-led EEU, China's Belt and Road Initiative, and America's New Silk Road.

It is important to note, however, that the United States in particular and the West in general could soon lose interest in Central Asia, rendering the C5 states vulnerable to either an era of Russian and Chinese hegemony not witnessed since the days of the Cold War or a period of instability and disorder. Such possibilities exist because Washington and other European capitals may grow frustrated with the general unwillingness of the Central Asian republics to reform themselves. So far, Kazakhstan has put forth a detailed plan with regard to reforming its economy, but its political system (like those found within most of the other Central Asian republics) remains inward-looking and highly authoritarian. This is troublesome because Central Asia's elites may prefer to maintain their respective holds on power, instead of executing modernizing schemes designed to empower ordinary citizens. For years, Kazakhstan has professed the argument that it takes time for democracy to bloom (Tokaev 2004: 95). The truth of the matter is that political reform has never been a top priority for Kazakhstan's elites, and the uncertainty surrounding the impending political succession magnifies this deficiency. As such, if Astana does not exercise sound judgment and assume a leading role in the adoption of significant reforms, then Kazakhstan will likely let this opportunity to reinvent its foreign policy slip away. The key to revising multivectorism lies with Kazakhstan's rulers guiding the processes of economic modernization and political liberalization by respecting the rule of law, attracting foreign investment, and diffusing political power. With Kazakhstan spearheading this effort and encouraging neighboring states to carry out similar reforms, hopefully the other Central Asian republics will take notice and decide to follow in Astana's footsteps.

Conclusion

Multivectorism is the best foreign policy that Kazakhstan can adhere to in the interest of safeguarding its stability, development, and sovereignty. However, in light of worsening Great Power relations and the possibility of declining Western interest in Central Asia, it is essential that Astana overhaul its foreign policy. By establishing a framework for sustained cooperation with Western countries and carrying out political and economic reforms within the Central Asian republics (namely through the C5+1), Kazakhstan can transform the "reactivity" of its foreign policy to "proactivity" once again. In adhering to such a strategy, however, it is important that Kazakhstan (in the interest of preserving a degree of harmony between the Great Powers) maintain formal economic and political-military ties to Russia and China. After all, "the fact that Russia has revealed coercion to be a viable option for achieving its foreign policy goals makes multi-vectoring even more attractive, while at the same time making it a high-risk project" (Holmquist 2015). Kazakhstan's success therefore is predicated on Astana's ability to triangulate among the Great Powers through participating in competing regional initiatives and assuming a more hands-on role in stimulating regional development. Astana should thus advance a foreign policy under the strategic umbrella of proactive multivectorism, in the hopes of reviving the spirited degree of Great Power competition that the doctrine of multivectorism so requires. In closing, Central Asia's future is fraught with many challenges and balancing Great Power interests in the twenty-first century amounts to a Herculean task. Yet Kazakhstan stands to greatly benefit from renewing its old brand of multivectorism. As such, Astana needs to focus on staving off the end of a foreign policy era.

References

Ambrosio, T., and W.A. Lange. 2014. Mapping Kazakhstan's Geopolitical Code: An Analysis of Nazarbayev's Presidential Addresses, 1997–2014. *Eurasian Geography and Economics* 55 (5): 537–559.

Baizakova, K. 2010. Energy Security Issues in the Foreign Policy of the Republic of Kazakhstan. *American Foreign Policy Interests* 32 (2): 103–109.

Barnard, A., and R. Gladstone 2017. Russia Reaches Deal for Syria Safe Zones, But Some Rebels Scoff. *The New York Times*, 4 May. https://www.nytimes.com/2017/05/04/world/middleeast/russia-iran-turkey-syria-de-escalation-zones.html?smpr&_r=1.

Barnard, A., and H. Saad. 2017. Iran, Russia and Turkey Agree to Enforce Syria Cease-Fire, But Don't Explain How. *The New York Times*, 24 January. https://www.nytimes.com/2017/01/24/world/middleeast/syria-war-iran-russia-turkey-cease-fire.html?_r=0.

Clarke, M. 2015. Kazakhstan's Multi-Vector Foreign Policy: Diminishing Returns in an Era of Great Power 'Pivots'? *The Asan Forum*, 9 April. http://www.theasanforum.org/kazakhstans-multi-vector-foreign-policy-diminishing-returns-in-an-era-of-great-power-pivots/.

Cooley, A. 2011. The Kyrgyz Crisis and the Political Logic of Central Asia's Weak Regional Security Organizations. *PONARS Eurasia*, Policy Memo 140 (May). George Washington University. http://www.ponarseurasia.org/node/5241.

———. 2012. *Great Games, Local Rules: The New Great Power Contest in Central Asia*. New York: Oxford University Press.

Cooper, H. 2014. Five Guantanamo Prisoners are Released to Kazakhstan. *The New York Times*, 30 December. https://www.nytimes.com/2014/12/31/world/middleeast/five-guantnamo-prisoners-are-released-to-kazakhstan.html.

Cornell, S., and N. Swanström. 2006. The Eurasian Drug Trade: A Challenge to Regional Security. *Problems of Post-Communism* 53 (4): 10–28.

Embassy of the Republic of Kazakhstan in USA. 2017. Syria Peace Talks. http://www.kazakhembus.com/content/syria-peace-talks.

Eurasian Economic Union is Not Responsible for Economic Hardships in Kazakhstan. 2015. *Tengri News*, 11 February. https://en.tengrinews.kz/politics_sub/Eurasian-Economic-Union-is-not-responsible-for-economic-258949/.

Ford, M. 2014. Kazakhstan's President is Tired of His Country's Name Ending in "Stan". *The Atlantic*, 7 February. https://www.theatlantic.com/international/archive/2014/02/kazakhstans-president-is-tired-of-his-countrys-name-ending-in-stan/283676/.

Goldstone, J.A. 2008. Pathways to State Failure. *Conflict Management and Peace Science* 25: 285–296.

Hanks, R.R. 2009. 'Multi-Vector Politics' and Kazakhstan's Emerging Role as a Geo-Strategic Player in Central Asia. *Journal of Balkan and Near Eastern Studies* 11 (3): 257–267.

Holmquist, E. 2015. Kazakhstan After Crimea: 'You Cannot Choose Your Neighbors'. *RUFS Briefing No. 26*, FOI Swedish Defense Research Agency Memo 5246.

İpek, P. 2007. The Role of Oil and Gas in Kazakhstan's Foreign Policy: Looking East or West? *Europe-Asia Studies* 59 (7): 1179–1999.

King, C. 2008. The Five-Day War. *Foreign Affairs* 87 (6): 2–11.

Kucera, J. 2013. Why Did Kazakhstan Give Up Its Nukes? *Eurasia Net*, 15 May. http://www.eurasianet.org/node/66967.

MacFarquhar, N. 2015. Ukraine's Latest Peace Plan Inspires Hope and Doubts. *The New York Times*, 12 February. https://www.nytimes.com/2015/02/13/world/europe/ukraine-talks-cease-fire.html.

Morozov, V. 2015. Kazakhstan and the "Russian World": Is a New Intervention on the Horizon? *PONARS Eurasia*, Policy Memo 364 (June). George Washington University. http://www.ponarseurasia.org/memo/kazakhstan-and-russian-world-new-intervention-horizon.

Najibullah, F. 2014. Putin Downplays Kazakh Independence, Sparks Angry Reaction. *Radio Free Europe/Radio Liberty*, 3 September. https://www.rferl.org/a/kazakhstan-putin-history-reaction-nation/26565141.html.

Omelicheva, M.Y. 2016. "Checks and Balances" on Kazakhstan's Quest for Military Independence. *Russian Analytical Digest—ETH Zurich Center for Security Studies* 188 (Aug.): 5–10.

Orazgaliyeva, M. 2016. Washington C5+1 Ministerial Meeting Launches Five Projects Worth $15 Million. *The Astana Times*, 5 August. http://astanatimes.com/2016/08/washington-c51-ministerial-meeting-launches-five-projects-worth-15-million/.

Potter, W. C. 1995. The Politics of Nuclear Renunciation: The Cases of Belarus, Kazakhstan, and Ukraine. *Occasional Paper 22* (April). The Henry L. Stimson Center.

Putin, V. V. 2013. A Plea for Caution from Russia. *The New York Times*, 11 September. http://www.nytimes.com/2013/09/12/opinion/putin-plea-for-caution-from-russia-on-syria.html.

Roberts, S. R. 2015. The Ukraine Conflict and the Future of Kazakhstan's Multi-Vector Foreign Policy, *PONARS Eurasia*, Policy Memo 388 (September). George Washington University. http://www.ponarseurasia.org/node/7938.

Robinson, P. 2016. Russia's Role in the War in Donbass, and the Threat to European Security. *European Politics and Society* 17 (4): 506–521.

Roth, A. 2015. Details of the Ukraine Cease-Fire Negotiated in Minsk. *The New York Times*, 12 February. https://www.nytimes.com/2015/02/13/world/europe/ukraine-cease-fire-negotiated-in-minsk.html.

Schenkkan, N. 2016. Kazakhstan with Russia: Smiling through Gritted Teeth. *Russian Analytical Digest—ETH Zurich Center for Security Studies* 188 (Aug.): 2–5.

Sullivan, C. J. 2015. The Coming Fall of Kabul. *PONARS Eurasia*, Policy Memo 386 (September). George Washington University. http://www.ponarseurasia.org/memo/coming-fall-kabul.

Sullivan, C.J. 2016. State-Building: America's Foreign Policy Challenge. *U.S. Army War College Quarterly—Parameters* 46 (1): 51–65.

———. 2017. State-Building in the Steppe: Challenges to Kazakhstan's Modernizing Aspirations. *Strategic Analysis* 41 (3): 273–284.

Tashkinbayev, R. 2014. Kazakhstan Toughens Punishment for Separatism. *Tengri News*, 8 April. https://en.tengrinews.kz/laws_initiatives/Kazakhstan-toughens-punishment-for-separatism-252777/.

Taylor, A. 2017. Kazakhstan and Kyrgyzstan Deny Reports They Are in Talks with Russia to Send Troops to Syria. *The Washington Post*, 23 June. https://www.washingtonpost.com/news/worldviews/wp/2017/06/23/kazakhstan-and-kyrgyzstan-deny-reports-they-are-in-talks-with-russia-to-send-troops-to-syria/?utm_term=.b679166a53ed.

Tokaev, K. 2004. Kazakhstan: From Renouncing Nuclear Weapons to Building Democracy. *American Foreign Policy Interests* 26: 93–97.

CHAPTER 4

The Environmental Legacy of the Soviet Regime

Beatrice Penati

Introduction

One of the first impressions a foreign visitor has of many cities in Kazakhstan is the high level of atmospheric pollution, which is disproportionately high relative to population density. From the heights of Ust-Kamenogorsk (Öskemen), one can see dense smog hovering above the city; in the former capital, Almaty, air pollution is mostly due to car traffic, but the air has been equally—if not more—unbreathable for the past three decades. Train travelers to Ekibastuz to the east and to the former GULag center, Karaganda, can recognize that their stop has come by sensing the smell of coal powder that meets them just out of their carriages. Not far from Karaganda, in the metallurgical city of Temirtau, residents are busy cleaning away the reddish dust that deposits itself on their cars and windows. To the north, coal powder is used for centralized heating in Astana, the new capital, although strong steppe winds contribute to dispersing the smoke.

Air pollution, especially in the form of dusts and other particles, which derives from the presence of heavy industry and from the reliance on coal powder for heating and energy production, is one of the many ways in

B. Penati (✉)
University of Liverpool, Liverpool, UK
e-mail: Beatrice.Penati@liverpool.ac.uk

J.-F. Caron (ed.), *Kazakhstan and the Soviet Legacy*,
https://doi.org/10.1007/978-981-13-6693-2_4

which the legacy of Soviet development policies is still having an impact on the natural environment and on people's health. This chapter explains how, from the viewpoint of the environment, the Soviet past is not at all "a foreign country": on the contrary, it is still continually present—or at least *perceived* as present—in the daily life of Kazakhstanis in three distinctive ways. First, there are situations in which Soviet policies with significant fallouts on the environment have indeed been interrupted (sometimes before 1991), but their consequences are still visible, for instance, on human and animal health. These will be the object of the first section of this chapter. Then, as in the case of the usage of coal powder, productive solutions initiated before independence have not been discontinued or substantially reformed, which leads to the perpetuation of their obnoxious effects in a very different socioeconomic context. The second section will provide examples of this type. Each of these two kinds of heritage underpins distinct issues of political responsibility, coping strategies, and memorialization. Finally, the Soviet environmental legacy also exists in a third and subtler form, namely in the political discourse about ecological problems, both officially and at the grassroots level. Such discourse—and the relative economic policy assumptions—was shaped not only by Soviet decision-making patterns but also by the emergence of ecological movements in the last two decades of the USSR.

In other words, the Soviet environmental legacy extends beyond the material domain (where it is visible both as direct continuity in practices and as long-term consequences of past policies) to include ideology and decision-making processes. In chronological order, the first great initiatives to shape the landscape in order to increase output—and thereby foster the consolidation and expansion of socialism—date to the late 1940s. They must be understood in the context of the early Cold War and of growing competition between the US and the USSR models of development, not only for either of these two countries but also for propaganda purposes in Asia and Africa. Stalin's "plan for the transformation of nature", launched in 1948 and paralleled by his "Great Communist Construction" (Gestwa 2005; Josephson 2013: 119–128), did not reach the degree of *hybris* and absurdity of Mao's "war against nature" (Shapiro 2001), and was less a tool for overall societal mobilization as Khrushchev's "Virgin Land campaign" would be half a decade later. Yet, such "transformation" entailed several important projects in Central Asia, which would have a direct or indirect impact on the natural and anthropic landscape in Kazakhstan, namely, the Karakum Canal (which actually started in 1947) and the Major Turkmen Canal (never accomplished), as well as the "diversion of Siberian rivers". While the "gigantism" of Stalin's "transformation of nature" was rejected under Khrushchev in favor of a more nuanced, "cybernetic" approach that took into account the environment's "feedback" on human initiatives, the idea of manipulation of nature for productive goals was never fundamentally shaken (Chida 2013).

At the beginning, all these construction projects were prompted by the "center", but later on and in particular under Brezhnev, initiatives for the "transformation of nature" were increasingly discussed at the republican level and became an opportunity for national party and Soviet elites to build their power. This was true not only for the revival of the unaccomplished "diversion of Siberian rivers" but also for decisions about the Balkhash-Ili basin, and even on the creation of the Medeu Dam to prevent mud floods. In other words, political decisions that entailed the direct manipulation of the environment became a terrain of confrontation between "center" and "peripheries" and underpinned the establishment of patronage networks between politics and expert scientific knowledge. In this, all the episodes reported in the next pages embody the Soviet technocratic approach (Chida 2013; Elie 2013). Not unlike policies in the field of military or industrial development, what these decisions were not really taking into account were negative externalities (desiccation, pollution, loss of biodiversity, etc.): what mattered was output, and in particular output on the short- or medium run. These three characteristics—environmental questions as a political arena, technocracy, and the emphasis on production—seem to be weighing on the way environmental issues are still dealt with in independent Kazakhstan.

The Soviet Environmental Legacy

The heritage of the Soviet regime in Kazakhstan is conventionally associated with the so-called Aral Sea tragedy and the long-term nuclear contamination in the east of the country. Both these situations belong to the first category of circumstances mentioned earlier: both the shrinking and the ultimate disappearance of the Aral Sea and the Semipalatinsk (Semey) atomic testing polygon belong to the pre-independence period, but their consequences are still very much present now.

The decline of the level of the Aral Sea is related to the demand for water for the expansion of the cultivation of cotton in southern Central Asia, particularly in what used to be the Uzbek Soviet Socialist Republic

(SSR) and the southern Kazakh SSR. Historically, the oases of southern Central Asia had been growing cotton (*Gossypium herbaceum*, locally known as *ghuza*) well before the Russian conquest of the region in the second half of the nineteenth century. The introduction of long-staple American cotton varieties (*Gossypium hirsutum*, especially *Upland*) in the 1870s, however, marked the beginning of a first "cotton boom", which was made possible by a combination of objectively favorable fiscal policies and the abundance of available labor in local small-holding peasant households (Penati 2013). This phase, however, can scarcely be compared to what followed in the Soviet era: in 1929, Stalin enunciated cotton autarky as one of the goals of the first five-year plan. The collectivization campaign in the oases of southern Central Asia aimed first and foremost at maximizing the cotton output through the establishment of larger mechanized farms than it had hitherto been the case. The expansion of both cotton acreage and output in the Soviet period was particularly intense in three periods: during the first five-year plan (1928–1932), with the opening of "virgin lands" for cotton under Nikita Khrushchev, and above all after 1966, as a consequence of the renewed mechanization effort, the further expansion of new irrigation, and the presence of more persuasive economic incentives under Brezhnev. At that point, water that should have ended up in the Aral Sea was being diverted not only for cotton but also for rice in southern Kazakhstan (Glantz 1999).

Some variability in the level of the Aral Sea was well known before the Soviet period: chronicles on the emergence and consolidation of the Khiva khanate in the Amu-Darya delta, for instance, suggest that variations in the discharge of rivers and even in their courses were not uncommon, and ultimately determined the volume of water that reached the Aral Sea each year (Abdurasulov 2017). Already at the beginning of the twentieth century, many observers discussed whether "Central Asia is drying up" on the basis of glaciers and the water level in rivers and in the Aral Sea (Berg 1905). Since then, Soviet and post-Soviet archaeological and historical scholarship has shown that indeed the Aral Sea (as other Central Asian lakes) expanded for the last time in the seventeenth to nineteenth centuries, while the situation changed by the beginning of the twentieth century (Narama et al. 2010). This variability, together with years of relatively abundant water around the middle of the century, may explain some reticence in engaging from the beginning with the shrinkage of the Aral Sea as a consequence of the increased diversion of water for irrigation. More generally, because all the water that ended up in the Aral Sea was regarded as wasted, it is not surprising that for a long time the diminution of the sea level did not cause much worry. Information was not lacking: the Aral Sea was constantly monitored, and since 1939 one of the first Kazakhstani natural reserves was located on its shores (Gunin and Neronov 1986: 175). Yet, since 1960 the water level had been plummeting, to the point that by 1987 the surface was three-fifths and the volume one-third of what it used to be at the beginning of the period (NASA 2016; P. P. Micklin 1988; Glantz 1999). This was essentially due to the opening of newly irrigated land in southern Kazakhstan and Uzbekistan, in the so-called Hungry Steppe, and to the digging of the Karakum Canal in Turkmenistan (Obertreis 2008). A massive diversion of the Ob and Irtysh Rivers was under study as early as the 1970s: although its first goal was to expand the irrigated surface in cotton-producing regions, this project could have helped "save" the Aral Sea. The project, known as *Sibaral* ("from Siberia to the Aral"), was generally welcomed by the republican Soviet and Party leadership; Russian observers and segments of the Soviet scientific community, instead, expressed substantial doubts. This led to a slowdown in the initial plans and ultimately to the dismissal of the project in the mid-1980s (P. P. Micklin 1988).

Although the health effects of the desiccation of the Aral Sea were not unknown to Soviet authorities and were indeed named in *perestroika* publications, and despite the fact that since independence the region has been receiving abundant attention in scientific circles and media, in 2001 *Médecins sans Frontières* observed with some alarm that the "tragedy" of the sea (that is, its disappearance) has obscured the "tragedy" which the five million people who live along its shores have experienced (Small et al. 2001). Studies in physical geography, zoology, botany, and climate science have long been more abundant than reliable analyses of the impact of desiccation on human health—a first step in building up advocacy. Such impact is both direct, because desiccation induced salinization and greater concentrations of pesticides and cotton fertilizers in water and food, and indirect, because of the increased incidence of dust and salt storms. Furthermore, the desiccation has led to the disappearance of the two major sources of income enjoyed by the riparian population: fishing and, to a lesser extent, hunting of muskrats (Glantz 1999). In sum, the region shows—and is still producing—high rates of morbidity and mortality because of infectious diseases (especially tuberculosis), chronic illnesses of the heart, kidneys, and lungs, and cancer. For instance, the rate of esophageal cancer in the autonomous province of Karakalpakstan is 25 times higher than the world average (Synnott 2015).

Nowadays, scarce awareness of what environmental risk is, the unavailability of venues for discussing it, and the exasperation of an "assessment fatigued" population that for a long time has seen no tangible measures taken to improve its condition have important social consequences: while focus on more compelling problems (e.g. unemployment) has averted the danger of a fight over the (very less) water left in the Aral (Koch 2016), more than a decade ago health practitioners had noticed a significant level of somatized posttraumatic stress, more characteristic of acute environmental disasters than of exposure to environmental risk. In other words, ten years after independence the riparian population had not yet developed the psychological coping strategies that occur among those subject to a long-term obnoxious condition (Small et al. 2001).

The current situation is similar, but not at all identical, at the opposite end of Kazakhstan, close to what used to be the Semipalatinsk nuclear test site (or "polygon"). For around 40 years starting in 1949, the population was exposed to radiation as a consequence of over- and underground nuclear explosions. Around 450 tests were performed at the polygon, around one-fourth of which in the atmosphere or "surface", until the Limited Test Ban Treaty of 1963 (Holloway 1996; Werner and Purvis-Roberts 2006). Data on the effects on people were surreptitiously collected under the cover of zoonosis prevention, but were considered as top secret until the late 1980s. Around 1.6 million people were exposed to potentially dangerous radiation levels, but very rarely residents were evacuated or even simply warned about what was taking place (Werner and Purvis-Roberts 2006). It was with Mikhail Gorbachev's "Lenin's policy" and the growing availability of *fora* where public health worries could be voiced that information started leaking. Unsurprisingly, the lead belonged to recognized Soviet intellectuals and WWII (World War II) veterans, who had a relatively higher ability to engage in public debates; in particular, the poet and writer Olzhas Suleymenov emerged as the main voice that requested transparency (*glasnost*) on this matter. Rallies sprung up from 1989 in several cities in the Kazakh SSR, so that at some point the movement changed its name from *Nevada-Semipalatinsk* to *Nevada-Kazakhstan* and collected snowballing grievances not only from East Kazakhstan but also from Baykonur (where the Soviet—now Russian—facilities for space exploration and satellite launch were located) and other localities. An account was opened to collect funding, and the movement tried to reach out not only to those protesters who, in Nevada, had successfully blocked the local testing ground but also to the United Nations and global NGOs, such as Greenpeace. In this respect, it has been argued that *Nevada-Semipalatinsk* was an "eco-internationalist" movement (Schatz 1999); in the light of its own propaganda, one may add that *Nevada-Semipalatinsk*'s internationalism echoed the Soviet "peace" rhetoric of the same years—and even more the Soviet emphasis on "friendship of the people", as embodied by Kazakhstan's ethnically mixed population. The *Nevada-Semipalatinsk* movement and Olzhas Suleymenov's role in it represent a foundational moment in the consecrated history and memory of Kazakhstan's "path to independence", almost on a par with the repression of the demonstrations against the appointment of Gennady Kolbin as first secretary of the republican Party December (*Zheltoqsan*) 1986 in Almaty. For sure, the reference to the movement and to the nefarious consequence of the tests was a cornerstone of Nazarbayev's nuclear "clean-up" policy (Werner and Purvis-Roberts 2006). Yet, one should stress with Schatz (1999) that in no way the polygon has been depicted, either by Suleymenov or by Nazarbayev, as a foreign "colonial" installation. This, as explained below, has a parallel in the way scholarship has evolved.

Nowadays, although the measurements of background radiation are a matter of controversy, the remaining inhabitants (mostly Kazakh, because most Russians have left since 1991) present high rates of morbidity and mortality, in particular for solid and blood cancers (Carlsen et al. 2001; Alexander 2016). As in the case of the riparian population of the Aral Sea, one observes "the residents' failure to demand state action", while "their political demobilization is further exacerbated by limited access to social welfare and the local emergence of free-market capitalism" (Stawkowski 2016). Around the polygon, though, the population seems to have elaborated by now its own coping strategy, which consists in claiming that one has "adapted" to radiation, to the point of not being able to live healthily without it (Stawkowski 2016). This does not mean, though, that residents did not acknowledge risk or underestimate it—an attitude they apparently share with local physicians, although not with other "experts" (Purvis-Roberts et al. 2007). Another difference between the two sites is visible in the different degree to which the Kazakhstani state machinery has engaged itself in putting a remedy to the direct and indirect consequences of the Cold War on the Aral and in the east of the country respectively: while Astana, with World Bank support, has sponsored the restoration of the

Small Aral and is considering further schemes to advance the same design (P. Micklin 2016), around Semipalatinsk the cause of "cleaning up" the site is murkily bundled up with the priority to extract uranium and other valuable underground resources, or even with a new technocratic emphasis on the postindependence renaissance of science in the country, and possibilities for expressing a public memory of the trauma are somewhat hampered (Stawkowski 2016; Alexander 2016; Brunn 2011). More generally, Werner and Purvis-Roberts (2006) have noted that the emphasis which the president of Kazakhstan Nursultan Nazarbayev has put on nuclear disarmament as a founding principle of the country's foreign policy has not led to a correspondingly high investment of resources to the benefit of those most affected by the consequences of the tests. The very recent discussions about the opening of a nuclear reactor in Kurchatov, within the perimeter of the former polygon, further contribute to the fundamental ambiguity of Kazakhstan's current "nuclear culture" (WNN 2016).

While medics, nuclear experts, and (more recently) several anthropologists have cast considerable light on the consequences of the nuclear tests that took place at the Semipalatinsk polygon, we are still lacking the kind of careful study of the decision-making process which, from the 1940s onward, has led to the current situation. Questions of agency and historical responsibility are still largely unanswered. In this respect, the study of the Semipalatinsk polygon is lagging behind, relative to research about Soviet development policies that similarly had a significant impact on the environment and, through it, on public health. As discussed earlier, we know that the Aral Sea tragedy was caused by an ideological parallelism between Soviet social engineering and "Great Communist Construction", as well as by a general emphasis on material output (in this case, agricultural) without the ability to account for negative externalities. Beyond these ideological premises, historians have also found that republican Soviet and Party elites played a key role in the underlying decision-making process, in particular in parallel to Brezhnev's "trust in the cadres" policy. This will be even clearer from the cases discussed in the next section. Instead, research on the decision-making process that led to the establishment of the Semipalatinsk polygon and on its subsequent activity—in particular on the mutual relations between authorities in the Kazakh SSR and in Moscow—is still underdeveloped. As noted earlier, lack of clarity on questions of agency in the past has objectively allowed a public discourse in which the "fault" for the contamination has been laid on the Cold War in general, and the international community (rather than Kazakhstan itself or, even less, the Russian Federation) is supposed to play a key role in "cleaning up" after it and compensate the victims (Werner and Purvis-Roberts 2006).

The Kazakhstani Way

The Semipalatinsk polygon is different from most other sites of environmental degradation in the Kazakh SSR, in that it is not related to development policies, but primarily to the Cold War and the armament race. In this respect, the only other similar site is the Baikonur space base in the center of the republic: as in Semipalatinsk, a portion of territory has been fenced off for the benefit of the "industrial-military complex"—an argument that we find in Olzhas Suleymenov's rhetoric. The consequences for human health are more modest: even now, residents of Kyzyl-Orda would lament the anomalous sand-carrying whirlwinds that reach their city a short time after every launch, while the Karaganda Ecomuseum (one of the first NGOs in the country to foster ecological awareness in the general public) displays "space rubbish" that has fallen on the steppe. What the Semipalatinsk polygon has in common with the Aral Sea tragedy, though, is the fact that the cause of the degradation is perceived as belonging to the past, at least as far as Kazakhstan is concerned: for the polygon this is very clear, while in the Aral Sea this impression depends on the relative success of Kazakhstani efforts to refill part of what is left of the basin (P. Micklin 2016). In both cases, the search for responsibility for what had happened is largely limited to the past or, for the most recent developments on the Aral Sea, fault is to be found outside the boundaries of Kazakhstan. This intellectual operation is evidently more arduous for the other category of environment-damaging activities mentioned in the introduction: what if the factories, mines, and plants that produced high level of air pollution and contamination of water and soil before 1991 are still in operation, and still represent an important component of the national economy, for instance by supplying energy or attracting foreign investments? The section that follows is going to discuss a few symptomatic cases of this kind.

The first case is that of Ust-Kamenogorsk in the east of the country. The area was one of the first to witness the exploitation of underground mineral resources, with the discovery of the first copper ores and the establishment of the Ridder lead, silver (and later zinc) mines as early as the late eighteenth century (Peck 2003: 10). The Altay region was also one of the first where the Russian imperial government actively promoted the arrival of peasant settlers, in order to create a food supply basis for the mines themselves. Through time, the exploitation of the region's many polymetallic ores intensified, first with foreign capital and then, under Soviet rule, thanks to the state's impulsion. With another locality in the Altay region of Kazakhstan, Zyryanovsk, Ust-Kamenogorsk was responsible for two-thirds of the Soviet production of rare metals just before independence. At the same time, both Zyryanovsk and Ust-Kamenogorsk were among the 68 Soviet cities with the highest air pollution, which was distinctly associated with nonferrous metallurgy. In the second half of the 1970s, lead in Ust-Kamenogorsk's air was 14 times higher than the maximum permitted concentration, but in nearby Leninogorsk it was 30–40 times higher, and on specific days this could peak by a factor of ten (Pryde 2009: 95). The same was true for water pollution: the concentration of heavy metals (copper, but also zinc and other substances) in the rivers of the Irtysh basin and in the Irtysh itself was the highest in the republic. The only exception to this sad primacy was chrome, the concentration of which in the western Ilek River was 60–230 times higher than in the east. This was due to the exploitation of polymetallic ores in Aktyube, which was itself initially linked to the availability of forced labor from the nearby GULag camp (Mnatsakanian 2002).

This long-term situation knew a sudden acceleration in 1990, in what represent the still understudied closest Kazakhstani equivalent to the Chernobyl disaster in Belarus in 1986. Ust-Kamenogorsk did not only host nonferrous smelting facilities: the Ulba plant (which is still active, as explained below) was responsible for a sizeable proportion of the Soviet production of nuclear fuel, which included the processing of beryllium. On 12 September, a blast at the plant generated a "poisonous cloud" and massive fallout of contaminated particles. Although in principle beryllium was not radioactive but "merely" toxic, foreign observers interpreted the episode as a nuclear incident. Surely the measures taken to reduce contamination after the blast were quite dramatic: roads should be "washed" four times a day, street-sweeping was blocked, and fears were expressed that road traffic may contribute to the spread of pollutants. Local authorities declared Ust-Kamenogorsk a disaster area, and Nursultan Nazarbayev, at the time president of the Kazakh SSR, asked for this status to be recognized by Moscow, for all those damaged to be indemnified, and for a commission with foreign participation to be established to ascertain the situation (Clines 1990; Mnatsakanian 2002: 121). Although there is basically no research on this episode, its public health consequences, and above all its political significance, a few striking resemblances with Chernobyl can be highlighted: first, the suddenness of the incident and the fact that it was related to some sort of productive (rather than military) activity; second, and more significant, Nazarbayev's requests appeared framed as a compensation from the "center" to the affected "periphery", defined in national terms. This was similar to what had occurred in Chernobyl: instead, the protests surrounding the Semipalatinsk polygon had assumed an "internationalist" tonality, even when the parallel with Chernobyl was made to emphasize the seriousness of the damage (Schatz 1999).

It is instead in its post-Soviet legacy that one can find a similarity between the polygon and the Ust-Kamenogorsk blast of 1990: in both cases, the memory of what had happened in the Soviet period has been sidelined in favor of a more general nuclear agenda that privileges disarmament and high-tech industry (both largely directed to a foreign audience) to a thorough local "clean-up". In Ust-Kamenogorsk, this means that the same Ulba plant entered in 2009 into a partnership with the French group Areva (which had already been participating in the extraction of uranium at Muyunkum for five years) to produce nuclear fuel. In both cases, the French side owns 51% of the shares (Nuklear Forum Schweiz 2004, 2009). More recently, the Ulba plant is handling the establishment of the International Atomic Energy Agency's (IAEA) low-enriched uranium bank. These measures are surely useful now that demand for nuclear fuel (and for beryllium for electronic components) is growing. To add a further layer of symbolic significance, the Ulba plant is also where all the metallic coins in circulation in Kazakhstan come from. Ust-Kamenogorsk's nuclear legacy is thereby turned into a bright future, despite the residual palpable fears of the residents (Uatkhanov 2016; Urankayeva 2016).

How does this outcome compare with other sites where the legacy of Soviet industrial development policies is still continuing at the expenses of the environment, but no major accident occurred and no (or only recent) link to the nuclear question exists? One can consider two examples, namely, the Balkhash Lake and the homonymous city, on the one hand, and the industrial area of Karaganda and Temirtau, on the other. In both these cases, problems of pollution have continued to exist across the 1991 divide, but unlike the case of the Ulba plant, attempts to modernize the local industrial landscape have been far less successful. While one may argue that Ust-Kamenogorsk's bright future lies on paper only, even such a moderate claim would sound implausible for these two sites.

Historian Kate Brown (2001) has presented the industrial city as the physical embodiment of measures to control people's lives through the imposition of a rigid spatial "grid", whereby ethnic categories were reinforced, hierarchies of social exclusion were reproduced, and the efficient mobilization of forced labor was ensured without obstruction. Brown argues that this kind of spatial organization bears strong resemblances with other sites of rapid industrialization based on the exploitation of underground resources and the pouring of settlers into a supposedly "empty" land, for instance, the city of Billings in the American state of Montana. This powerful thesis somewhat neglects the fact that the very existence of Karaganda, unlike Billings, was premised on coercion. Karaganda was the center of the homonymous camp (KarLag), the economic activity of which revolved around the extractive industry and around agriculture (to feed the workers of the latter) (Khlevniuk 2004). While copper and coal ores around Karaganda were known well before the Bolshevik Revolution, it was with Soviet accelerated industrialization that production took off, particularly during WWII, when a steel mill was built, iron extraction was started, a rain link northward was established, and coal started to be used not only for smelting copper but also for power generation for ferrous metallurgy. A fundamental factor for the development of the Karaganda basin overall was the availability of forced labor, which allowed to compensate for the higher costs related to logistic constraints that had marred earlier development plans. Some detainees and forced settlers of the Karaganda area moved on to the Virgin Lands (see below), while others stayed in the area after the closing of the GULag in the second half of the 1950s, to be employed in the mines. In addition, Karaganda's coal had the relative advantage of being located close to where electricity was needed for smelting. This made their exploitation desirable, even when, from the 1950s onward, the USSR switched to the "coal-by-wire" program. The latter entailed the construction of coal-burning power plants as close as possible to the sources of fuel, for instance in Aksu, not far from the huge open-pit coal mines of Ekibastuz. In any case, the cost per kilowatt hour in Karaganda remained much lower than in the rest of the USSR, and even lower than elsewhere in Kazakhstan (Peck 2003: 15–17, 43, 51, 184).

Continuous industrial development meant that Karaganda was the second biggest city in Kazakhstan in terms of population on the eve of independence—and the first for concentration of nitrogen dioxide and formaldehyde (Mnatsakanian 2002: 121–122). In the postindependence period, the odd traveler could (and can) smell the legacy of the forced-pace growth of heavy industry in Karaganda—and apprehend its sociopolitical underpinnings by looking at the urban landscape. If the situation has improved, it is not because of greater investments in devices for capturing gases and particulates, but rather because of the sharp decline of the metallurgical and coal industry in the area. A more subtle, often-forgotten environmental legacy of the same phenomenon, though, is represented by the accumulation of billion cubic meters of coal tailings, which represent a continual source of pollution and "crowd out" land that could be destined to other usages. No quick fix is possible for coal tailings, the costs of which are likely passed on to the next generations (Peck 2003: 193).

While it would be tempting to identify the center of a GULag camp as large as France as a major site of environmental degradation, too, the situation in Karaganda was not (and *is* not) as bad as in nearby Temirtau. In Karaganda on the eve of independence the rate of capture of air pollutants was 81.5%: this was probably an optimistic estimate, but nonetheless in line with the republican average and higher than on the oil fields of the West. By contrast, the Temirtau blast furnace did not possess any filters *at all*—and accounted for only one half of the total air pollution (Mnatsakanian 2002: 121). Temirtau, the name of which literally means "Iron Mountain" in Kazakh, swelled up into a major industrial center in the postwar period, thereby gaining the status of "city" (with all the perks that went with it in the Soviet hierarchy of consumption and investments) and becoming the second biggest steel-producing site in the whole of the USSR. As in Karaganda, pollution was driven by quick-pace heavy industrialization, which in Temirtau revolved around the entire cycle of production of steel: before WWII, there were no steel mills in the Kazakh SSR, while the first one—evacuated to Shymkent to save it from the German advance—could roll steel out of pig iron, but not smelt iron ore to obtain the latter. Again, as in Karaganda metallurgy was accompanied by the production of electrical energy from coal. What was radically different was the sheer dimension of air pollution: total gas and particulate emissions in 1989 were almost four times greater in Temirtau than in nearby Karaganda, and far higher than anywhere else in the republic, including the coal-mining center of Ekibastuz in the east. Mercury and phenols contaminate not only the Nura River, but also underground waters, to the point that no local source can be used to provision the city of Temirtau (Mnatsakanian 2002: 122, 125).

As in Karaganda, the end of the Soviet economic system—premised, as explained below, on the "soft budget constraint"—and the privatization of industrial assets in the 1990s led to a reduction of output. In 1995, the government conferred the Karaganda Metallurgical Combinat (Karmet), which controlled the coal mines in Karaganda as well as the steel plant in Temirtau, to a company controlled by Lakshmi Mittal. This happened after two failed attempts to involve other Western companies and at a moment when output had hit rock bottom, Karmet was heavily indebted, and workers on several of its sites were protesting or going on strike to receive arrear salaries and better work conditions. In these conditions, Mittal got away with a very good deal; additionally, while post-Soviet privatization "packages" usually included guarantees for the workers and securities for the activities that had depended on a combinat in the Soviet period (e.g. flats, sanatoriums, kindergartens), Mittal could lay off a substantial proportion of employees and transfer responsibility for those parallel activities to the not-so-well-off municipality. Only at the beginning of the 2000s Mittal took back control of some services, including a hotel, the hot water system, and the tramway (itself a symbol of Temirtau's Soviet glory). In this context of severe social precariousness, the city has been plagued by social problems of all kinds, including drug addiction: the sad primacy in air pollution of the 1980s has been replaced by the highest rate of HIV infection in Kazakhstan (Peck 2003: 114–116).

In turn, the dramatic urgency of such social issues has been masking the gravity of environmental problems and their effects on public health. A pioneering study by Xeniya Prilutskaya (2016) has shown that the population of Temirtau, while generically aware of the risk posed by air pollution and contamination of water and soil, is unable to articulate such threat in a scientifically informed way. The mechanisms for the transmission of this sort of information having broken down, residents are left in a vulnerable position and are largely alienated from the providers of specialist knowledge, and in particular from "ecologists" by profession. For instance, residents of Temirtau have never heard about the potential presence of dioxin in the soil and, consequently, in the food chain. Rather than empowering them, they have been often patronized and even stigmatized for their supposed ignorance. In this respect, the situation has not significantly improved across the independence divide: through the 1980s and into the early 1990s a more open discussion of the environmental consequences of industrial decisions (e.g. establishing a new slag-processing plant) left the citizens with the impression that ecological questions did not have a clear-cut, easy solution. In short, if before *perestroika* people were left in the dark, as a consequence of it they were simply more puzzled (Prilutskaya 2016). Forced to cope with economic instability, lack of trust, and soaring social problems of various kinds, Temirtau residents have elaborated their own coping strategies: similar to their fellow citizens close to the Semipalatinsk polygon, they claim to have developed some sort of "immunity" to pollutants (Stawkowski 2016). Yet, Temirtau residents enjoy far lower visibility and have had little, if no, opportunity of posing as "victims" with a right for moral or monetary compensation (Werner and Purvis-Roberts 2006). As in many postindustrial sites, the choice is between unemployment (or emigration, followed by possible unemployment) and the tolerance of a "domesticated" threat on human health (Prilutskaya 2016).

Another site which is still bearing the consequence of Soviet industrial development strategies is Balkhash. As it is known, the homonymous lake is one of the largest in Eurasia and it possesses two different levels of salinity in each of its halves, which allowed for an incredibly rich and diverse flora and fauna and—historically—a locally important fishing and muskrat hunting industry. The main inflow of the Balkhash Lake is the Ili River. In the Soviet period, decision-makers had to balance two conflicting priorities: on the one hand, nonferrous (copper) metallurgy in the city of Balkhash on the northern shore; on the other hand, the usage of water from the Ili River for irrigation and hydroelectric power. Copper ores were discovered close to Balkhash as early as in the late 1920s, although proper exploitation started only later, after the completion of a railroad that made the evacuation of black copper possible, and in particular during WWII: in this, the trajectory of Balkhash was similar to that of Karaganda and other localities (Peck 2003: 40). Plans to expand irrigation on the Ili for the production of grain and rice also started in the early Soviet period, to become a priority after the deportation of Koreans in 1937 (Chida 2013).

Ferrous and nonferrous metallurgy, together with the concentration of an urban population of workers in need for drinking water, required abundance of fresh water. In this respect, not only fish and muskrat reserves, but also the industrial development of Balkhash would be negatively affected by projects that would shrink the inflow, reduce the volume of the lake, and increase salinity. Historian Tetsuro Chida (2013) has projected the debates on the expansion of establishment of the Kapchagai reservoir and hydropower station (in operation since 1970) on the backdrop of two concurrent wider dynamics: first, the generalized skepticism about "gigantism" and a more cautious approach to the idea of "transformation of nature" in the post-Stalin period; second, the circumstance that development plans of this kind were crucial for the establishment and preservation of local power structures under Brezhnev. As for the construction of the Medeu Dam to protect Alma-Ata from mud floods (Elie 2013), one of the keys to Dinmukhamed Kunaev's political success as a first secretary of the Kazakhstan Communist Party was his ability to present himself as a patron of (modestly) beneficial construction projects. In the case of the Balkhash basin, though, Kunaev's ability consisted more in balancing contradictory interests: the expansion of agriculture around Kapchagai *versus* the need for fresh water in Balkhash city (Chida 2013).

This fundamental tension between incompatible priorities, combined with the partial recognition of the need to account for their "negative" consequences and with the "trust in the [republican] cadres" that marked the Brezhnevian period, led to a no-win situation: the Kapchagai hydropower station was never efficient, and by the mid-1980s less than one-half of its generators were working. At the same time, the Kapchagai reservoir never filled up completely and the programmed water release scheme failed. In the end the newly irrigated surface was much less than forecast, and rice production was never comparable to the one on the Syr Darya. From another viewpoint, though, the salinity increased (to the point that experts considered the possibility of building a dam between the two halves of the lake) and Balkhash city became dependent on a pipeline for its drinking water (Chida 2013). The reduction of the volume of water in the Balkhash Lake led to a diminution in biodiversity and greater concentration of pollutants.

As anticipated in regard to Ust-Kamenogorsk, the smelting of nonferrous ores is responsible for a huge share of air and water pollution in Kazakhstan, and the Balkhash combinat (which handles copper, zinc, and lead) is no exception. After the Baykal Lake and the Volga and Kama Rivers, in 1969 Lake Balkhash was the object of one of the first large campaigns against water pollution (Moor-Stahl and Allaman 2000: 33). In 1989, the city had the highest concentration of particulates in the whole of the republic, while the concentration of copper in water was between 38 and 238 times higher than the limit (Mnatsakanian 2002: 122). Copper, zinc, and lead powder still floated on the water of the lake in large amounts more than a decade later (Kozlova 2006). Around Balkhash, smelting plants, ores, and subsidiary activities (including provision of basic services to local communities) are owned by the copper-producing Kazakhmys Corporation (run by Cuprum Holdings), which received them in 2014 from Kazakhmys PLC (2014). Until 2004 the latter was controlled by Samsung and gathered together all the copper-related activities which this South Korean giant of electronics had acquired throughout Kazakhstan up until 1997 (Peck 2003: 89–90). As it happened elsewhere, pollution temporarily declined in the 1990s because of the diminution in output; later on, Kazakhmys made efforts to install capturing systems (Reuters 2012). The attention of Balkhash's residents and activists, though, has been captured for the last decade by another question, namely, the possibility of opening a nuclear power plant to generate electricity for the area south of the lake (Kozlova 2006; WNN 2016).

Conclusion

Environmental issues in Ust-Kamenogorsk, Balkhash, Temirtau, Karaganda, and elsewhere ultimately originate from the same problem, which we have hinted at before: the inability of the planned economy to take into account negative externalities. As it is true that environmental problems in the USSR were not substantially different from those of other industrialized countries, including the US (Goldman 1972; Pryde 2009: 292), it is also true that this inability is not as such a characteristic of the Soviet system only, but a shortcoming to be observed in policymaking worldwide. In the USSR, though, this was a clear-cut consequence of considering land, air, and water as "socialist property", which made it impossible to consider costs related to their degradation. The idea of an "environmental tax" was considered in the 1970s but soon discarded. "Socialist property"—which meant, in practice, state property—perpetuated and reinforced the "delusion of abundance", which some observers identify as a trait of Russian views on nature already before 1917 (Moor-Stahl and Allaman 2000: 59).

This theoretical shortcoming had even more serious effects when the damage to the natural environment did not result from something that could be instrumentally measured, for instance, as air pollution or water contamination, but simply from its depletion. The degradation of rangeland because of overgrazing (Robinson et al. 2003; Mirzabaev et al. 2016), soil erosion (deflation) as a consequence of the Virgin Land campaign (Pryde 2009: 198–202; Josephson 2013: 152), and salinization in the south of the republic are all part of the environmental legacy of Soviet policies in the Kazakh SSR, although their economic consequences "only" translate into loss of productive capacity. Pollutants could not, after all, be ignored: the diminution in the productive capacity of the land because of overusage, by comparison, was more difficult to grasp and conceptualize. Even when this was possible, the theoretical underpinnings evoked earlier meant that, legally speaking, these phenomena could be considered only as violations of "state property" on land and water, in the same category as unauthorized buildings or the neglect of field boundaries (AN KSSR 1988). Even after the USSR had embraced the international notion of "biosphere" in the 1970s, the measurement of the degradation of flora and fauna in the steppe—and, hopefully, their protection—posed specific problems: in the USSR, natural reserves and monitoring "stations" were set up where the density of species was the highest, which privileged mountain and forest environments rich in water against the steppe and deserts. This made phenomena such as desertification not only difficult to handle with the toolbox of Soviet economics but also hard to acknowledge and measure (Filonov 1986; Gunin and Neronov 1986).

In line with the bulk of studies on the functioning of the Soviet planned economy in general, one may argue that this deficiency was aggravated by several entangled circumstances: first, on the demand side, the fact that in a planned economy prices do not send any significant "signal"; second—and related, but from the supply side—, the focus on output measures in *material* terms, rather than in value (which would have been difficult, given the absence of meaningful prices); third, the soft budget constraint, which allowed state-run companies to disregard costs of production, too (Gregory and Stuart 2000). (The cost of labor, in particular, was long made meaningless by the presence of the GULag and, consequently, the availability of forced workers.) In addition, secrecy about the plan and compartmentalization in the definition of input-output plans (i.e. the waste of sector A could not become a raw material for sector B) represented further obstacles to environment-savvy economic decisions (Moor-Stahl and Allaman 2000: 62). While an inquiry on the continuity of budgeting and planning practices in Kazakhstan across the independence divide goes well beyond the scope of this survey, some similarities exist in the importance of symbolic and ideological considerations in the decision-making process. This is particularly clear in the way the legacy of the Semipalatinsk polygon has been handled and, by contrast, in the way "nuclear culture" plays into plans for the future industrial development of Ust-Kamenogorsk.

What, on the other hand, seems to have survived the 1991 divide is the emphasis on technical-scientific knowledge as the most important (if not the only) way to identify, manage, and solve environmental issues. As in the Soviet period, environmental questions are the purview of engineers and natural scientists or, at the most, economists. In the *Kazakhstan 2050* strategy, "Ecology" is still articulated as "management of natural resources" and most "actions" refer to punctual construction projects (Strategy 2050 2016). The emphasis is on technical solutions, which are perceived as politically neutral and as possessing a higher epistemic status than decisions involving social scientists, or founded on the participation of "laymen". This approach is quite clear if one looks at the capital Astana. The new city is presented as energy-savvy and ecologically sound. The official discourse presents its growth as natural and "organic" (Melnikov 2016). All these represent a departure from the "mechanicism" of the Soviet period, but only on the surface: the city is environmentally friendly because it is "smart". Digital computation has replaced the machine, but the solution to the problems of human society in relation to the environment is still a *technical* one. A similar emphasis is to be seen in the "Future Energy" theme of the 2017 Expo, where issues of sustainability are formulated with no or very little regard for crucial social questions, such as equal access to energy itself (Expo-2017 2016). As recent studies on "smart cities" in India show (Datta 2012, 2015), Kazakhstan is not alone: indeed, that "smartness" is an international trend, including in countries that Kazakhstan regards as models, and it represents a further layer of legitimization, on the top of the delusions of neutrality and epistemic superiority mentioned earlier (Fauve 2015).

Last but not least, the legacy of the Soviet system is also visible in the way one of the typical questions of USSR politics is articulated and responsibility (or simply agency) is attributed. All in all, one keeps on asking: "who is guilty?" The continuities, however, are not just in the question *as such*, but also in its political and practical consequences—or lack thereof: first, as it happened already in the Kazakhstani variant of de-Stalinization (Wojnowski 2016), criticism of individuals rarely turned into a criticism of the systemic underpinnings of their behavior and choices. Furthermore, the identification of the "guilty" part does not necessarily lead to a solution or improvement of the problem at hand. For example, Prilutskaya (2016) has found that, together with the emergence of less unambiguous notions about ecology, in Temirtau residents gradually shifted the blame from the factory management to "experts" (including the Society for the

Protection of Nature) during the *perestroika* period. Still, her findings confirm to what extent such "experts" are alienated from the citizenry. From another viewpoint, studies on the Semipalatinsk polygon discussed earlier (Schatz 1999; Werner and Purvis-Roberts 2006; Stawkowski 2016) show how responsibility has been shifted to the "outside" (in the past, outside Kazakhstan). This, in the end, is not very different from Olzhas Suleymenov's "internationalization" of the Semipalatinsk question in the late 1980s: by stating that nuclear experiments did not happen *only* in the USSR, those experiments ended up having *nothing* to do with the way decisions were taken in the USSR. More recently, if the responsibility for what happened belongs to an outside "nuclear club" or Cold War actors, then the "solution" is nuclear disarmament—although this has very little bearings on the residents' situation. The third and last shortcoming of a focus on individual guilt derives from the number and gravity of environmental issues at hand. This sad overabundance made (and still makes) it easy to shift responsibility by pointing at something else, which is more urgent or closer to everyday experience. In 1988, how could someone worry about pesticides and heavy metals in water, when 21% of tap water in the Kazakh SSR was at risk of fecal contamination (AN KSSR 1988: 4–5)? For the same reason, "experts" blame Temirtau's parents for letting their children play near car exhausts, thereby avoiding saying much about industrial pollution (Prilutskaya 2016). To sum up, asking who is guilty in a context in which knowledge of the problems themselves among the public is imprecise and accountability is fuzzy is unlikely to lead to solutions, but rather to further patronizing, mere interinstitutional battles, or political "sublimation" of the issues at hand.

References

Abdurasulov, U. 2017. The Aral Region and Geopolitical Agenda of the Early Qunghrats. *Eurasian Studies* 13 (1–2): 3–36.

Alexander, C. 2016. Nettoyer et Tourner La Page: La 'renaissance Nucléaire' du Kazakhstan. In *Les Chantiers Du Nucléaire*, ed. by Romain Garcier and Françoise Lafaye. Paris: Archives Contemporaines.

AN KSSR. 1988. *Effektivnost' Prirodookhranitel'nogo Zakonodatel'stva (Na Materialakh Kazakhskoi SSR)*. Alma-Ata: Nauka.

Berg, L.S. 1905. Vysykhaet Li Sredniaia Aziia? *IRGO*. In *Turkestanskii Sbornik, t. 490*, pp. 1–15, 41 (3).

Brown, K. 2001. Gridded Lives: Why Kazakhstan and Montana are Nearly the Same Place. *The American Historical Review* 106 (1): 17–48.

Brunn, S.D. 2011. Fifty Years of Soviet Nuclear Testing in Semipalatinsk, Kazakstan: Juxtaposed Worlds of Blasts and Silences, Security and Risks, Denials and Memory. In *Engineering Earth*, ed. Stanley D. Brunn, 1789–1818. Springer Netherlands. https://doi.org/10.1007/978-90-481-9920-4_101.

Carlsen, T.M., Leif E. Peterson, Brant A. Ulsh, Cynthia A. Werner, Kathleen L. Purvis, and Anna C. Sharber. 2001. Radionuclide Contamination at Kazakhstan's Semipalatinsk Test Site: Implications on Human and Ecological Health. *Human and Ecological Risk Assessment* 7 (4): 943–955.

Chida, T. 2013. Science, Development and Modernization in the Brezhnev Time. *Cahiers Du Monde Russe* 54 (1–2): 239–264.

Clines, F.X. 1990. Disaster Zone Is Urged After Soviet Nuclear Blast. *The New York Times*, 29 September 29, sec. World. http://www.nytimes.com/1990/09/29/world/disaster-zone-is-urged-after-soviet-nuclear-blast.html.

Datta, A. 2012. India's Ecocity? Environment, Urbanisation, and Mobility in the Making of Lavasa. *Environment and Planning C: Government and Policy* 30 (6): 982–996.

———. 2015. New Urban Utopias of Postcolonial India 'Entrepreneurial Urbanization' in Dholera Smart City, Gujarat. *Dialogues in Human Geography* 5 (1): 3–22.

Elie, M. 2013. Coping with the 'Black Dragon': Mudflow Hazards and the Controversy over the Medeo Dam in Kazakhstan, 1958–66. *Kritika: Explorations in Russian and Eurasian History* 14 (2): 313–342.

Expo-2017. 2016. Project Concept. Accessed 7 December. https://expo2017astana.com/en/energy/zamyisel-proekta.

Fauve, A. 2015. Global Astana: Nation Branding as a Legitimization Tool for Authoritarian Regimes. *Central Asian Survey* 34 (1): 110–124.

Filonov, K.P. 1986. Razvitie Printsipov Zapovednogo Dela v SSSR. In *Itogi I Perspektivy Zapovednogo Dela v SSSR*, 13–47. Moskva: Nauka.

Gestwa, K. 2005. Das Besitzergreifen von Natur Und Gesellschaft Im Stalinismus. *Saeculum* 56 (1): 105–138.

Glantz, M., ed. 1999. *Creeping Environmental Problems and Sustainable Development in the Aral Sea Basin*. Cambridge: Cambridge University Press. https://www.cambridge.org/core/books/creeping-environmental-problems-and-sustainable-development-in-the-aral-sea-basin/87385456B63B99DE479F8BACDF5BE383.

Goldman, M.I. 1972. *The Spoils of Progress: Environmental Pollution in the Soviet Union*. Cambridge, MA: MIT Press.

Gregory, P.R., and R.C. Stuart. 2000. *Russian and Soviet Economic Performance and Structure*. 7th ed. Boston: Prentice Hall.

Gunin, P.D., and V.N. Neronov. 1986. Ekologicheskie Printsipy Okhrany Genofonda I Problemy Organizatsii Monitoringa Opustynivania v Aridnoi Zone Azii. In *Itogi I Perspektivy Zapovednogo Dela v SSSR*. Moscow: Nauka.

Holloway, D. 1996. *Stalin and the Bomb: The Soviet Union and Atomic Energy, 1939–1956: Soviet Union and Atomic Energy, 1939–56*. New ed. New Haven, CT and London: Yale University Press UK SR.

Josephson, P. 2013. *An Environmental History of Russia*. Cambridge and New York: Cambridge University Press.

Kazakhmys, P.L.C. 2014. Proposed Transfer of Certain of the Company's Subsidiaries Owning Mature Assets. 23 March. https://www.kazminerals.com/media/2658/shareholder_circular_english_2014.pdf.

Khlevniuk, O.V. 2004. *The History of the Gulag: From Collectivization to the Great Terror*. New Haven, CT: Yale University Press.

Koch, N. 2016. Why No 'Water Wars' in Central Asia? Lessons Learned from the Aral Sea Disaster. *PONARS Eurasia*, Policy Memo.

Kozlova, M. 2006. Lake Balkhash's Disappearing Act: Is Central Asia's Second-Largest Lake Destined to Become Another Aral Sea? *Transitions Online*, December: 1–1.

Melnikov, D. 2016. From the Virgin Lands City to Astana: Toward the Afterlife of Soviet Utopia? Paper presented at the 17th Annual CESS Conference, 3–6 November.

Micklin, P.P. 1988. Desiccation of the Aral Sea: A Water Management Disaster in the Soviet Union. *Science* 241: 1170–1176.

Micklin, P. 2016. The Future Aral Sea: Hope and Despair. *Environmental Earth Sciences* 75 (9): 844.

Mirzabaev, A., M. Ahmed, J. Werner, John Pender, and Mounir Louhaichi. 2016. Rangelands of Central Asia: Challenges and Opportunities. *Journal of Arid Land* 8 (1): 93–108.

Mnatsakanian, R. 2002. *L'héritage écologique du communisme dans les Républiques de l'ex-URSS*. Paris: Editions Frison-Roche.

Moor-Stahl, J., and J. Allaman. 2000. *L'exception écologique russe: Systèmes et acteurs de 1917 à nos jours*. Paris: Editions L'Harmattan.

Narama, C., J. Kubota, V.I. Shatravin, M. Duishonakulov, G. Moholt, K. Abdrakhmanov, and Kicengge. 2010. The Lake-Level Changes in Central Asia during the Last 1000 Years Based on Historical Map. In *Reconceptualizing Cultural and Environmental Change in Central Asia: An [Sic] Historical Perspective on the Future*, ed. M. Watanabe and J. Kubota. Kyoto: RIHN. http://archives.chikyu.ac.jp/archives/AnnualReport/Viewer.do?prkbn=R&jekbn=E&id=49.

NASA. 2016. World of Change: Shrinking Aral Sea. Accessed 17 November. http://earthobservatory.nasa.gov/Features/WorldOfChange/aral_sea.php.

Nuklear Forum Schweiz. 2004. Lancement Du Projet France-Kazakhstan En Production D'uranium. NuklearForum Schweiz. http://www.nuklearforum.ch/fr/actualites/e-bulletin/production-duranium-nouvelle-collaboration-entre-la-france-et-le-kazakhstan.

———. 2009. Production D'uranium: Nouvelle Collaboration Entre La France et Le Kazakhstan. NuklearForum Schweiz. http://www.nuklearforum.ch/fr/actualites/e-bulletin/production-duranium-nouvelle-collaboration-entre-la-france-et-le-kazakhstan.

Obertreis, J. 2008. Der "Angriff Auf Die Wüste" in Zentralasien. Zur Umweltgeschichte Der Sowjetunion. *Osteuropa* 58 (4–5): 37–56.

Peck, A.E. 2003. *Economic Development in Kazakhstan: The Role of Large Enterprises and Foreign Investment.* London and New York: Routledge.

Penati, B. 2013. The Cotton Boom and the Land Tax in Russian Turkestan (1880s–1915). *Kritika: Explorations in Russian and Eurasian History* 14 (4): 741–774.

Prilutskaya, X. 2016. Juggling Risk: Lay Perceptions of Ecological and Health Risk in post-Soviet Industrial Temirtau. Master diss., Nazarbayev University, Astana.

Pryde, P. 2009. *Environmental Management in the Soviet Union.* Cambridge and New York: Cambridge University Press.

Purvis-Roberts, K.L., Cynthia A. Werner, and I. Frank. 2007. Perceived Risks from Radiation and Nuclear Testing Near Semipalatinsk, Kazakhstan: A Comparison between Physicians, Scientists, and the Public. *Risk Analysis* 27 (2): 291–302.

Reuters. 2012. KAZAKHSTAN: Copper Plant Tries to Reduce Pollution of Lake Balkhash. 20 June. http://www.itnsource.com/en/shotlist/RTV/2012/06/20/RTV1916312/?v=2.

Robinson, S., E.J. Milner-Gulland, and I. Alimaev. 2003. Rangeland Degradation in Kazakhstan during the Soviet Era: Re-Examining the Evidence. *Journal of Arid Environments* 53 (3): 419–439.

Schatz, E.A.D. 1999. Notes on the 'Dog That Didn't Bark': Eco-Internationalism in Late Soviet Kazakstan. *Ethnic and Racial Studies* 22 (1): 136–161.

Shapiro, J. 2001. *Mao's War against Nature: Politics and the Environment in Revolutionary China.* Cambridge and New York: Cambridge University Press.

Small, I., J. van der Meer, and R.E.G. Upshur. 2001. Acting on an Environmental Health Disaster: The Case of the Aral Sea. *Environmental Health Perspectives* 109 (6): 547–549.

Stawkowski, M.E. 2016. 'I Am a Radioactive Mutant': Emergent Biological Subjectivities at Kazakhstan's Semipalatinsk Nuclear Test Site. *American Ethnologist* 43 (1): 144–157.

Strategy 2050. 2016. Strategia Kazakhstan 2050—Ekologia. Accessed 7 December. http://strategy2050.kz/en/news/category/125/.

Synnott, M. 2015. Sins of the Aral Sea: For Millennia the Aral Sea Reigned as One of the Planet's Largest Inland Bodies of Water, Straddling What Is Now Kazakhstan and Uzbekistan. Today Its Decline Serves as a Cautionary Tale. *National Geographic* 227 (6): 114–131.

Uatkhanov, Y. 2016. Ulba Metallurgical Plant Leads in World Uranium Production. *The Astana Times*, 26 July. http://astanatimes.com/2016/07/ulba-metallurgical-plant-leads-in-world-uranium-production/.

Urankayeva, Z. 2016. Building Low Enriched Uranium Bank at Ulba Metallurgical Plant to Cost $150 Million. *The Astana Times*, 25 October. http://astanatimes.com/2016/10/building-low-enriched-uranium-bank-at-ulba-metallurgical-plant-to-cost-150-million/.

Werner, C., and K. Purvis-Roberts. 2006. After the Cold War: International Politics, Domestic Policy and the Nuclear Legacy in Kazakhstan. *Central Asian Survey* 25 (4): 461–480.

WNN. 2016. Kazakhstan Mulls Construction of Two Nuclear Plants. Accessed 6 December. http://www.world-nuclear-news.org/NP-Kazakhstan-mulls-construction-of-two-nuclear-plants-26011501.html.

Wojnowski, Z. 2016. De-Stalinization and the Failure of Soviet Identity Building in Kazakhstan. *Journal of Contemporary History* 52 (4): 999–1021.

CHAPTER 5

Trials and Tribulations: Kazakhstan's Criminal Justice Reforms

Alexei Trochev and Gavin Slade

Introduction

Many observers characterize Kazakhstan's political regime as soft authoritarianism (Matveeva 2009; Koch 2013; Omelicheva 2015) that relies more on the "means of persuasion than on the means of coercion, although coercion remains a part of the ruling elite's arsenal" (Schatz 2009: 203). Others view Kazakhstan's political regime as neopatrimonial noting that since gaining independence in 1991, Kazakhstan has been led by the same patronal network with President Nursultan Nazarbayev on top and maintained through exchanges of concrete benefits and punishments between him and his clients (Isaacs 2011; Olcott 2010; Laruelle 2012; Peyrouse 2012; Schiek and Hensell 2012; Hale 2015; Nurumov and Vashchanka 2016). In short, most researchers emphasize stability of political system that Nazarbayev has built through the skillful use of three mechanisms—coercion, persuasion and clientelistic bargaining. Criminal justice lies at the heart of these three mechanisms. It offers legal instruments of coercion through the imposition of criminal punishment. This is meted out through various mechanisms including the prison system. Criminal laws arguably

A. Trochev (✉) • G. Slade
Nazarbayev University, Astana, Kazakhstan
e-mail: atrochev@nu.edu.kz; gavin.slade@nu.edu.kz

J.-F. Caron (ed.), *Kazakhstan and the Soviet Legacy*,
https://doi.org/10.1007/978-981-13-6693-2_5

deter crime and disobedience by persuading people not to commit crimes while criminal procedure grants law-enforcement officials and attorneys persuasive powers over victims, witnesses, defendants and clients. Finally, criminal justice is a fertile environment for rent-seeking and patron-client bargaining through made-to-order prosecutions, exchanging compromising materials, selling sentences, shorter jail times and early releases from prisons, and distributing prestigious law-enforcement posts. As a result, reforming criminal justice is problematic in any political regime because it is a large bureaucracy consisting of competing interests and institutions, whose actions directly and frequently impact state-society relations.

Yet the Kazakhstani paradox is that criminal justice system is also a double-edged sword for Nazarbayev's regime. The criminal justice system can also damage this regime for the following reasons. It is unpopular among the elite and the public, as capital flight and public opinion, victimization and corruption surveys show. It is a poor feedback mechanism for the regime because it offers distorted information about actual crimes (Titaev et al. 2018; van Dijk et al. 2018) and it processes criminal cases instead of solving them and paying attention to crime victims (Trochev 2017). It weakens the legitimacy of the regime by generating hundreds of thousands of complaints to the president and international human rights watchdogs about police behavior, prison torture and unfair prosecutorial actions and court judgments every year. It fails to implement one of the key functions of law in authoritarian regimes—monitoring the discipline of lower-level government officials (Moustafa 2014)—who instead enjoy impunity for scandalous behavior through informal agreements or protections from their colleagues and cronies on top (Amnesty International 2016). Existing explanations of Nazarbayev's Kazakhstan tend to exaggerate the servility of the criminal justice system and tend to overlook the ability of the system to resist unfavorable reform proposals and its agility in transforming reforms to serve its own needs rather than the needs of regime.

In this chapter, we examine both continuity and change of these three mechanisms—coercion, persuasion and patron-client exchanges—by examining Kazakhstan's attempts at criminal justice reforms in the past two decades. We argue that the mix of Soviet legacies and post-communist incentives, which enable and disable reform ideas as various institutions debate them, explains why certain elements of criminal justice, such as pro-accusation bias, have persisted since Soviet times while others, such as high prison population rates, have disappeared. First, we define the two types of legacies of late Socialism—what we call fragmentation and embedded ways of thinking and behaving—that we observe in Kazakhstan's criminal justice system. Then, we analyze how each type of legacy shapes the performance of criminal justice agencies—police, state prosecutors, criminal judges and prisons—and their acceptance, ignorance or rejection of criminal justice reforms. Next, we explore how the interplay between these legacies and post-Soviet incentives perpetuates the dysfunctions of the criminal justice system in Kazakhstan. Finally, we explore how the Soviet legacy shapes interactions between citizens and police and argue that the public today is highly skeptical of the criminal justice system. We conclude with insights about the agency of criminal justice institutions in authoritarian neopatrimonial regimes.

Two Soviet Legacies as Relationships in Kazakhstan's Criminal Justice

Following Beissinger and Kotkin (2014: 11), we view Soviet legacies as long-term causal relationships between earlier Soviet institutions and practices and those of the present in the wake of the collapse of the USSR. This relationship-centered approach is helpful to explain mechanisms of coercion, persuasion and patron-client exchanges in today's criminal justice system in Kazakhstan. We emphasize the "Soviet" in order to separate them from pre-Soviet organizations, beliefs and practices, such as departmentalism, localism, corruption, eyewash and kinship, which have been existing in the steppe prior to the arrival of the Bolsheviks. We focus on two types of Soviet legacy relationships. The first one is legacy as fragmentation. This is how Soviet-era organizations, such as the GULAG system of punishment and law-enforcement agencies, remain as fragments. An example is the penal colony, a remnant of the Soviet era that still exists despite reformist intentions. Fragmentation is evidenced by cosmetic changes to formal rules and organizations as well as resistance of these Soviet-era organizations to serious reform. The second type of legacy is an embedded way of Soviet thinking and behaving. This type of legacy has a strong informal component and may be reflected in the agendas and practices of criminal justice actors. Evidence of this legacy includes pre-existing norms and relationships among these actors and between them and the public, such as the punitiveness assumed by the prison system, pro-accusation bias and ignorance of the victims in criminal proceedings, domination of police detectives and procurators over judges, telephone "justice" and over-reliance on quantitative indicators of law enforcers at the expense of actual concerns of citizens.

Soviet Legacy as Fragmentation in Kazakhstan's Criminal Justice

The first type of legacy as fragmentation refers to minimal changes in the work of formal organizations. As the breakup of Soviet Union in December 1991 took the leaders of the Kazakh SSR by surprise, the immediate choice of the Kazakhstani rulers was to keep the old guard in charge. They renamed "people's" courts into the "district" courts, removed the word "labor" from the title of penitentiary system in March 1995, renamed the KGB as the KNB in July 1992 and the *militsiia* into "police" in December 1998 (Beissinger and Kotkin 2014: 12). They also removed the word "socialist" that used to precede "legality". But the essential task of criminal judges and prison chiefs remained the same: to support police detectives and procuracy in their function of maintaining law and order (Trochev 2014).

The new law-enforcement agencies, prisons and courts of post-Soviet Kazakhstan were, in effect, the fragments of previous Soviet-era agencies and courts and closely resembled their predecessors. According to Snajdr (2006: 180–181), "even more than a decade after the transition from Soviet rule, the basic composition of Kazakhstan's Ministry of the Interior (MVD) has remained more or less intact". This means in essence a highly centralized Soviet-style police force, enforcing a Criminal Code from 1997 that had been modeled on Soviet-era criminal codes. When, in August 2018, President Nazarbayev demanded the drastic reform of police and threaten to purge it using the model of police reform in Saakashvili's Georgia, the MVD Minister responded by rejecting the purge and ordered to design a new police uniform. Similarly, according to Bastemiev (2009: 139), the author of the only monograph on the history of Kazakhstani penitential system, "nothing has changed … no new types of penitentiaries have been set up … no changes in structure, architecture and geographic location". Indeed, "penitentiary" is a misleading word—today penitentiaries are penal colonies built in the 1960s–1980s "in conditions of totalitarianism" (181). In an attempt to break away from this Soviet legacy, in 2004, President Nazarbayev transferred the prison system from the Ministry of Interior, which had supervised prisons since Soviet times, to the Justice Ministry. However, in 2011, after a series of prison riots and right after Kazakhstan's chairmanship of the Organization for Security and Co-operation in Europe (OSCE) had ended, the prison system was transferred back to the MVD under the pretext that the Justice Ministry was unable to maintain law and order in the penitentiaries.

The judiciary has been no different. As late Justice Minister Shaikenov complained in 2001, the courts of post-Soviet Kazakhstan have worked much worse than the Soviet-era judiciary (*ZonaKz.Net*, 19 March 2001) even though one US-based observer noted some positive changes (Davis 2002). As President Nazarbayev publicly admitted in 2015: "we need to get rid of the Soviet judicial system, we need to cultivate new judges" (*Strategy2050.KZ*, 6 March 2015) and complained as late as October 2018 that judges were still Soviet and lacked professionalism (*KazTAG*, 5 October 2018). Finally, the General Procuracy kept its Soviet-era investigatory, prosecutorial and general supervisory powers until the 1995 Constitution, which took away its pre-trial investigatory powers and transferred it to the newly created State Investigation Committee modeled after the US FBI. Once the drafting of the 1995 Constitution had been completed, President Nazarbayev received a letter from the General Procuracy of Russia with request not to reduce Procuracy's powers. He rejected this request (*ZonaKz.Net*, 19 March 2001) and ordered the creation of the separate State Investigation Committee, which took investigatory powers over grave crimes away from the KNB and MVD together with their best cadres. However, this Committee lasted only two years and was disbanded in November 1997 due to incessant efforts of the MVD, KNB and the Procuracy, which wanted their powers back and blamed the Committee for its inability to investigate crimes. Meanwhile, the Procuracy's power of general supervision of legality was abolished only in 2017.

The new office holders, trained in Soviet institutions, continued to occupy Soviet-era buildings, practiced Soviet-style recruitment and preserved the organizational inertia of late Socialism, perpetuating the legacy relationship in the form of fragmentation (Beissinger and Kotkin 2014: 13). This legacy has been especially strong in Kazakhstan's criminal justice system, where officials have gained a high degree of discretion once the supervision by the Communist Party and ideological monopoly had disappeared. Criminal justice officials glorify their Soviet-era accomplishments, performing Soviet-era roles and protecting their Soviet-era benefits. President Nazarbayev has the formal power of appointing and dismissing judges (except those on the Supreme Court), ministers and other senior government officials. He continued the Soviet practice of rotating senior law-enforcement officials across different ministries similar to other top officials (Siegel 2018) and of judicial chiefs across prestigious courts. Unlike Vladimir Putin in Russia, Nazarbayev chose not to recreate the myth of honorable, patriotic and fearless KGB officers and had 13 KNB chiefs between 1992 and 2018, with two of them convicted of grave crimes. In the same period, he had at least eight Chiefs of the Penitentiary System, ten Ministers of Internal Affairs, nine General Procurators and seven Supreme Court Chief Justices (see Tables 5.1 and 5.2).

Table 5.1 Career paths of the Chairs of the Supreme Court of Kazakhstan

Name	*Birthplace province*	*Supreme Court Chair*	*Prior Appellate Court Chair?*	*Prior work in the executive branch/ Presidential Administration?*	*Post-court career*
Tamas Aitmukhambetov	Astrakhan	1984–1993	No	No	Demoted to the diplomatic and educational jobs
Mikhail Malakhov	Kuibyshev	1994–1996	Yes	Yes	Dismissed on corruption charges, became a notary public in Astana
Maksut Narikbayev	Almaty	1996–2000	No	Yes	Demoted to educational job, Chair of the Higher Judicial Council (2003–2006), unsuccessfully ran in parliamentary elections in 2004 and 2007
Kairat Mami	Zhambyl	2000–2009	Yes	Yes	Rotated to Procurator General (2009–2011), Chair of the Senate (2011–2013), Supreme Court Chair (2013–2017)
Musabek Alimbekov	Zhambyl	2009–2011	Yes	No	Demoted to serve on the Court of Eurasian Economic Community (2011–2014), Karagandy Province Chair (2014–present), Chair of the Union of Judges (2016–present)
Bektas Beknazarov	Zhambyl	2011–2013	Yes	No	Demoted to be a Chair of the Higher Judicial Council (2013–2014), Vice-Chair of the Senate (2014–present)
Kairat Mami	Zhambyl	2013–2017	Yes	Yes	Rotated to Constitutional Council Chair (2018–present)
Zhakyp Asanov	Kyzyl-Orda	2017–present	No	Yes	

Table 5.2 Career paths of the Chairs of Province-Level Courts in Kazakhstan, 2017

Province	*Birthplace province/city*	*Current Chair appointed*	*Years on the bench prior to current appointment*	*Served as a Chair of a different Appellate Court/ Collegium? (period)*	*Served on the Supreme Court? (period)*
North Kazakhstan	Almaty City	06/2016	21	Yes (2010–2016)	No
Kostanay	Pavlodar	12/2015	12	Yes (2014–2015)	No
Atyrau	Almaty City	02/2015	19	Yes (2007–2014)	No
West Kazakhstan	South Kaz.	05/2014	20	Yes (2004–2014)	No
South Kazakhstan	Pavlodar	03/2012	17	Yes (2010–2012)	No
Akmola	Zhambyl	12/2013	16	Yes (2002–2005, 2009–2013)	Yes (2005–2009)
Mangistau	Atyrau	03/2015	21	Yes (1994–1999, 2006–2011)	Yes (2001–2006)
East Kazakhstan	Zhambyl	03/2015	26	Yes (2002–2015)	No
Aktobe	Semipalatinsk	06/2016	15	Yes (2005–2016)	No
Karaganda	Zhambyl	09/2014	32	Yes (1999–2006)	Yes (2006–2011)
Almaty Province	Almaty	12/2013	16	Yes (2007–2013)	No
Pavlodar	Almaty	02/2015	20	Yes (1995–2014)	No
Almaty City[a]	South Kaz.	12/2013	27	Yes (1992–2005, 2009–2013)	Yes (2005–2009)
Zhambyl	Almaty City	02/2015	11	Yes (2012–2014)	No
Kyzyl-Orda	East Kaz.	07/2012	12	Yes (2009–2012)	No
Astana City	Almaty	12/2013	21	Yes (1999–2013)	No

[a]Chair of the Almaty City Court passed away in May 2017

Soviet Legacy as Thinking and Behaving, Soviet Style, in Kazakhstan's Criminal Justice

One would expect that legacy as fragmentation would disappear once the old guard leaves the criminal justice system and society goes through generational change. However, another type of legacy—embedded ways of thinking and behaving Soviet style—has remained strong despite the shocks of new statehood, the introduction of a market economy, rejection of official ideology and Kazakhisation of the new state apparatus (Karin and Chebotarev 2002). In this section, we aim to show how the institutions of justice are still structured in a Soviet-style way such that criminal justice actors lack incentives to change embedded ways of thinking and behaving. We first look at pro-accusation bias among judges, police and prosecutors. We then discuss the issue of improper and informal influence before examining changes to the system of punishment.

Judges, for example, despite constitutional promises of the separation of powers and judicial independence, are part and parcel of the law-enforcement world both in practice and in the view of the public. Police detectives still torture suspects to obtain confessions of guilt, as in the Soviet era, in this way reporting back high clearance rates for grave crimes. For minor crimes, the police began to register most reported offenses only once they stopped using the clearance rate for minor crimes as a key performance indicator in 2012. State prosecutors are also motivated by Soviet-era quantitative performance indicators and still view denials of arrests and court acquittals as unacceptable failures (Titaev et al. 2018). They do their best to overturn acquittals on appeal and often succeed. Appellate judges overturn a much higher proportion of acquittals than convictions and themselves acquit a very small number of defendants. The message to the trial-level judges has been clear: convict or have your Soviet-era indicator of "stability of sentences" lowered, with subsequent disciplining by the court chair (Trochev 2014). The pro-accusation bias of judges is evident in the wholesale approval by judges of pre-trial detention requests, in the less than 1% rate of acquittals and of acquitted and exonerated defendants, and in the resistance to the expansion—ordered by President Nazarbayev in 2015—of the jury trial courts, which acquit much more often than ordinary courts (Titaev et al. 2018; Trochev 2017).

Meanwhile, the so-called practice of telephone justice—a Soviet-era practice of telephoning police chiefs, prosecutors and judges with orders or requests of making favorable legal decisions—has also been proliferating.

While in the Soviet period it was the Communist party officials who made these orders and requests, in the post-Soviet period this can be any elite person outside the judicial branch. Unlike measuring the pro-accusation bias described above, studying this informal practice systematically is difficult. A strong public perception that this practice is growing may be more important than the phone calls themselves. As Table 5.3 shows, in the World Justice Project Rule of Law Index the "improper government influence" score for Kazakhstan has been the worst among all criminal justice indicators between 2014 and 2017. President Nazarbayev told the 2016 Congress of Judges that he knew about cases of improper interference in the administration of justice, but he did not name the perpetrators. Instead he proposed to announce their names publicly in order to shame them in front of the entire nation (*Kapital.Kz,* 21 November 2016). In August 2017, Nazarbayev announced that he wanted courts in which litigants would receive a "fair judicial decision without a telephone call, without any interference", as in the courts of Germany, France and Great Britain (*KazInform*, 21 August 2017). Meanwhile, the Freedom House *Nations in Transit* rated Kazakhstan as lacking independent courts (see Table 5.4).

Prisons are, in effect, still governed by the Soviet-era practices through secrecy, fear and violence by the prison guards and among inmates. The collapse of the Soviet Union did not see a decrease in the use of incarceration as a form of punishment. Despite state weakness, high crime rates and impoverishment in the 1990s contributed to increasing prison rates across the former Soviet region. Unexpectedly, after 2000, prison rates started to decline across the region. This decline was notable in Kazakhstan. The trends in prison rates are shown in Fig. 5.1.

As can be seen in Fig. 5.1, from 2000 onward Kazakhstan, along with a number of other former Soviet countries, has gone against the trend of the 1990s. By the year 2000, it was fully expected that the countries of the former Soviet Union would continue to incarcerate more people proportionately than other countries in Europe and Asia. Soviet legacies were considered to weigh heavily as a major obstacle to removing the centrality of the prison as the most common form of punishment in the region. King and Piacentini (2005) as well as Christie (2000) argued that inertial pressures within the penal systems of the countries of the former Soviet Union would make decarceration unlikely. One such legacy was a penal culture, developed during Soviet times, which placed labor colonies as a central part of economic and social progress on the Soviet route to modernity (Kharkhordin 1999; Viola 2007; Barnes 2011). Moreover, the administrative structure and tradition of prison departments, usually attached to

Table 5.3 Criminal justice indicators in the Rule of Law Index for Kazakhstan, 2014–2017

Year	*No corruption in the judiciary*	*Effective investigations*	*Timely and effective adjudication*	*Effective correctional system*	*No discrimination*	*No corruption*	*No improper gov. influence*	*Due process of law*
2014	0.40	0.38	0.56	0.48	0.24	0.45	0.29	0.45
2015	0.39	0.48	0.64	0.38	0.28	0.46	0.26	0.44
2016	0.41	0.40	0.64	0.37	0.30	0.41	0.28	0.44
2017	0.48	0.39	0.61	0.40	0.29	0.47	0.28	0.44

Source: World Justice Project (2018)

0 = No rule of law; 1 = rule of law

Table 5.4 Judicial framework and independence in Kazakhstan, 1999–2018

Year	*'99–2000*	*'01*	*'02*	*'03*	*'04*	*'05*	*'06*	*'07*	*'08*	*'09*	*'10*	*'11*	*'12–17*	*'18*
Score	5.5	5.75	6	6.25	6.25	6.25	6.25	6.25	6.25	6	6.25	6.25	6.5	6.75

Source: Freedom House (2018)

1 = independent judiciary; 7 = no independent judiciary

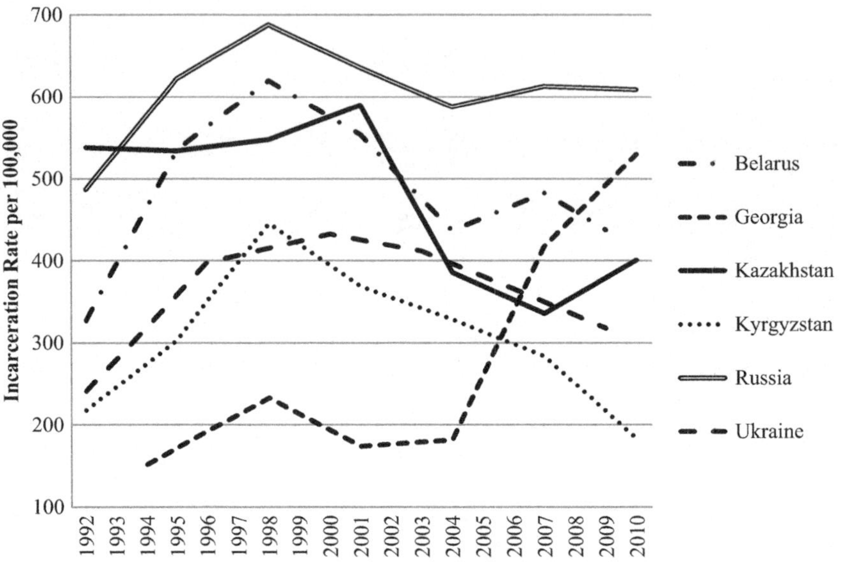

Fig. 5.1 Incarceration rates in selected post-Soviet countries, 1992–2010. Source: International Centre for Prison Studies

the Ministry of the Interior, as well as prisons themselves, were designed for a large prison population. Reform of these structures would mean downsizing and redundancies. The Soviet penal system had been designed for production and could still be used to exploit cheap labor; continuing such exploitation might be tempting for cash-strapped post-Soviet governments. Finally, these governments also lacked resources to make substantive reforms to penal institutions; prisons were often low down the list of priorities. As Piacentini and Slade (2015) argue, there was a capacious perception of incarceration as more than just punishment but an integral part of solving the moral, economic and social woes of former Soviet countries. This had become manifested in the culture, traditions and structure of prisons and prison departments themselves.

In terms of the legacies just outlined, Kazakhstan had a bigger obstacle to overcome than most. The country was presented with the biggest penal inheritance of all the former Soviet republics other than Russia. Kazakhstan had been one of the major sites for the Gulag labor camps along with Siberia and the northern Ural mountains. The Kazakh government upon independence had huge amounts of penal space at its disposal and high numbers of prisoners working in labor colonies. By the end of the 1980s there were 91 penal institutions in the country containing roughly 100,000 people (Posmakov 2001). The Soviet government occasionally attempted to decrease the numbers of prisoners but this was done through amnesties, such as in 1987 to mark the 70th anniversary of the October Revolution when 7000 people were released from Kazakh colonies. Despite this, Kazakhstan maintained the highest rates of incarceration in the Soviet Union, excluding Russia. At the beginning of the 1990s, of 700,000 prisoners in the collapsing Soviet Union, 100,000 were in Kazakhstan, with prisoners from all over the Union. Numbers did not reduce with the collapse of the Soviet Union. The number of people incarcerated in Kazakhstan for the period 1976–1985 was the same as for the period 1986–2000. In both periods, every 18th person between the ages of 18 and 50 had spent time in prison (Posmakov 2001:10).

Around the year 2000, incarceration rates in Kazakhstan started to decline. In 2000 there were 520 prisoners per 100,000 of the population; by 2014 this stood at 289, a 45% decrease; and by 2018, this declined even further to 189. Whereas in much of the post-Soviet space declines in prison populations can occur through amnesties which powerfully express state power to enact "commanded forgetting" (McEvoy and Mallinder 2012) and enable state-society bargaining in undemocratic regimes, Kazakhstan has eventually eschewed the use of amnesty. Instead, the decreases are part of a concerted policy to institutionalize the reduction of the prison population through consistent non-custodial sentencing and the development of and investments in viable alternatives to prison.

There are specific reasons for this move away from the use of prison as a form of punishment. In response to pressures from above, in 2013, the General Prosecutor's office set out ten steps to reduce the prison population, based, in the words of the General Prosecutor himself, "on the advanced standards and innovations, successfully applied in countries abroad" (Daulbayev 2016: 18). Humanization is rarely mentioned as an incentive in and of itself for reducing the use of imprisonment. Reading policy documents and analyzing the official forum discussions that took place among the top civil servants in charge of this process, two rationales are clear: an economic rationale, and a performative rationale. In terms of the economic rationale, there was clearly an incentive not to exclude large numbers of potentially productive workers in decrepit colonies that no longer played a role in Kazakhstan's modernizing economy. The economy and productivity had been growing quickly since 2000. As the General Prosecutor put it, a lack of penal reform had created "an unjustifiable increase in expenditure" (Daulbayev 2016: 19). The political economic theory of punishment suggests that where economic conditions improve, exclusionary and highly punitive policies are resisted—Kazakhstan's decarceration drive provides support for this theory.

Yet, there is also a performative element to this—the "10 steps to reduce the prison population" policy is largely based on Kazakhstan's image as a "normal" country for investment and anxiety about the incarceration rate league table itself. This is in line with Heathershaw's (2014) argument that Central Asian states are "global performance states" which act out their legitimacy through participating in international networks and systems of rankings. As Daulbayev argued: "completing these measures will allow us to take our country out of the top 50 leading countries by incarceration ... and in the long term to compare with indicators from advanced European countries (the UK 101th [place in the world], Portugal 111th, Italy 139th)... a low prison rate will bring about not only a smaller budget expenditure, but show the effectiveness of criminal justice, the security of society, and the investment attractiveness of the state" (Daulbayev 2016:20). Human rights turn out to be an unintended consequence of the quest for foreign direct investment and healthier state budgets (Posmakov 2002).

Despite these important reforms to the overall quantity of prisoners in Kazakhstan, the quality of the prisons for the prisoners that remain is still marked by legacies of the Soviet past. Kazakhstan's places of detention are run overwhelmingly as Soviet-style penal colonies. As such, prisoners live and work communally. Prisoners are held in barracks that are split up into local sectors and further into prisoner "detachment". Each detachment in Soviet times worked together, and they were collectively responsible for the productive output. Today, the word is still used to denote a group of prisoners living together in dormitories in a sector. Sectors are staffed by the "head of detachment" who is responsible for oversight and order as well as educational and rehabilitative work. Overall order in a colony is still maintained through Soviet-style institutions. Most important of these from the perspective of order is the use of the operative section in prisons to gather information. This is done through the recruitment of prisoner-informants and the transmission of information about what is happening in colonies through networks of these informants. The reliance on such networks is in large part due to a lack of staff inside the colonies. Instead officers patrol prison walls, their main duty being to prevent escape.

As staff are untrusted information and monitoring, vital to good order, relies on the secretive networks of the operative sector. What this also means is that the colonies remain an extension of law enforcement. Prisoners are pressured to provide not only information about infractions and crimes committed inside the prison but evidence concerning unsolved crimes outside it. Staff employed to provide rehabilitative services are undermined by competing objectives. Only two out of three positions of prison doctors had been filled in 2018, and the numbers of psychologists and social workers were also minimal. For example, there are around 300 prisoners for one psychologist. The concept of rehabilitation then, while commonly used in reformist circles, remains far from the agenda.

Inside the penal colonies, the old prisoner subculture that arose in Soviet times, often referred to as the *vorovskoi mir* or thieves' world, still exists. Prisoners produce self-governance, collecting and redistributing resources, operating a black market for various goods and producing collective forms of decision-making, conflict resolution and protection. A status hierarchy is also maintained and policed by prisoners themselves. The connection of this subculture to elements of organized crime such as forced gambling for the purposes of organized extortion, drug dealing and racketeering makes it an object of government intervention. As mentioned above, in 2011, the prison system was moved back from the Ministry of Justice, where it had been since 2004, to under the Ministry of Interior. The change in administration served to make prisons more securitized and lower the influence of the prisoner subculture. However, since 2011 a new form of security threat emerged in the form of religious radicalization in prisons. This problem was to some degree created and exacerbated by the Soviet-style procedural, administrative and architectural structuring of the penal colonies. This is manifested most overtly by the lack of staff control inside the colonies, the deliberate sowing of distrust among prisoners by prison administrations and the communal living that produces prisoner monitoring, control and influence over one.

A final factor that may be seen as contributing to the maintenance of the prison subculture and the problem of radicalization in prison is the use of violence and torture from the side of prison administrations. While not specifically a Soviet legacy, this type of violence is structured by the remnants of Soviet prison management and staff subculture. Hundreds of cases of torture are reported each year. Since changes in the law to ensure the police register reported crime in 2012, the numbers of known cases of torture increased. In 2014, they reached a peak of 1282 for the year. An analysis of 475 cases of torture in the half year between June 2015 and 2016 revealed that within the criminal justice system police cells and remand prisons had the highest levels of complaints of torture (Prosecutor's Office of Kazakhstan 2017). This can be explained by a policing system that relies on confessions to clear cases, as explained above. Cases within the post-conviction prison system were fewer. This may be due to a lack of reporting in these closed institutions and the use of the informal prisoner hierarchies to do the work of maintaining prison order including the use of violence. The "culture of impunity" (Amnesty International 2016) for torturers continues to undermine the operation of the penal system, producing an "us versus them" culture within prisons that empowers alternative sources of power, whether radical extremists or organized criminals. President Nazarbayev called for further reduction of the prison population and admitted that Soviet-style prisons hurt the legitimacy of his regime in November 2018: "As well all know, a normal person does not come out of [prison]. There we are not cultivating a [human being], to the contrary we are pushing a person to the other side" (*Zakon.Kz*, 28 November 2018).

Mixing New and Old Incentives to Resist Criminal Justice Reform

The post-communist transformation added new incentives to those already discussed in relationship to Soviet legacies. For the top law-enforcement officials the display of loyalty both formally and informally to President Nazarbayev has been the key to preserving their place at the top and the ability to build their own clientelist subnetworks. For example, in 2005, the Supreme Court arranged a meeting of the Congress of Judges, which President Nazarbayev had opened. The Congress declared that all judges had to carry out the directives which president had outlined in his annual State of the Union address. As in pre-Soviet times and the Soviet period, top law-enforcement officials compete for the favor of the leader among themselves preparing for him compromising materials against each other and engaging in what experts called "bulldog fights under the carpet" (Satpayev 2008). Scholars often portray Nazarbayev as a respected referee in these rivalries (Junisbai 2010). Even though he has been continuing the Soviet practice of rotating top-level officials, some of them—through loyalty—managed to stay in their positions for unusually long periods of time like Minister of Internal Affairs Kassymov who has been in office since April 2011 until February 2019. Keep in mind that Nazarbayev allowed the rotated top officials to bring along their own loyal subordinates to the new posts, thus making loyalty to the superiors a litmus test for career protection through all rungs of the criminal justice.

If in the Soviet era key local actors could exploit tension between the Communist Party leaders in Moscow and Almaty (Gleason 1991), the previous capital city, today there is only one power center located in the Akorda—the seat of the Kazakhstani president in the 20-year-old capital city of Astana. In exchange for public and private displays of loyalty, top officials obtain broad powers, a large degree of discretion in exercising them and political protection that allows abusing them. These public displays of loyalty to Nazarbayev help even those who had appeared to have fallen out of favor with the president (see Table 5.5). For example, in December 2015, the former Prime Minister Serik Akhmetov was tried together with 20 accomplices for multiple corruption-related offenses. In his final word in the courtroom he publicly asked President Nazarbayev for forgiveness. Akhmetov paid out 2.2 bln tenge compensation and initially received a ten-year prison sentence. However, due to an amnesty, he was released from prison in September 2017, which meant that in effect he had spent in confinement less than two years.

For the lower-level law-enforcement officials and judges the key need is to protect one's career on the bench, as the job of a prosecutor and a judge is better paid, more prestigious and attracts more applicants. Unlike in the socialist period when judges often switched between professions, generous salaries and retirement benefits of post-communist judges are too attractive for them to change their careers. Judges who often disagree with state prosecutors over detention or conviction are blamed for incompetence, suspicious leniency and selling judicial decisions to the accused, all of which are bases for potential dismissal and criminal charges from the very same state prosecutors. Facing widespread general public distrust in the police and judiciary, politicians' haste to blame someone else for corruption and the media's sensationalism over judicial bribery, recalcitrant judges have nowhere to turn for protection against unfounded accusations. Appellate judges, who preserved their power to overturn acquittals thanks to the massive lobbying efforts of law-enforcement elites, will not praise judges who acquit or portray them as heroes protecting judicial independence. As

Table 5.5 Apologies to President Nazarbayev in Criminal Trials, 2011–2018

Name of apologizer	*Post*	*Charges*	*Date of sentence*	*Sentence*	*Outcome*
Doskaliyev	Minister of Healthcare	Bribery 673 mln tenge	August 2011	7 years in prison	Pardoned by president and released in March 2012
Baimaganbetov	Chief of Customs Committee	Bribery 80,000 USD	January 2013	10 years in prison	Released in February 2015
Aryn	Governor of Pavlodar Province	Bribery 7.5 mln tenge	November 2014	3 years of conditional imprisonment	Appointed to lead the Institute of Spiritual Renewal at the Eurasian National University in March 2018
Ospanov	Chief of the Anti-Monopoly Agency	Bribery 300,000 USD	February 2015	Fine 6 mln USD	Paid in October 2015
Abdishev	Governor of Karagandy Province	Abuse of office and illegal business	December 2015	5 years in prison	Reduced to 3 years on appeal and released in May 2016
Akhmetov	Prime-Minister	Bribery and abuse of office	December 2015	10 years in prison	Reduced to 8 years on appeal and released in September 2017
Bishimbayev	Minister of Economy	Bribery 293,000 USD	March 2018	10 years in prison	

a result, trial judges engage in risk-averse behavior by strengthening their already existing relationships, loyalties and friendships with state prosecutors and appellate judges. Court chairs, who began their careers in the USSR and remain important figures in the judicial system (see Table 5.4), tend to recruit judicial candidates from the pool of trusted court clerks and judges' assistants—insiders in the judicial system who are already imbued with a sense of conformity to the orders of judicial bosses and state prosecutors in criminal proceedings. In short, as one judicial chief in the Karagandy province told her judges to contribute to the country's global performance: "How do we evaluate the work of a court? If the court is quiet in public, if it does not cause us any problems, then, [the court] is working well" (*Zerkalo*, 23 July 2018).

In contrast, the job of a rank-and-file police officer and prison guard is much less prestigious, and the regime has trouble filling the low-level vacancies in police and finding guards for 69 penal colonies and 17 jails. In 2016, the starting salary of traffic police was 60,000 tenge per month, while that of precinct officers was 140,000 tenge per month, as compared to a monthly salary of 200,000 tenge that district judges begin their career on the bench with. As result of low pay and difficult working conditions, police chiefs estimated that in 2016 between 6000 and 6,500 police officers quit or have been let go from their jobs. The starting salary of a prison guard in 2018 was still below 100,000 tenge and even less for civilians working in prisons. Low salaries and lots of overtime work contribute to the willingness to engage in abuse of office and corruption. Moreover, as with judges and prosecutors, the work of police and prison guards is still evaluated on the basis of Soviet-era quantitative indicators, such as the crime rate and clearance rate of crimes as compared to the previous year (Titaev et al. 2018). And this goes on despite President Nazarbayev's demand made at the 2016 Congress of Judges that the work of judges "should not be tied to quantitative indicators and statistics" (*KazInform*, 21 November 2016).

Yet the volume of reporting paperwork in the criminal justice system has increased dramatically from the 1980s, as the leadership of the country insisted on knowing what lower-level officials are doing on the job. Relying on the old practices of eyewashing and falsifying official documents, criminal justice officials have been reporting strong records of achievements every year, thus distorting the information about actual crime levels in the country. Officially, crime rate grew from 198 per 10,000 population in 2014 to 221 in 2015 and then fell to 203 in 2016 to 175 in 2017 and to 159 in 2018. Yet many distrusted these statistics produced by the MVD. For example, the Procurator General publicly announced in 2016 that he did not trust data on economic crimes and accused law-enforcement officials of faking criminal prosecution of businesses in order to extort money from them in return for dropping criminal charges against them. In 2017, the Procuracy announced that police lost 3500 criminal case files between 2015 and 2017. While the top clearly distrusts the street-level criminal justice officials, it lacks any other source of information outside the state apparatus. Competition among the law-enforcement agencies further generates distrust horizontally within the criminal justice system, which sometimes spills into mass media. Media leaks are now used by the rival law enforcers to leak compromising materials against each other, something that did not exist under the total censorship of the Soviet period. This distrust in official statistics made President Nazarbayev finally announce at the end of 2018 that he would use public trust in courts and other law-enforcement agencies as the main indicator for evaluating their performance.

The Soviet Legacy in Citizen-State Interactions in Kazakhstan's Criminal Justice

Criminal justice is a key site of citizen-state interaction. In Kazakhstan, similar to Soviet times ordinary citizens display an attitude of mistrust and avoidant behavior toward criminal justice institutions and actors. The police try in vain to enlist volunteer assistants while court chairs frequently complain that citizens refuse to show up for jury duty. A 2018 International Crime Victims Survey (ICVS) of 4000 Kazakhstanis, which was conducted shortly before the murder of the Olympic figure skater Denis Ten in Almaty, revealed 60% of people claimed to trust the police. This is low by world standards, but higher than some might have predicted. Yet, this figure is also contradicted by the behavior of crime victims toward criminal justice institutions. The survey found that only one out five crime victims actually reported crimes to police (Van Dijk et al. 2018). This level of reporting is very low by world standards, though in line with the post-Soviet region. Moreover, those who report crime are highly dissatisfied with the work of the police. Only a third of those who had reported were satisfied with the way police treated them. Of those who had experienced and reported a theft from their car in Kazakhstan only 26% were satisfied or very satisfied with the work of the police. This is a lot lower than most countries in Western Europe, where satisfaction with the police for this sort of crime is 50% and higher. It is low even for the former Soviet Union. These statistics persist even though Kazakhstan has drastically expanded the use of reconciliation between crime victims and defendants prior to and during trials. Kazakhstani prosecutors and judges close more criminal cases on this basis than they send cases to trial and issue sentences (Trochev 2017). In theory, if reconciliation is a victim-centered process, crime victims would be more satisfied with the outcome because they could demand faster and fuller compensation in informal settings, which they could control. But in practice, criminal justice professionals have bureaucratic priorities in mind and often help the defendants rather than victims in order to process criminal cases faster with little concern for a victim's well-being (Trochev 2017).

According to a survey of 1600 Kazakhstanis conducted in 2014, only one out of five respondents said that she or he had a duty to stop a violation of public order, only one out of four personally knew their precinct police officer, only a half of respondents expressed readiness to help police fight crime, and among those only a quarter expressed readiness to be a witness in a criminal case (*ZonaKz.Net*, 21 November 2016). This survey also found that the key barriers to people's cooperation with police were specific to criminal justice: 38% of respondents did not wish to serve as a witness, 29% did not trust the police and 23% were afraid of being labeled "stukach" or snitch—a derogatory nickname for a police informer that had been inherited from the criminal world of the Soviet period. This labeling barrier was the highest among young Kazakhstanis (18–24 and 35–44 years old), indicating the strength of Soviet-style thinking and behaving among people who were born after the collapse of the USSR (*ZonaKz.Net*, 21 November 2016). Indeed, this fear of being shamed for cooperation with police goes hand in hand with the romanticization of the criminal underworld and popularity of gang culture as well as the recent growth in crime and conviction rates among juveniles, who tend to commit crimes in groups (*Aktobe Times*, 15 December 2017; *Rezonans*, 21 February 2018; *Ustinka*, 26 June 2018; *Altyn-orda.kz*, 30 October 2018). The UNICEF-sponsored survey of 1358 students in 40 secondary schools from four regions of the country that was conducted in 2012 confirmed that schoolchildren used the term "stukach" in a variety of violent activities among their peers (UNICEF Kazakhstan 2013: 46).

Thus, skepticism and distrust of law enforcement, partly a legacy of Soviet regime–policing rather than citizen-oriented policing (Shelley 1999; Marat 2018), are still present. A recent nationally representative household survey (National Analytical Center 2018) of 3000 persons aimed to understand the interaction between police and citizens. Since 2014, the Kazakhstani government has promoted a policy of "zero tolerance" to petty crime which involves encouraging citizens to work with police in reporting anti-social behavior. Elements of the campaign are reminiscent of Soviet policies that pushed citizens to report on each other (LaPierre 2012). Due to such policies, Soviet citizens attempted to prevent forms of snitching and collaboration with the authorities through informal pressure that included ostracism. For example, if anyone with a history of snitching went to prison they would be demoted down the informal prison hierarchy and suffer worse conditions than those with no history of snitching. The NAC survey included questions on attitudes to "snitching" today in

Kazakhstan and reasons for non-collaboration with the police. The survey finds that 45% of respondents mention a perception of their fellow citizens as simply apathetic to the hassle of providing help to the police in their top three answers as to why people do not help the police. A further 44% cite a perception that their fellow citizens do not trust the police enough to help them in their top three. Moreover, 39% think fear of revenge from the side of the lawbreaker is a top three reason for not helping the police. Around 16% named a fear of being known as a "snitch" as one of the main three reasons people in Kazakhstan might not go to the police and 30% of people said that reporting crime to the police is not approved of or respected in their area of residence. These results suggest a continuing distance and distrust, framed in a distinctly Soviet idiom, between police and the citizens they are supposed to serve. In August 2018, President Nazarbayev aptly summed up this this relationship when he publicly asked: "A police officer abroad is a friend but who is our police officer?"

Conclusion

Kazakhstani criminal justice system is in many ways different from the late Soviet era. Yet Soviet legacies of fragmentation and the embedded ways of thinking and behaving, Soviet style, still shape these differences in both the tempo and substance of criminal justice reforms and formal and informal performance of criminal justice actors. Clearly, these actors have agency and are strong enough to modify and resist reform proposals announced by President Nazarbayev and even engage in counter-reforms that reverse his initiatives. Concerned with building his own legacy, Nazarbayev openly admits mistakes in his earlier choices of not purging the law-enforcement apparatus, repeats his dissatisfaction with the current state of the criminal justice system and insists on its radical overhaul using public trust rather than bureaucratic performance indicators as criteria of successful reforms. Yet he is clearly constrained by the system, which is built on Soviet-era law-enforcement institutions and ways of thinking and behaving. We have explored how these formal institutions and informal norms and practices constrain the powerful and popular president and delegitimize his regime, contrary to what scholars of law and courts of authoritarianism usually argue about their contribution to legitimacy and bureaucratic discipline (Ginsburg and Moustafa 2008). While legacies and patron-client regimes usually imply stability and continuity, we have shown that they may produce dynamic relationships among criminal justice actors who set their own priorities and act on incentives structured by both Soviet legacies and post-Soviet realities under the broad cover of displays of loyalty to President Nazarbayev. As a result, criminal justice reforms in authoritarian regimes must be analyzed on the subnational level, as one police precinct or a court or a prison may be different from another. As we have shown, the view of reforms from the top is very different from the view from the bottom, and further research on the ground is needed to shed light on how and why exactly some reforms are accepted, while others are ignored yet others are rejected.

References

Amnesty International. 2016. *Dead End Justice: Impunity for Torture in Kazakhstan*. London: Amnesty International.

Barnes, S. 2011. *Death and Redemption: The Gulag and the Shaping of Soviet Society*. Princeton, NJ: Princeton University Press.

Bastemiev, S.K. 2009. *Ispravitelnye uchrezhdeniia Kazakhstana: istorichesko-pravovoi aspekt*. Pavlodar: Kereku.

Christie, N. 2000. Dangerous States. In *Dangerous Offenders*, ed. Mark Brown and John Pratt. London: Routledge.

Daulbayev, A. 2016. *10 Steps to Reducing the Prison Population: Address to the Prison Forum of Kazakhstan*. Astana: General Prosecutor's Office.

Davis, K. 2002. Purging the System: Recent Judicial Reform in Kazakhstan. *University of California Davis Journal of International Law and Policy* 8 (1): 255–273.

Freedom House. 2018. *Nations in Transit 2018: Kazakhstan*. Washington, DC: Freedom House.

Ginsburg, T., and T. Moustafa. 2008. Introduction: The Functions of Courts in Authoritarian Politics. In *Rule by Law: The Politics of Courts in Authoritarian Regimes*, ed. T. Ginsburg and T. Moustafa. New York: Cambridge University Press.

Gleason, G. 1991. Fealty and Loyalty: Informal Authority Structures in Soviet Asia. *Soviet Studies* 43 (4): 613–628.

Hale, H. 2015. *Patronal Politics: Eurasian Regime Dynamics in Comparative Perspective*. New York: Cambridge University Press.

Heathershaw, J. 2014. The Global Performance State: A Reconsideration of the Central Asian 'Weak State'. In *Ethnographies of the State in Central Asia: Performing Politics*, ed. J. Rasanayagam. Bloomington, IN: Indiana University Press.

Isaacs, R. 2011. *Party System Formation in Kazakhstan: Between Formal and Informal Politics*. London: Routledge.

Junisbai, B. 2010. A Tale of Two Kazakhstans: Sources of Political Cleavage and Conflict in the post-Soviet Period. *Europe-Asia Studies* 62 (2): 235–269.

Karin, E., and A. Chebotarev. 2002. The Policy of Kazakhization in State and Government Institutions in Kazakhstan. In *The Nationalities Question in post-Soviet Kazakhstan*, ed. Oka Natsuko. Chiba, Japan: IDE-JETRO.

Kharkhordin, O. 1999. *The Collective and the Individual in Russia: A Study of Practices.* Oakland, CA: University of California Press.

King, R., and L. Piacentini. 2005. The Russian Correctional System During the Transition. In *Ruling Russia: Law, Crime, and Justice in a Changing Society*, ed. W.A. Pridemore. Lanham, MD: Rowman & Littlefield Publishers.

Koch, N. 2013. Sport and Soft Authoritarian Nation-Building. *Political Geography* 32): 42–51.

Kotkin, S., and M.R. Beissinger. 2014. Historical Legacies of Communism: An Empirical Agenda. In *Historical Legacies of Communism in Russia and Eastern Europe*, ed. M.R. Beissinger. New York: Cambridge University Press.

LaPierre, B. 2012. *Hooligans in Khrushchev's Russia: Defining, Policing, and Producing Deviance during the Thaw*. Madison: University of Wisconsin Press.

Laruelle, M. 2012. Discussing Neopatrimonialism and Patronal Presidentialism in the Central Asian Context. *Demokratizatsiya: The Journal of Post-Soviet Democratization* 20 (4): 301–324.

Marat, E. 2018. *The Politics of Police Reform: Society Against the State in Post-Soviet Countries.* New York: Oxford University Press.

Matveeva, A. 2009. Legitimising Central Asian Authoritarianism: Political Manipulation and Symbolic Power. *Europe-Asia Studies* 61 (7): 1095–1121.

McEvoy, K., and L. Mallinder. 2012. Amnesties in Transition: Punishment, Restoration, and the Governance of Mercy. *Journal of Law and Society* 39 (3): 410–440.

Moustafa, T. 2014. Law and Courts in Authoritarian Regimes. *Annual Review of Law and Social Science* 10: 281–299.

National Analytical Center. 2018. *Attitudes to Criminal Justice in Kazakhstan.* Astana: NAC. On file with authors.

Nurumov, D., and V. Vashchanka. 2016. Constitutional Development of Independent Kazakhstan. In *Semi-Presidentialism in the Caucasus and Central Asia*, ed. R. Elgie and S. Moestrup. London: Palgrave Macmillan.

Olcott, M. 2010. *Kazakhstan: Unfulfilled Promise?* Washington, DC: Carnegie Endowment for International Peace.

Omelicheva, M. 2015. *Democracy in Central Asia: Competing Perspectives and Alternative Strategies.* Lexington, KY: University Press of Kentucky.

Peyrouse, S. 2012. The Kazakh Neopatrimonial Regime: Balancing Uncertainties Among the "Family" Oligarchs and Technocrats. *Demokratizatsiya: The Journal of Post-Soviet Democratization* 20 (4): 345–370.

Piacentini, L., and G. Slade. 2015. Architecture and Attachment: Carceral Collectivism and the Problem of Prison Reform in Russia and Georgia. *Theoretical Criminology* 19 (2): 179–197.

Posmakov, P. 2001. *Prison Syndrome*. Baspa: Almaty.

———. 2002. From a Totalitarian Prison System in Kazakhstan to a System Based on Human Rights. *Corrections Today* 64 (1): 58–63.

Prosecutor's Office of Kazakhstan. 2017. *Report on the Results of Research into Cases of Torture*. Astana: General Prosecutor's Office.

Satpayev, D. 2008. Under the Carpet Bulldog Fighting in *Excluziv.kz*. Accessed 13 December 2018. http://www.exclusive.kz/expertiza/antresoli/11045/.

Schatz, E. 2009. The Soft Authoritarian Tool Kit: Agenda-Setting Power in Kazakhstan and Kyrgyzstan. *Comparative Politics* 41 (2): 203–222.

Schiek, S., and S. Hensell. 2012. The 'Dilemma of Inclusion' in Kazakhstan. In *Presidents, Oligarchs and Bureaucrats: Forms of Rule in the Post-Soviet Space*, ed. Susan Stewart, Margarete Klein, Andrea Schmitz, and Hans-Henning Schröder. Farnham: Ashgate.

Shelley, L. 1999. *Post-socialist Policing: Limitations on Institutional Change*. London: UCL Press.

Siegel, D. 2018. The Political Logic of Cadre Rotation in Post-Soviet Central Asia. *Problems of Post-Communism* 65 (4): 253–270.

Snajdr, E. 2006. Creating Police Partnerships in Kazakhstan through U.S.-Funded Domestic Violence Training. In *Democratic Policing in Transitional Societies*, ed. Nathan W. Pino and Michael D. Wiatrowski. New York: Ashgate.

Titaev, K., T. Bocharov, A. Dmitrieva, A. Knorre, V. Kudriavtsev, and D. Kuznetsova. 2018. *Opravdanie i reabilitatsiia v Kazakhstane*. Astana: EUCJ.

Trochev, A. 2014. Soviet Legacies in Postcommunist Criminal Justice. In *Historical Legacies of Communism in Russia and Eastern Europe*. New York: Cambridge University Press.

———. 2017. Between Convictions and Reconciliations: Processing Criminal Cases in Kazakhstani Courts. *Cornell International Law Journal* 50: 107–124.

UNICEF Kazakhstan. 2013. *Evaluation of Violence Towards Children in Schools in Kazakhstan*. Astana: UNICEF Kazakhstan.

Van Dijk, J., J. Van Kesteren, G. Slade, and A. Trochev. 2018. *Issledovanie "Otsenka urovnia bezopasnosti naseleniia idoveriia k pravookhranitelnym organam"*. Astana: EUCJ.

Viola, L. 2007. *The Unknown Gulag: The Lost World of Stalin's Special Settlements*. New York: Oxford University Press.

World Justice Project. 2018. *The World Justice Project Rule of Law Index*. Washington, DC: WJP.

CHAPTER 6

Comparing Political and Economic Attitudes: A Generational Analysis

Barbara Junisbai and Azamat Junisbai

Introduction

One of our co-authors recently taught an undergraduate politics course at a major university in Kazakhstan. At the end of the semester, students wrote self-reflection papers in response to two questions. How have politics affected my life, and how have I affected politics? Many themes emerged, but the one that stood out was the idea that the young generation stood apart from their parents' generation, exhibiting more westernized and even "post-materialist" and "self-expression" values (Inglehart and Welzel 2005). Not having directly experienced the Soviet past or the trials of the immediate years following independence, students saw themselves as members of a qualitatively different age cohort. This cohort, what might be called the "Nazarbayev generation," came into political awareness during a time when the country's first and only president, Nursultan Nazarbayev, faced no serious contenders for power, when his policies went publicly uncontested, and when the economy had long since been transformed from stagnant backwater to regional giant. The period of

B. Junisbai • A. Junisbai (✉)
Pitzer College, Claremont, CA, USA
e-mail: Barbara_Junisbai@pitzer.edu; Azamat_Junisbai@pitzer.edu

J.-F. Caron (ed.), *Kazakhstan and the Soviet Legacy*,
https://doi.org/10.1007/978-981-13-6693-2_6

presidential consolidation during which these young people entered their "impressionable years" of preference formation marked them, so much so that they could be said to constitute a discernable political generation (Alwin and Krosnick 1991; Beck and Jennings 1991; Corning and Schuman 2015; Dinas 2013; Funk et al. 2013; Kedem and Bar-Lev 1989; Mannheim 1952; Markus 1986; Osborne et al. 2011; Sears and Funk 1999; Tessler et al. 2004).

President Nazarbayev underscored the distinctiveness of this generation in his 2012 state of the union address:

> Young people today have not witnessed interethnic wars and conflicts and the chaos of the 1990s. Many view the stability and comfortable life in Kazakhstan as their birthright... We created a modern educational system, intellectual schools, a world-class university in Astana. Every year we send thousands of students to the best universities in the world... I count on you, the new generation of Kazakhstanis. You must become the driving force... You grew up under the conditions of independence—something that we [the previous generation] did not have. Your independent thinking is a factor that will lead our country to new goals, goals that today seem distant and unattainable.[1]

The assumption that the so-called Nazarbayev generation constitutes a distinct political cohort—and the idea that members of this cohort are somehow more independent and pluralistic in their thinking than their predecessors—struck us as a testable hypothesis. Empirically, do the attitudes of those who came into political consciousness/maturity following President Nazarbayev's consolidation of power atop the political hierarchy (post-2001) differ from the generations that came before?[2] If so, are generational differences indicative of a rise in "independent thinking" (e.g., the expression of economic and political views that are distinguishable from prior generations)? If so, does it also entail the expression of views that challenge government policy? That is, should young people in Kazakhstan be regarded as "the vanguard of revolutionary... change," as implied by the president's statement above (Beck and Jennings 1991: 760)?

To explore these questions, this paper analyzes original data from a nationally representative public opinion survey carried out in 2012. The

[1] http://www.akorda.kz/ru/addresses/addresses_of_president/page_poslanie-prezidenta-respubliki-kazakhstan-n-nazarbaeva-narodu-kazakhstana-14-dekabrya-2012-g_1357813742.

[2] See Hahn and Logvinenko (2008) for a study along similar lines, in which they ask, are the attitudes, values and beliefs of those who came of age politically after the fall of the Soviet Union significantly different from those who did so in the Soviet period?

analysis shows that the Nazarbayev generation (aged 18–29 in 2012) is indeed distinct, but not necessarily in ways that fit popular narratives. Compared to older Kazakhstanis (those aged 30 and above), young people are more accepting of social inequality and less likely to hold views associated with economic egalitarianism. They are also less likely to make demands on the welfare state in favor of the poor and unemployed. In this sense, the Nazarbayev generation shares the ethos of economic liberalism common to youth the world over. This economic liberalism, however, does not go hand in hand with political liberalism; in fact, youth are less likely than older generations to express democratic attitudes. They are more politically passive, less likely to see the value of questioning government decisions, and more trusting in (certain) state and state-affiliated institutions. Finally, they are less likely to be troubled by political nepotism and family rule.

The attitudes that distinguish the Nazarbayev generation, it turns out, are rarely in the direction of greater pluralism and contestation. Instead of advocating for political and economic alternatives, young people's views tend to mirror the status quo.[3] In other words, their views reflect the reality of Kazakhstan's limited welfare state, its personalist political system, and the policies and practices associated with these.[4] In line with Karl Manheim's (1952) impressionable years theory of preference formation, it appears that the current political environment has left a deeper imprint on the Nazarbayev generation than on those who matured under an earlier and different set of conditions.

Generational Attitudes, With a Focus on Kazakhstan's Youth

Historically, studies of generation-specific attitudes focused on the advanced industrial democracies of North America and Western Europe.[5] In recent years, however, there has been a shift to other parts

[3] See Kwong (1994) for a similar argument regarding youth in the People's Republic of China. Pro-government/pro-regime attitudes among Russian youth are also reported in Levintova and Butterfield (2010), Mendelson and Gerber (2006), and Whitefield (2005).

[4] Note that we focus in this chapter on the effect of domestic policy and political/economic climate and exclude the influence of foreign policy. For a study that looks at how foreign policy changes affect public attitudes in Malaysia, see Howell (1986). For a study that focuses on how US political attitudes are shaped by public policy directly affecting one's personal life chances, see Erickson and Stoker (2011).

[5] For notable exceptions see Iyengar (1979) and Verba (1965)

of the world—notably China, the Middle East and North Africa, and Russia (Jennings and Zhang 2005; Nikolayenko 2008; Tessler 2002; Tessler et al. 2004). Kazakhstan is an excellent venue to extend our understanding of how public opinion differs, and fails to differ, by political generation. The country's political and economic experience is in many ways typical of transitioning/post-colonial/newly independent states. First, its system of governance—personalist rule in which a strong president monopolizes formal and informal power—is the most common form of authoritarianism in the world today (Svolik 2012). Kazakhstan's powerful executive dominates politics, while other actors and institutions are deliberately weakened so as to manage political contestation and prevent alternative sources of power from cropping up (Geddes 1999; Hale 2015). Second, the government's experimentation with privatization and a much-reduced role of the state in the economy are typical of the global turn to market capitalism. The dismantling of the Soviet welfare state began early in Kazakhstan and many services once provided by the government have since been taken over by the private sector.

Finally, the leadership's emphasis on political stability and domestic legitimacy echoes similar concerns in many parts of the world. Kazakhstan's political elites rely upon a mix of foreign and domestic policies to promote international recognition and attract foreign investment, technology, and know-how; establish the country's democratic bonafides abroad while restricting political competition at home; and cultivate popular support and mobilize citizens behind the regime. Such efforts are familiar, as all are closely intertwined with nation and state building. Nation and state building are ongoing as Kazakhstan celebrates its 25th year of independence from the Soviet Union. And a primary target of the regime's efforts is the country's youth. As Sidney Verba, a foundational figure in the study of political attitudes and civic culture, noted more than half a century ago, this is true of every country:

> There is in the first place the need to create citizens out of each new generation. Even where the pattern of political attitudes ... remains relatively stable from generation to generation, each society must socialize young people into this pattern. But even stable nations do not merely transmit a set of political attitudes from generation to generation; they are also faced with the problem of the creation of new political attitudes. (1965: 130)

Our emphasis on Kazakhstanis aged 18–29[6] follows in this spirit, building on numerous empirical studies that find late adolescence and early adulthood to be a crucial "formative period for individual socialization" (Tessler et al. 2004: 186).[7] While we are interested in the ways that young people are attitudinally distinct, we also hope to go beyond statements about *how* political generations differ and offer thoughts as to *why* these differences exist. As institutionalists, we seek to draw causal inferences regarding the intersection of the "larger political environment" (Highton and Kam 2011: 205) and generation-specific preferences. Our explanation thus flows from institutions—the practices, policies, and values associated with personalist rule—to the formation, reproduction, and modification of attitudes and values at the societal level (Braungart and Braungart 1986; Carmines and Stimson 1989; Erikson et al. 2002; Tessler 2002).

Data and Methods

In fall 2012, we organized and oversaw a nationally representative public opinion survey in Kazakhstan, with the goal of producing an internationally comparative dataset. (See Appendix for information on the selection of respondents.) All questions were culled from well-established surveys, including the International Social Justice Project (ISJP), the International Social Survey Program (ISSP), the World Values Survey, and Afrobarometer. The use of pre-tested and commonly used questions was an intentional component of the study's design, as it both helps ensure reliable and valid measurement and enables comparisons with data collected elsewhere. The questionnaire covers a broad range of socio-political and economic topics that reflect theoretical and empirical debates in sociology, political science, and area studies. These include questions that tap into citizens' religious practice, patterns of media consumption, political attitudes, perceptions of social and economic inequality, ideas about the role of government in the economy, trust in institutions, and inter-generational social mobility.

A total of 1500 face-to-face interviews with respondents aged 18 and older were completed, with a response rate of 60.1%. According to the

[6] Our lower threshold is 18 years because that is the age of the youngest respondents. The upper threshold of 29 years aligns with the government of Kazakhstan's definition of youth, as specified in the Law on Youth.

[7] See also Funk et al. (2013), Hooghe and Wilkenfeld (2008) and Rekker et al. (2015) for recent empirical studies supporting this view.

research organization that implemented the surveys, this response rate is typical and can be attributed to growing weariness with survey researchers brought about by the recent proliferation of marketing studies. There was also some difficulty in accessing the wealthiest households, but this problem is endemic to survey research the world over, as it is nearly impossible to survey the most well off in any society.[8] Ninety-seven interviewers conducted the interviews in 150 sampling points covering all 14 provinces (*oblasts*). The average interview duration was 45 minutes.

We use two primary methods of analysis to determine whether the Nazarbayev generation is truly (i.e., significantly) different in their political and economic attitudes. In the first empirical section, entitled "Results Series 1," we report the results of cross tabulations of responses to specific survey questions by age group. We specify two groups, designating those aged 18–29 the "Nazarbayev generation" and those 30 and above "other." We check for statistically significant differences between the two groups using *chi-square* tests. This method gives us a feel for the presence or absence of generational differences, without controlling for other factors.

Following the initial series of crosstabs, in the second empirical section, we use regression analysis to see if the inter-generational differences we found in the first section still hold after control variables are introduced. We add nuance to the analysis by dividing the "other" age category into three generational cohorts: the "transition generation" (those aged 30–40), the "Gorbachev generation" (41–49), and the "Soviet generation" (50 or older). For details, see the second empirical section, entitled "Results Series 2."

Results Series 1: Cross Tabulations for Individual Survey Items

In this section, we use cross tabulations to test whether Kazakhstan's youth are indeed different in their economic and political attitudes than non-youth. We are interested in areas of consensus, in which there are no statistically significant differences by age group, as well as where the attitudes of the Nazarbayev generation differ from those who entered late adolescence and early adulthood prior to the period of presidential consolidation. The data are presented in Tables 6.1–6.6. Wherever a result is found to be significant at the 0.05 level or better, this is indicated in

[8] For an impressive exception to this rule in the US context, see Page et al. (2013).

Table 6.1 Economic outlook and youth optimism

Survey item and responses (%) by generation (youth vs. other)	*Is the generational difference statistically significant?*
Material condition of R's family 5 years from now will improve it will be better or much better: 60% of others vs. 76% of youth it will be much better: 23% of others vs. 36% of youth	+ (significant at the 0.001 level)
Percentage of poor in KZ will decline in the next 5 years agree somewhat or strongly: 24% of others vs. 36% of youth	+ (significant at the 0.001 level)
In our country, people have the same/equal opportunities to get ahead disagree somewhat or strongly: 49.7% of others vs. 42.9% of youth agree somewhat or strongly: 34.4% of others vs. 38.1% of youth	(not statistically significant)

Table 6.2 Views about economic inequality

Survey item and responses (%) by generation (youth vs. other)	*Is the generational difference statistically significant?*
Government should give more educational opportunities to low-income children agree somewhat or strongly: 90.4% of other vs. 90.3% of youth	(not statistically significant)
In our country, people get what they need disagree somewhat or strongly: 54.5% of other vs. 50% of youth agree somewhat or strongly: 21.4% of other vs. 22.8% of youth neither agree nor disagree: 24.1% of other vs. 27.2% of youth	(not statistically significant)
In our country, hard work is rewarded disagree somewhat or strongly: 33.8% of other vs. 28.2% of youth agree somewhat or strongly: 40.5% of other vs. 41.6% of youth neither agree nor disagree: 25.7% of other vs. 30.2% of youth	(not statistically significant)
Current income differences in KZ are too large agree somewhat or strongly: 92.7% of others vs. 87.5% of youth disagree somewhat or strongly: 7.3% of others vs. 12.5% of youth	– (significant at the 0.001 level)
Income inequality is acceptable only if people had equal opportunities to earn money agree somewhat or strongly: 83.7% of others vs. 78% of youth disagree somewhat or strongly: 4.7% of others vs. 8.9% of youth	– (significant at the 0.05 level)
Fair that rich people can use higher quality medical services agree somewhat or strongly: 33.7% of others vs. 37.8% of youth disagree somewhat or strongly: 53.2% of others vs. 42.9% of youth	+ (significant at the 0.05 level)

(*continued*)

Table 6.2 (continued)

Survey item and responses (%) by generation (youth vs. other)	*Is the generational difference statistically significant?*
Fair that rich people can purchase higher quality housing disagree somewhat or strongly: 25.7% of others vs. 20.4% of youth agree somewhat or strongly: 55.7% of others vs. 60.3% of youth	+ (significant at the 0.05 level)
Large income differences needed to stimulate initiative agree somewhat or strongly: 48.4% of others vs. 58.4% of youth disagree somewhat or strongly: 51.6% of others vs. 541.6% of youth	+ (significant at the 0.05 level)

Table 6.3 Views about root causes of wealth and poverty

Survey item and responses (%) by generation (youth vs. other)	*Is the generational difference statistically significant?*
How often is dishonesty responsible for wealth/material success in our country? often or very often: 65.1% of others vs. 56.9% of youth	– (significant at the 0.01 level)
How often is hard work responsible for wealth in our country? never or rarely: 20.1% of others vs. 13.7% of youth often or very often: 52.4% of others vs. 57.8% of youth	+ (significant at the 0.05 level)
In our country intelligence and professional mastery/skill are rewarded disagree somewhat or strongly: 29.8% of others vs. 23.9% of youth agree somewhat or strongly: 39.4% of others vs. 47.7% of youth	+ (significant at the 0.05 level)
How often is the unfair economic system responsible for poverty in our country? often or very often: 60.5% of others vs. 50.2% of youth	– (significant at the 0.01 level)
How often is an unfair economic system responsible for wealth/material success in our country? often or very often: 56.2% of others vs. 49.3% of youth never or rarely: 14.4% of others vs. 14.4% of youth	(not statistically significant)
How often is the fact that not all people have the same opportunities responsible for poverty in our country? often or very often: 85.3% of others vs. 82.3% of youth	(not statistically significant)
How often are better starting conditions/opportunities among some responsible for wealth/material success in our country? often or very often: 86.1% of others vs. 84.8% of youth	(not statistically significant)
How often are connections responsible for wealth/material success in our country? often or very often: 89.8% of others vs. 88.5% of youth	(not statistically significant)

Table 6.4 Attitudes toward the welfare state and the role of government in the economy

Survey item and responses (%) by generation (youth vs. other)	*Is the generational difference statistically significant?*
Government should provide everyone with a guaranteed standard of living disagree somewhat or strongly: 4.1% of others vs. 8.4% of youth agree somewhat or strongly: 89.4% of others vs. 82.1% of youth	– (significant at the 0.001 level)
Government should reduce the income gap between rich and poor disagree somewhat or strongly: 16.8% of others vs. 20.9% of youth agree somewhat or strongly: 61.1% of others vs. 50.6% of youth completely agree: 27.1% of others vs. 16.6% of youth	– (significant at the 0.001 level)
Government should provide a decent standard of living for the unemployed disagree somewhat or strongly: 16.5% of others vs. 22.3% of youth agree somewhat or strongly: 59.4% of others vs. 50.9% of youth	– (significant at the 0.05 level)
Government should impose an upper limit on the amount of money a person can make disagree somewhat or strongly: 28.9% of others vs. 33.5% of youth agree somewhat or strongly: 50.9% of others vs. 45.4% of youth	– (significant at the 0.05 level)
Role of government in business and industry should be increased agree somewhat or strongly: 79.2% of others vs. 70.4% of youth	– (significant at the 0.05 level)
Government should cut assistance/benefits to the poor agree somewhat or strongly: 12.4% of others vs. 17.4% of youth disagree somewhat or strongly: 70% of others vs. 70.1% of youth strongly disagree: 49.4% of others vs. 38% of youth	+ (significant at the 0.001 level)
A market economy is necessary for economic development agree somewhat or strongly 89.9% of others vs. 93% of youth	(not statistically significant)
Government should provide employment to all who want to work disagree somewhat or strongly: 92.7% of others vs. 90% of youth	(not statistically significant)

Table 6.5 Democratic values

Survey item and responses (%) by generation (youth vs. other)	*Is the generational difference statistically significant?*
How important is it to live in a democratic country? somewhat or very important: 81.5% of all respondents very important: 29.5% of all respondents somewhat important: 52.3% of all respondents not very important: 15.0% of all respondents not at all important: 3.3% of all respondents	(not statistically significant)
Laws should reflect the will of the people agree somewhat or strongly: 86.7% of all respondents	(not statistically significant)
Fair elections are important for the wellbeing of my family agree somewhat or strongly: 89.3% of all respondents	(not statistically significant)
Fair elections are important for the economic development of the country agree somewhat or strongly: 95.6% of all respondents	(not statistically significant)
Most important political goals maintain order in the country: 78% of all respondents fight inflation: 35% of all respondents give people more opportunities to influence government decisions: 13% of all respondents protect freedom of speech: 5% of all respondents	(not statistically significant)
Role of citizens: People should question gov't more actively agree somewhat or strongly: 87.6% of others vs. 85.1% of youth disagree somewhat or strongly: 14.9% of other vs. 12.5% of youth agree strongly: 32.1% of other vs. 24.2% of youth	– (significant at the 0.05 level)
Mass media should constantly investigate and report on government corruption and mistakes agree strongly: 44.0% of others vs. 35.0% of youth disagree somewhat or strongly: 23.8% of others vs. 28.0% of youth agree somewhat or strongly: 90.9% of others vs. 91.3% of youth	– (significant at the 0.05 level)
Leaders should not favor their families or specific groups agree somewhat or strongly: 76.1% of others vs. 72% of youth strongly agree: 37.0% of others vs. 28.0% of youth	– (significant at the 0.05 level)
What kind of regime is KZ today? a true democracy: 8.5% of all respondents we don't have democracy: 15.7% of all respondents democracy with minor deficiencies: 36.6% of all respondents a democracy with major deficiencies: 30.5% of all respondents I do not know what democracy is: 8.7% of all respondents	(not statistically significant)

Table 6.6 Trust in formal institutions

Survey item and responses (%) by generation (youth vs. other)	*Is the generational difference statistically significant?*
Most trusted	
93% of all respondents trust the president	(not statistically significant)
84% of all respondents trust their provincial	(not statistically significant)
government (*akimat*)	(not statistically significant)
83% of all respondents trust the national government	(not statistically significant)
82% of all respondents trust universities and colleges	(not statistically significant)
80% of all respondents trust the mass media	(not statistically significant)
79% of all respondents trust parliament	(not statistically significant)
77% of all respondents trust the provincial governor	(not statistically significant)
73% of all respondents trust the army	
Moderately trusted	
62% of all respondents trust banks (59.9% of others vs. 64.8% of youth)	+ (significant at the 0.001 level)
61% of all respondents trust religious organizations	(not statistically significant)
57% of all respondents trust pro-government political parties	(not statistically significant)
Least trusted	
50% of all respondents trust law enforcement agencies (<50% of others vs. 58.5% of youth)	+ (significant at the 0.05 level)
50% of all respondents trust judicial system/courts (47.9% of others vs. 53.3% of youth)	+ (significant at the 0.01 level)
45% of all respondents trust opposition parties	(not statistically significant)

Column 2 with a positive (+) or a negative (−) sign. The former means that youth are more likely than others to support or agree with the statement; the latter means that youth are less likely than others to do so. The phrase "not statistically significant" indicates no meaningful differences between the two age groups. A summary of the breakdown of responses (%) by age group can be found in Column 1.

Economic Outlook and Youth Optimism

We look first at economic outlook and optimism about the future. Projecting ahead to the next five years, do Kazakhstanis expect the economy and their own conditions to improve, remain the same, or worsen? Survey responses reported in Table 6.1 indicate that those 29 and under are significantly more optimistic about the economy and their own family's future wellbeing than those aged 30 and over. Among those in 18–29 age group in 2012, 36% feel that economic conditions of their own families, as well as of the country as a whole, will be "much better." In contrast, less than a quarter of those 30 and above shares this sentiment. These findings are consistent with other studies. In a variety of contexts, young people tend to be future-oriented, providing a more positive economic prognosis than those who are older (Hahn and Logvinenko 2008; Kwong 1994).

At the same time, our surveys highlight interesting variation, including some areas in which youth optimism may be inhibited. While hopeful about the economy in the next five years, young people are divided in their assessments of the fairness of the economic system. While 38% of youth agree that there is a level playing field, with the same opportunities open to all, another 43% disagree that this is so. This division between believers and skeptics reflects that found within Kazakhstani society as a whole. Only 34% of respondents, irrespective of age, agree that there is equal opportunity to get ahead, while almost 50% disagrees. Interestingly, pessimistic views are not limited to assessments of economic opportunity in Kazakhstan. A degree of pessimism resurfaces in young people's perceptions of and attitudes toward economic inequality, as well.

Views About Economic Inequality

Overall, Kazakhstanis appear generally more economically egalitarian and more in favor of equal opportunity than not, at least in the abstract (Table 6.2). This is true across society, including among young people. For example, about 90% of all those surveyed agree that the government should provide low-income children with greater opportunities to receive a higher education. Similarly, about 80% of all respondents are willing to accept economic inequality "only if people have equal opportunities to earn money." Yet, as we saw above, only 35% of respondents believe that equality of opportunity obtains. Moreover, only about one-fifth of all respondents agree that people in Kazakhstan "get what they need." One half—irrespective of age—disagree. It makes sense, then, that the overwhelming majority of respondents (90%) consider the current gap between rich and poor to be "too large."

We observe similarly critical views regarding the degree to which Kazakhstan is meritocratic. While a little over 40% of respondents agree somewhat or strongly that "in our country, hard work is rewarded," another 30% disagree. (The last 30% neither agree nor disagree.) Note that there is no statistically significant difference between the two age cohorts' responses either to this question or to the question about people's needs being met. This suggests some limits to youth optimism. In contrast to economic wellbeing, in a number of areas, young people are no more likely to see the economic system through rose-colored glasses as compared to those who are older.

As the above analysis shows, Kazakhstani society is generally pro-egalitarian, with many people expressing pessimism about how meritocratic claims play out in reality. Despite broad support for economic egalitarianism, important generational differences emerge. The Nazarbayev generation seems better able to stomach economic inequality and this difference is statistically significant. For example, the Nazarbayev generation is significantly less likely to view income differences as "too large." They are also less likely to agree that "income inequality is acceptable only if people have equal opportunities to earn money." Finally, the Nazarbayev generation appears better able to stomach material manifestations of inequality. They are less troubled by the idea that the better off benefit from access to superior healthcare and housing. They are more likely to agree that inequality is beneficial: 52% agree that "large income differences are necessary to stimulate initiative," as compared to 42% of older respondents.

These statistically significant differences by age suggest that generational cohort matters. The Nazarbayev generation mirrors (or, one could argue, is defined by) the socioeconomic and political environment particular to Kazakhstan since the early 2000s. This is the country's first generation to enter adulthood under the post-Soviet economic system, in which previous rights to free higher education and healthcare are but a distant memory, rather than a lived, personal experience. In contrast to those who matured when the government provided a wide array of services and support or was in the process of shifting away from doing so, this generation knows only a privatized system in which most public goods have been commodified and access depends on one's ability to pay.

Views about the Causes of Wealth and Poverty

A bundle of questions focusing on the perceived causes of wealth and poverty helps us further understand how youth attitudes differ from older Kazakhstanis, as well as align with the general public (Table 6.3). The Nazarbayev generation tends to focus less on negative sources of wealth generation (such dishonesty) and is more likely than others to believe that positive individual-level characteristics (such as hard work and intelligence) are what determine who gets ahead in their country. Young people are also less likely to look to systemic roots of poverty. As an illustration, the Nazarbayev generation is less likely to blame the "unfair economic system" for poverty in Kazakhstan. Those 30 and over, on the other hand, are more likely to hold the economic system responsible for both poverty and wealth—although the difference in responses between younger and older people is only statistically significant for the former. Such generational differences could be the result of typical life-cycle effects, as young people are generally less inclined to pay attention to structural impediments to success and tend to believe that individual drive and hard work matter more. In this way, the Nazarbayev generation again reflects similar views to their peers elsewhere.

When presented with additional causes of wealth and poverty, we observe broad societal agreement. Irrespective of age, over 80% of respondents believe that Kazakhstan's differential opportunity structure often or very often leads to poverty. Over 80% also believe that better starting opportunities for some are responsible for unequal economic outcomes. Finally, there is nearly universal agreement among people of all ages that connections are often or very often responsible for wealth and success. For the most part, it appears, young people are only marginally less harsh in their assessments of what generates poverty and wealth. Widely shared cynicism about who gets what and why is striking, especially in the face of narratives—carefully cultivated by the government—about Kazakhstan's dynamic economic growth and burgeoning middle class (Daly 2008).

Attitudes toward the Welfare State and the Role of Government in the Economy

Younger Kazakhstanis favor a relatively smaller role for government in the provision of social welfare. While there is broad consensus regarding an active role for government in the economy, the Nazarbayev generation is still less likely to support proposals to expand the welfare state (Table 6.4). As we know, most people feel that the gap between rich and poor is too large. Yet, only about half of young people agree that the government should step in and reduce inequality. In contrast, 60% of older people support more government action in this area, and the difference between responses by age groups is statistically significant. Statistically significant differences between youth and non-youth extend to other proposals for greater government intervention, ranging from providing "a decent standard of living for the unemployed" to imposing "an upper limit on the amount of money a person can make." The only policy that young people are more likely to strongly support—by 11 percentage points—is to cut government assistance targeting the poor and unemployed.

The generation gap is clearest when it comes to proposals to increase the "role of government in business and industry." While almost 80% of those 30 and older agree that the government should intervene in the economy, 70% of young people agree with this statement. This 10 percentage-point gap suggests a far more laissez-faire stance among younger Kazakhstanis. The Nazarbayev generation, like youth across the globe, including in Eastern Europe and neighboring Russia, leans more toward economic liberalization and market reforms than their older counterparts (Grosjean et al. 2013; Whitefield 2005).

These responses indicate that, compared to prior generations, the Nazarbayev generation places fewer demands on the government to provide a social safety net. Again—as with our earlier discussion of economic inequality and egalitarianism—the difference in welfare-state attitudes is relative. Kazakhstanis on the whole tend to agree that the government should play an active role in taking care of its citizens. However, young people are less supportive of this vision for the state than older respondents, and the difference is statistically significant. Our findings echo survey results from Russia, going back as far as the late 1990s and early 2000s, in which youth showed themselves to be "more anti-welfare" (Whitefield 2005: 139).[9] In our assessment, young Kazakhstanis' expectations of government are more modest precisely because they are accustomed to a living under a more modest welfare state than their predecessors.

Interestingly, although older respondents are more likely to desire a more robust welfare state, they are just as accepting of capitalism as younger respondents. We find a strong societal consensus that a market economy is a good thing. Just over 90% of youth and 90% of non-youth agree somewhat or strongly that "a market economy is necessary for economic development." There is also resounding rejection of the Soviet model of full-employment in which the state ensures that everyone is given a job: 90% of youth and 93% of non-youth reject this alternative. Responses to both questions confirm widespread acceptance of capitalism

[9] See also Hahn and Logvinenko (2008).

and private enterprise. Unlike in Russia, the Nazarbayev generation is ***not*** more pro-market or pro-capitalist than older people, even if they are similar to their Russian counterparts in their views about economic inequality and a limited welfare state (Whitefield 2005; Hahn and Logvinenko 2008).

We now shift from economic to political attitudes, with a focus on questions designed to tap into democratic values and the degree to which people trust formal institutions. Based on the survey results analyzed above, it is clear that the vast majority of Kazakhstanis rejects fundamental tenets of communism and the Soviet command economy. We can also conclude that the idea—promulgated by the government—of capitalism as crucial to Kazakhstan's development has been successfully internalized. In this section we ask, does the consensus on economic freedom extend to politics? Does greater economic liberalism among youth translate into greater political liberalism, for example, in the form of pro-democratic views and desire for political alternatives (Colton 2000; Niemi et al. 1978; O'Kane 1970; Tezcür et al. 2012; Tilly 2002)? Is the Nazarbayev generation more supportive of democracy and the rights and responsibilities associated with it? Are they more critical of the political regime and political institutions (Glazer 1966)? Such questions are central given the debate over the relationship between economic transformation (i.e., privatization) permitted or imposed by the state and subsequent demands from societal actors for political reform (i.e., democratization).

Democratic Values

When asked about the importance of democracy and features associated with it, such as free elections, laws reflecting the will of the people, and an active and critical citizenry, well over 80% of respondents express clear support for democracy as an ideal form of government. Moreover, 82% of all respondents state that it is somewhat or very important to "live in a democratic country," and 87% agree that "laws should reflect the will of the people." In addition, 89% believe that "fair elections are important for the wellbeing of my family" and nearly all (95%) express such elections to be "important for the economic development of the country." Combined, these response rates suggest overwhelming acceptance of democracy as being tied to economic success at both the micro and macro levels. They are also consistent with findings elsewhere, including in Russia. At least in the abstract, people tend to favor democracy over other political systems (Rose and Mishler 1996; Sen 1999).

Yet when probed further, responses reveal less support for democracy than might be assumed at first glance (Table 6.5). Nearly 80% of respondents, irrespective of age, selected "maintain order" as the most important political goal to be pursued. In contrast, less than 13% expressed desire for a greater say in government decision-making. Furthermore, while about 87% of all respondents agree that "people should question gov't more actively," it is the younger generation that is less likely to support the idea of an active citizenry. Turning to the most devoted democrats, those who strongly agree with the need for more active citizens, we find that 24% of youth—versus 32% of non-youth—selected this choice. The Nazarbayev generation is thus less likely than those 30 and older to believe in (their own) active role as democratic citizens willing to critically engage with government.

Likewise, views of the mass media differ by age group. If we look at somewhat and strongly agree responses combined, there is nearly universal agreement with the portrayal of mass media as a government watchdog. Yet, if we separate out at the most ardent responses, we find that young people are significantly less supportive of the idea that the media "should constantly report on government corruption and mistakes" than older respondents. Whereas 44% of non-youth strongly agree with this statement, only about a third of youth do so. It seems that youth are less likely to place value on civil society as a counterbalance to the state. We observe this trend in their attitudes about the role of citizens, as well as in their views of the mass media, when it comes to keeping leaders and government accountable.

The question of leadership accountability and representation is further explored in the statement, "Since leaders represent everyone, they should not favor their own family or group." Here, we find evidence that the Nazarbayev generation is significantly less likely than others to be bothered by political nepotism and family rule. Almost three-quarters of all respondents agree somewhat or strongly with this statement, but when we look at the strongly agree responses we again find an attitudinal gap between age groups. Among the respondents, 28% of youth compared to 37% of non-youth strongly agree that favoritism and narrow interests should not prevail.

Since younger Kazakhstanis have only lived under a system in which nepotism is in evidence at every level of government, it is understandable that they should be more accepting of it than older respondents. Although connections were also central to allocation of resources and power under the Soviet system, we argue that this has only become more pronounced post-independence. The highest-ranking political figures, for example, are all close allies and relations of the president—with this small circle of elites recycling in and out of posts. Researchers investigating elite politics in Kazakhstan have uncovered very little political turnover, especially in the last decade or so, with the presidential family and members of his clan predominant.

Finally, we turn to Kazakhstanis' perceptions of the regime type under which they live. As we reported earlier, over 80% responded that it is important to live in a democratic country. Yet, nearly half of those polled also understand that they live in something other than a democracy. There are no significant differences between the responses of youth and non-youth. When asked to characterize the current regime, 16% of all respondents selected the option "we don't have democracy," while another 31% described Kazakhstan as "a democracy with major deficiencies." Only about 8% believe their country to be "a true democracy," and another 8% replied that they do not know what a democracy is. Most (37%) describe Kazakhstan as "a democracy with minor deficiencies." Alternatively, we could divide responses into two categories: Kazakhstan as a democracy (true or one with minor deficiencies) and Kazakhstan as undemocratic (not a democracy or one with major deficiencies). Categorizing in this manner reveals a public opinion that is bifurcated, with 45% of respondents falling into the former and another 47% falling into the latter.

Trust in Formal Institutions

In contrast to the almost 50–50 split in how respondents characterize the current regime are strikingly high levels of trust in Kazakhstan's formal institutions (Table 6.6). Kazakhstanis, it seems, are trusting across the board, placing their faith in their national and regional governments and in large-scale institutions, including many institutions that are far removed from ordinary citizens (i.e., those that ordinary people are unlikely to directly encounter in their daily lives). The president, national and regional governments, parliament, universities, mass media, and the army enjoy the highest levels of trust, ranging from 93% for the president to almost three-quarters for the army. Institutions that we describe as moderately trusted based on our survey responses include banks (62%), religious organizations (61%), and pro-government political parties (57%). All three enjoy rates of trust near or in the 60% range and all three can to varying degrees be described as associated with government or the state, albeit not necessarily directly.

Lower rates of trust for banks and religious organizations are expected. Banks have in recent years experienced a number of scandals and the oligarchs who own private banks are often controversial figures. Religion in Kazakhstan is contentious, and state policy toward religion is ambivalent since the state supports official Islam and other major religions while simultaneously working to delegitimize and dampen the appeal of extremist views.

It is the moderate support for pro-government political parties that we find intriguing. Considering all of the effort and resources placed in cultivating and branding the party of power, one might expect that pro-government parties would engender higher levels of trust. It is even more puzzling considering the fact that the main pro-government party, Nur Otan, is closely identified with President Nazarbayev, easily the most trusted figure in all of Kazakhstani politics. This might suggest that the government's considerable party building efforts have yielded limited results in an environment characterized by a lack of genuine political contestation. Parties, as compared to other political institutions, may be seen as less central to political decision-making and representation.

Trailing far behind the rest are three institutions that people of all ages trust the least. These include, predictably, law enforcement (50%), the judicial system (49%), and opposition political parties (45%). Beginning with the least trusted of the three, it is noteworthy that it is only trust in opposition parties that dips significantly below 50%. All other institutions listed in the survey are trusted by at least half of all respondents, and most of the institutions listed have much rates of trust well above 50%. Mistrust and suspicion of opposition parties are understandable since Kazakhstan's opposition is small, unknown, fragmented, and has little to no experience governing at any level. It is also understandable given official discourse about opposition as radical and eager to undermine Kazakhstan's hard-won stability, as well as their lack of democratic credentials.

What is surprising is that nearly half of respondents trust such parties despite their failings and despite government repression against political opponents. It could be that Kazakhstanis' inclination to trust institutions generally is having a spill-over effect, working more in favor of the opposition than might be expected. Kazakhstan is often referred to as one of the politically most stable of post-Soviet Eurasian states and an unlikely setting for an opposition to come to power (McGlinchey 2011). Another interpretation is that there may be a degree of latent support for alternative political voices that has not yet been successfully tapped. Our results are only suggestive, and further research could look more systematically into support for the opposition. Questions such as who supports the opposition and whether support for the opposition is tied to democratic values, other economic and political values, or assessments of one's own wellbeing and/or government performance are theoretically engaging, but beyond the scope of this chapter.

Within the least trusted category, it is not patterns of support for the opposition, but support for law enforcement and the judicial system that we find curious. Unlike most of the state and state-related institutions we inquire about, it is precisely these two with which the average citizen is most likely to have direct experience. They are, in many ways, the face of the state. Based on our survey responses, institutions that are closest to the people (e.g., courts and law enforcement) appear to engender the lowest levels of trust, while those furthest removed from the people (e.g., parliament and the national government) appear to cultivate the highest.[10] We speculate that this is for one simple reason: Ordinary people are not only more likely to come face to face with the police and the courts (as compared to, e.g., governors or members of parliament), but they also understand that these have great power over their personal wellbeing and safety. Interactions with corrupt police and court officials may be, at best, an inconvenience involving bribery and wasted time, or, at worst, leave people with a very personal—and very visceral—experience with everyday forms of state predation.

Thus far we have discussed overall levels of trust, irrespective of age. If we revisit Table 6.6, we see that young people are significantly more likely to trust law enforcement and the court system than older Kazakhstanis. Both youth and non-youth are generally wary of the police and the courts, but youth less so, and this difference—while small—is statistically significant. Greater trust implies that the Nazarbayev generation may be more

[10] These findings contrast with patterns in U.S. politics regarding institutions. For example, Americans are known to dislike Congress and give the legislature low marks for trust, while at the same time giving their own Congressional representatives high marks. This bifurcation between local and national (or close and far) has also been uncovered in recent public opinion polls about public schools. People express dissatisfaction with public schools as an institution, but nevertheless tend to be satisfied with the local public school their children attend (see: http://www.npr.org/sections/ed/2016/08/23/490380129/americans-like-their-schools-just-fine-but-not-yours).

receptive to decisions handed down by representatives of state organs with wide discretion.

That this new generation is more trusting in and less critical and demanding of their government makes sense when we link back to our findings regarding perceptions of the need for active and critical citizens. Remember that younger Kazakhstanis were less likely than others to agree with the statement, "people should question government more actively." We infer from these patterns that the Nazarbayev generation is more, rather than less, compliant and passive than older generations. If an active and questioning citizenry is indeed central to the development and maintenance of democracy, young people may be far less inclined to hold their government to the fire as democratic theory demands. One implication is that Kazakhstan's chances for democratization are declining rather than growing—especially if we assume that the process of democracy building is bottom-up rather than top-down and requires citizen participation, criticality, and alternative viewpoints in order to take hold (Almond and Verba 1963; Inglehart 2000; Lipset 1959; Mainwaring 1999; Pateman 1970).

Results Series 2: Statistical Tests of Attitudinal Variation by Generational Cohort

We now delve deeper into the idea that generation matters in the formation of public preferences. Moving beyond simple cross tabs, in this section we run a series of regression models to see if the distinctiveness of the Nazarbayev generation still holds after control variables are introduced. We add complexity to our analysis by dividing the "other" age category into three generational cohorts, for a total of four political generations. The additional three cohorts include the "transition generation" (those 30–40 in 2012), the "Gorbachev generation" (41–49), and the "Soviet generation" (50 or older). Our rationale for distinguishing between generational cohorts is based on the idea that "the prevailing historical circumstances" (Tessler et al. 2004: 185) of an era—or the "tenor of the times" (Marwell et al. 1987)—heavily influence the political and economic attitudes of young people.[11] It is during late adolescence and early adulthood that attitudes and values "are hardened and internalized" (Tilly

[11] For researchers who advocate for and carry out comparisons by generational cohorts, see also Braungart and Braungart (1986), Nikolayenko (2008), Rose and Carnaghan (1994).

2002: 228) and, thus, that the political climate is most likely to have "an enduring impact" (Osborne et al. 2011: 87).[12] In other words, it is argued that distinct periods leave an "imprint" (Jennings and Zhang 2005: 1165), such that each political generation "may be distinguished from earlier or later generations who passed through their formative years under different circumstances" (Tessler et al. 2004: 186).

In line with prior research on generation-specific attitudes in a variety of national settings, we distribute survey respondents into one of the four generational cohorts listed above. All respondents were placed into the political era that they spent at least half of their formative or impressionable years of 15–25. It is generally accepted that political attitudes are established within this age range (Hahn and Logvinenko 2008; Jennings 1996; Jennings and Zhang 2005; Manheim 1952; Rintala 1963; Rose and Carnaghan 1994; Tessler et al. 2004), when individuals are "especially susceptible" to "the political climate of the times" (Beck and Jennings 1991: 759).

Each of the four generational cohorts is based upon our understanding of key political periods in Kazakhstan's history.[13] Following Rose and Carnaghan (1994) and Nikolayenko (2008), we made the generation that came to age under *glasnost'* and *perestroika* (1985–1991) its own cohort; we call them the Gorbachev generation. For simplicity's sake, we decided against dividing up respondents older than the Gorbachev generation into distinct cohorts and left them as an undifferentiated Soviet generation. Finally, we created a separate cohort of those who were 15–25 during the immediate post-independence years (1992–2001). This was the period of relative political pluralism and experimentation, during which waves of political opposition openly contested President Nazarbayev and/or his policies (Brill Olcott 2010; Junisbai and Junisbai 2005). Since 2001, there has been no serious organized opposition to the president, despite isolated protests and acts of civil disobedience.[14] Table 6.7 describes our break-

[12] See Pacheco (2008) for a sub-national study in the US that shows the lasting effect of political context (competitive versus noncompetitive electoral districts) on rates of youth political participation. For a critique of the "hardening" argument regarding adolescent attitudes, see Franklin (1984) and Niemi and Klingler (2012).

[13] For more on political periods and their effects on individual attitudes, see Fendrich and Turner (1989).

[14] Examples include the Shanyrak protests led by squatters forcibly removed from a district outside of Almaty in 2005, the Zhanozen riots in Western Kazakhstan in 2012, and protests against proposed land reform in 2016.

Table 6.7 Political eras in Kazakhstan's history and corresponding age cohort[a]

Political era	*Respondent's birth year*	*Respondent's age in 2012*
Soviet period (pre-1985)	before 1964	>48
Gorbachev era (1985–1991)	1964–1971	41–48
Transition period (1992–2001)	1972–1982	30–40
Nazarbayev/consolidation era (2002–2012)	1983–1991	18–29

[a]Table modeled loosely after Harmel and Yeh (2015)

down of Kazakhstan's history into these four political eras and the corresponding political generation.

The Outcomes of Interest: Meritocracy, Causes of Poverty and Wealth, and Democratic Attitudes

In the first empirical results section, we highlighted certain intergenerational differences in economic and political attitudes that we saw as key. These include (1) perceptions of how meritocratic Kazakhstan's economic system is, (2) perceptions of the causes of poverty and wealth, and (3) trust in institutions. Each of these areas is important because they tap into perceptions of system fairness and legitimacy, whether economic or political. Reliance on coercion and fear is generally not sufficient to encourage popular support for the regime. Thus Kazakhstan's leaders, as do members of the ruling elite everywhere, seek to reinforce among the population—and especially among youth—a belief that how power and wealth are distributed (and exercised) is legitimate and "right" or "natural."

Like many students of public opinion in nondemocracies, we are also interested in the degree to which young people value political participation and pluralism. Recall that the Nazarbayev generation, based on survey responses to individual items, appears more politically passive than older generations and less likely to express values associated with democracy—for example, a critical citizenry, a conception of media as watchdog, and wariness of nepotism. Do these findings still hold when we control for individual-level characteristics that have been found to influence attitudes and perceptions?

In designing our regression models, we created scales measuring perceptions of economic meritocracy, causes of poverty and wealth, and trust in government institutions. All of the scales are internally consistent, as indicated by their high Chronbach's alpha scores (see Table 6.8). This

Table 6.8 Dependent variable definitions

Variable	*Definition*
Economic meritocracy (scale)	A four-item index, based on the respondent's degree of agreement with the following statements: (1) In Kazakhstan people get rewarded for their intelligence and skill. (2) In Kazakhstan people get rewarded for their effort. (3) In Kazakhstan people get what they need. (4) In Kazakhstan people have equal opportunities to get ahead. Answers ranged from strongly disagree (1) to strongly agree (5). The scale was a mean of responses to these questions, with a higher score corresponding with the view of society's economic system as legitimate. Cronbach's alpha for the scale equals 0.83
Structural causes of wealth and poverty (scale)	A six-item index, based on the respondent's answers to the following questions: In your view, how often is each of the following factors a reason why there are rich people in Kazakhstan today: (1) Having the right connections (2) More opportunities to begin with (3) The economic system which allows to take unfair advantage In your view, how often is each of the following factors a reason why there are poor people in Kazakhstan today: (4) Prejudice and discrimination against certain groups in Kazakhstan (5) Lack of equal opportunity (6) Failure of the economic system Answers ranged from never (1) to very often (5). The scale is a mean of responses to these questions, with a higher score corresponding with the view that structural rather than individual factors are responsible for individual economic outcomes in Kazakhstan. Cronbach's alpha for the scale equals 0.74
Trust in government institutions (scale)	A nine-item index, based on the respondent's answers to the question "How much do you personally trust:" (1) Regional/local authorities (2) The army (3) Pro-government political parties (4) National government (5) Parliament (6) President (7) Regional governor (8) Legal/justice system (9) Police Answers ranged from definitely distrust (1) to definitely trust (4). The scale is a mean of responses to these questions, with a higher score corresponding with higher levels of trust. Cronbach's alpha for the scale equals 0.91

(*continued*)

Table 6.8 (continued)

Variable	*Definition*
Citizens should question government	= 1, if respondent strongly agrees with the statement: "Citizens should be more active in questioning the actions of leaders"; otherwise = 0
Leaders should not favor own families	= 1, if respondent strongly agrees with the statement: "Since leaders represent everyone, they should not favor their own family or group"; otherwise = 0
Media as watchdog	= 1, if respondent strongly agrees with the statement: "The news media should constantly investigate and report on corruption and the mistakes made by government"; otherwise = 0
Democracy preferable	= 1, if respondent believes that democracy is preferable to any other form of governance

gives us confidence that the individual survey items that make up each scale fit together and tap into the same attitude. For democratic attitudes, we focus on four individual survey items, to which respondents could indicate their level of support (from strongly disagree to strongly agree). These include the idea that: (1) citizens should question government, (2) leaders should not favor their own families, (3) media should serve as watchdog, and (4) democracy is preferable to other systems of government. On the four individual items, we created dummies to distinguish between those who strongly agree with each statement versus all others. We chose this strategy because we are primarily interested in those who seem to be the most ardent of democrats. We wish to find out, what makes this group of "democrats at heart" distinct from those who are not as passionate about or devoted to pluralistic ideals?

In total, there are seven outcomes of interest: two economic attitude scales, a scale measuring trust in institutions, and individual survey items designed to tap into democratic attitudes. These are described in Table 6.8. Table 6.9 lists the independent variables that we included in the analyses: our four generational cohorts, plus a series of control variables that have been used in similar studies. Controls range from ethnicity (Kazakh versus other), sex, education, and income to internet use (Jennings 1996; Nikolayenko 2008; Shanahan 2000; Tessler et al. 2004; Tilly 2002). We use ordinary least squares (OLS) regressions for the scales and logistic regression for the individual (binary response) items.

Table 6.9 Independent variable definitions

Variable	*Definition*
Nazarbayev generation	= 1, if respondent was between 18 and 29 in 2012; otherwise = 0
Transition generation	= 1, if respondent was between 30 and 40 in 2012; otherwise = 0
Gorbachev generation	= 1, if respondent was between 41 and 49 in 2012; otherwise = 0
Soviet generation	= 1, if respondent was 50 or above in 2012; otherwise = 0
Male	= 1, if respondent is male; otherwise = 0
Kazakh	= 1, if respondent is Kazakh; otherwise = 0
Urban	= 1, if respondent lives in an urban area; otherwise = 0
University degree	= 1, if respondent has completed higher education; otherwise = 0
Household income	= Standardized household income
Internet user	= 1, if respondent uses internet for news and information several times per week or more; otherwise = 0

The Results: How and Why the Nazarbayev Generation Differs from Its Predecessors

The results of the regression analyses are presented in Tables 6.10 and 6.11. Note that the reference (or omitted) category is the Nazarbayev generation, meaning that the output for each of the other three generations is in comparison to it. Note also that the overall model fit is poor, as indicated by the small degree of variation that our models explain (R^2). This, however, is not a major cause for concern, as we are less interested in constructing models that account for as much attitudinal variation as possible. Instead, our main goal is to test for differences between the Nazarbayev generation and the three older age cohorts when other potential causal factors have been taken into account. As will be shown below, the generational differences we find are striking and support our hunch that regime type and the political climate it engenders can leave a lasting imprint on economic and political attitudes.

Our first finding of note is that the Nazarbayev generation is significantly more likely to trust government institutions than all political generations prior to President Nazarbayev's consolidation of power (Table 6.10, Column 2). That is, those who were adolescents and young adults before 2002 trust government at significantly lower rates than those whose impressionable years coincided with the years 2002–2012. If a pattern of higher levels of trust among the Nazarbayev generation remains, and trust does not erode as young people age and gain more life experience, what

Table 6.10 Results of OLS regressions for quantitative dependent variables

	Trust in institutions	*Structural causes of wealth and poverty*	*Economic meritocracy*
Transition generation (Nazarbayev generation = reference)	−0.123*	0.079	−0.137
	(0.050)	(0.052)	(0.074)
Gorbachev generation	−0.152**	0.179**	−0.161
	(0.056)	(0.058)	(0.083)
Soviet generation	−0.126*	0.134*	−0.188*
	(0.052)	(0.054)	(0.077)
Male	−0.034	−0.021	−0.043
	(0.035)	(0.036)	(0.052)
Kazakh	0.104**	0.019	0.160*
	(0.036)	(0.037)	(0.053)
Urban	−0.066	−0.075*	−0.041
	(0.037)	(0.038)	(0.055)
University degree	0.037	−0.037	0.026
	(0.044)	(0.046)	(0.066)
Household income	−0.057**	−0.009	0.013
	(0.019)	(0.020)	(0.029)
Internet user	−0.115**	0.120**	−0.072
	(0.043)	(0.045)	(0.065)
Constant	3.071	3.840	2.968
R^2	0.037	0.013	0.017
N	1297	1299	1302

Standard errors are in parentheses

*Significant at the 0.05 level; ** significant at the 0.01 level

implications might follow? On the one hand, if one conceives of trust in institutions as a requisite for democratic governance, then high levels of trust among youth may suggest a healthy connection between those who govern and the citizenry. With greater trust may ensue increasingly open channels of communication and greater government responsiveness.

On the other hand, if very high levels of trust are conceived of as problematic for democracy, then consistently high rates of trust may reduce government accountability. Very high rates of trust may signal to leaders that citizens prefer a paternalistic role for government, forfeiting their right to inform policy and monitor outcomes. Insulated from criticism, appointed and elected leaders may then conceal information from the public and make decisions without consulting voters. Leaders would in that case take it upon themselves to make decisions on behalf of citizens, claiming that government knows best and that citizens should not meddle in matters of the public interest. This would prove contrary to democratic governance.

Table 6.11 Results of logistic regressions for binary dependent variables

	Citizens should question government	*Media as watchdog*	*Leaders should not favor own families*	*Democracy as preferred form of government*
Transition generation (Nazarbayev generation = reference)	0.269 (0.188)	0.333* (0.170)	0.204 (0.178)	0.262 (0.170)
Gorbachev Gen	0.467* (0.203)	0.455* (0.187)	0.286 (0.195)	0.455* (0.192)
Soviet Gen	0.726** (0.192)	0.432* (0.176)	0.422* (0.182)	0.220 (0.176)
Male	0.203 (0.124)	−0.216 (0.116)	0.048 (0.120)	0.116 (0.119)
Kazakh	0.236 (0.129)	−0.131 (0.120)	0.051 (0.125)	0.031 (0.124)
Urban	−0.148 (0.132)	0.275* (0.122)	−0.700** (0.127)	−0.145 (0.127)
University degree	−0.061 (0.159)	−0.141 (0.148)	−0.038 (0.156)	−0.066 (0.150)
Household income	0.025 (0.069)	−0.098 (0.064)	−0.015 (0.067)	−0.029 (0.066)
Internet user	0.290 (0.157)	0.251 (0.145)	−0.008 (0.153)	0.209 (0.150)
Constant	−1.475 (0.208)	−0.686 (0.188)	−0.537 (0.193)	0.009 (0.188)
Pseudo R^2	0.008	0.015	0.028	0.006
N	1302	1302	1302	1205

Standard errors are in parentheses

*Significant at the 0.05 level; **significant at the 0.01 level

Indeed, there is evidence in our survey data that youth conceive of its relationship with government as paternalistic. As compared to those who grew up in the Soviet Union, the Nazarbayev generation seems far less inclined to see the need for a critical and vigilant civil society (Table 6.11, Columns 2 and 3). Both the Gorbachev[15] and pre-Gorbachev generations

[15] According to Nikolayenko, people who were "...socialized during [the Gorbachev] period... witnessed [the] wave of political liberalization that... accelerated the collapse of communism and the dissolution of the Soviet Union. The new information policy spawned... a close scrutiny of the moribund political system... [Thus] the last cohort of the Soviet citizenry [is in the post-Soviet era] most prone to political action against the authorities" (2008: 442).

are more likely to strongly agree that citizens should actively question government decisions. They are also more likely than the Nazarbayev generation to strongly support a watchdog role for the mass media. In fact, all political generations that came before President Nazarbayev's consolidation of power are more likely to support the idea of a vigilant civil society—as denoted by a critical media and citizenry—than are young people today.

There are at least two possible reasons for this difference. First, young people may buy into the idea that they are freer and that the government is less repressive than the Soviet regime that came before it. They might thus not perceive a need for vigilance; if, compared to the USSR, the government of independent Kazakhstan is accountable and responsive to public opinion, why do we need higher levels of vigilance? Perhaps the pay off from heightened public caution is not worth the opportunity costs, energy, and effort that could be more productively spent elsewhere. Second, perhaps older generations who lived through the Soviet system place greater value on citizen input and criticality precisely because they were not previously afforded these. Of course, these reasons are not mutually exclusive, and it may be that both are working together to generate the distinction we find.

The third inter-generational difference of note is in understandings of the factors that affect one's economic life chances. According to our data, it is clear that the Nazarbayev generation downplays structural inequality in their understanding of the causes of poverty and wealth. Compared to all other political generations, the Nazarbayev generation is decidedly individualistic and non-structural in how it accounts for material success and failure. Referring to Column 3 in Table 6.10, we see that those who came into political maturity under the Soviet Union (both the Soviet and the Gorbachev generations) are significantly more likely to believe that systemic factors—including connections, unfair advantage, lack of equal opportunity, discrimination, and a failed economic system—are responsible for poverty and wealth in today's Kazakhstan.

The reason for this discrepancy, as previously noted, may simply be that young people, in general, tend to overlook structural impediments and causes and prefer to believe that their fate is in their own hands. Our data, which represent only one point in time, cannot tell us if over the course of a life span the Nazarbayev generation will shift to emphasize structure over individual factors. What is clear, however, is that downplaying structural causes has positive repercussions for those in power. As is commonly known, Kazakhstan's political leaders and associated elites have used their positions and connections to accumulate wealth and pass it on to their children.[16] This behavior could in theory cause young people to see the system as unfair and illegitimate. However, that they are less likely to hone in on structural causes of poverty and wealth takes at least some of the burden off politicians to address their role in the creation and maintenance of economic inequality. When poverty and wealth are interpreted as the outcomes of individual ability and hard work, rather than the end result of public policy or decision-making, government can be absolved from blame (Hacker and Pierson 2010). In this way, youth attitudes seem to favor the regime and promote its longevity.

Our interpretation is bolstered by generation-specific evaluations of how meritocratic the economic system is (Table 6.10, Column 3). Compared to the Nazarbayev generation, the Soviet generation—those Kazakhstanis who grew up prior to Gorbachev's political opening and attempt at economic reform—is much less likely to view the current economic system as meritocratic. They are thus more likely to question its legitimacy. This difference should not be surprising. Those who grew up in the USSR internalized the communist regime's emphasis on economic egalitarianism. They became accustomed not only to a relatively even distribution of resources across society, but the idea that government was responsible for eradicating poverty and preventing the concentration of wealth in the hands of a few.

One interpretation of this perception gap between the oldest and youngest cohorts is that it bodes well for the regime and current leaders. If it is primarily the very old who have a problem with how wealth and material rewards are distributed and by what criteria, their ability to mobilize others' discontent is limited. The government can, therefore, discount the views of older citizens as marginal or inconsequential and focus its attention on encouraging support among younger cohorts. Moreover, if young people are already more likely to perceive the economic system as meritocratic, fair, and legitimate, then the regime need not alter its policies or message about economic outcomes. Both appear to be working quite well—and finding resonance—as is.

[16]The Nazarbayev family is a case in point. Among Kazakhstan's richest people are the president's daughter, Dinara Kulibaeva, and her husband, Timur (see Forbes' Magazine's list of billionaires by country at: http://www.forbes.com/billionaires/list/-version:static_country:Kazakhstan). The Panama Papers document leak also revealed offshore interests held by the president's grandson, Nurali Aliev (see http://www.eurasianet.org/node/78086).

Finally, we turn to the last two attitudinal differences: rejection of political nepotism and support for democracy. Interestingly, there is no difference between the Nazarbayev and transition generations on either item; the opinions of those who came of age after the collapse of the Soviet Union are distributed across both populations in a similar manner. If we compare the Nazarbayev generation to our pre-independence generations, however, attitudinal differences come to the fore. The Soviet generation, made up those who lived the longest under communist rule, is much more likely to be troubled by nepotism than the Nazarbayev generation. They are significantly more supportive of the view that elected leaders should not represent the interests of their family or small group of supporters. Similarly, those who came of age during *glasnost'*—arguably the most politically open era in modern Kazakhstani history—are much more likely than today's young generation to strongly identify with democracy as their preferred form of government.

One of the messages propagated by President Nazarbayev is that Kazakhstan has come a long way politically since Soviet times and that the country is making strides toward democracy. Yet, these last two attitudinal differences by generation paint a different picture. If it is true that generation-specific values tend to reflect the overarching political environment and dominant discourse, then what views are being encouraged under the current regime? Based on our survey results, it appears that the climate of the times is reinforcing a vision of government that promotes narrow, personal interests over the public good and where elected officials pursue ends meant to primarily benefit their kin or connections. These realities may be channeling into expectations. Instead of rejecting these practices, the Nazarbayev generation seems to accept them as part of the usual course of politics and getting into power. It appears that the political lessons gleaned by the Nazarbayev generation are that nepotism is the norm and democracy much less valued (or valuable) in reality than in rhetoric. And, again, their assessment would be correct.

Conclusions

To explain the variation in attitudes between the Nazarbayev and other generations, we look to political context. In particular, we argue that the values that youth express are in many ways in line with—or a reflection of—policies and practices implemented by the Nazarbayev regime. For example, it is not surprising that younger people are less concerned with economic inequality than older Kazakhstanis; inequality is a fact of life, one with which those who grew up over the past couple of decades are all too familiar. Inequality is the direct result of pro-market reforms, including the shrinking of the welfare state. Neither should one be surprised that young people pay less attention to structural causes of poverty and wealth. After all, official discourse points to individual-level characteristics to explain away poverty, while giving the regime credit for creating conditions for the middle class to flourish.

Politically, as well, young people's expressed views are closely aligned with regime practices. We point to family rule and nepotism as a case in point. From the perspective of bureaucratic rationalization and the ideal of meritocracy, it might be normatively disturbing that the Nazarbayev generation is more accepting of elected officials acting on behalf of their family and close allies. Yet, if we think in terms of the reality of politics on the ground, greater acceptance of nepotism and placing private interests above other considerations makes complete sense. After all, the practice of favoring one's own and promoting one's personal group or clan—whether those from the same region, one's childhood friends, university mates, or family members—is so widespread that it can be considered a well-established and well-accepted, even if officially frowned upon, norm. Successful individuals lift up and share the perks of office with those who support them and those whom they trust most. This form of personalism and clan politics, from the very top of the political order down to its lowest rungs, is part and parcel of Kazakhstan's authoritarian system. And it is the only system that the Nazarbayev generation has known. As a result, this generation has had "no opportunity to evaluate [how things are currently done] relative to other forms of government" (Rose and Mishler 1996: 53).

Our analysis of the Kazakhstan survey data leads us to the conclusion that institutions—regime values, policies, and practices—have a strong effect on the value orientations of young citizens. We base our interpretation on a single country at a single point in time, an approach that has both advantages and downsides. A key advantage is that we are able to dig deep into a particular place and see how political generations differ across a broad range of economic and political attitudes. We come away with a layered understanding of how the current generation is distinct and offer contextual arguments that we believe account for the differences we find. There are limitations, however, to the lack of cross-national and longitudinal comparison. How can we know with certainty that our institutional explanation is better than alternatives? How can we be sure that the climate-mass attitude nexus that we find in Kazakhstan applies elsewhere?[17]

A number of indirect comparisons exist, and collectively they point to a similar conclusion. In studies of public opinion and youth attitudes in the 2000s in Iran, China, and the US, as well as in India in the 1970s, the main finding is that institutional context matters a great deal in determining public attitudes and political culture (Iyengar 1979; Harmel and Yeh 2015; Pacheco 2008; Tezcür et al. 2012). Moreover, all point to a particular type of context: institutions that allow some semblance of political choice, albeit in different ways. Competitive environments in which alternative ideas and agendas are publicly aired and argued—such as during competitive elections or through political parties, civic associations, local rallies, and protests—affect young people in lasting ways, imparting the values of political pluralism and voice that endure far beyond a particular electoral or protest cycle (Pacheco 2008).

This logic suggests that the converse is also true. Where competition is absent or deliberately constrained, it is difficult for young people to internalize the benefits of pluralism and the need to exercise their voice. In Kazakhstan, the Nazarbayev generation is coming of age in a system where one figure (the president) is dominant. Any vetting of policy takes place behind closed doors, without public debate or discussion. Elites and institutions appear firmly behind the president in whatever direction he decides to take. Under such conditions, it is unlikely that Kazakhstan's youngest citizens will develop an appetite for political competition and an appreciation for the virtues thereof. If institutions remain as they are currently configured, we speculate that there will be greater suspicion of political competition over time. Why might this be the case? Kazakhstani politics are designed to minimize public contestation over ideas and votes and do so in the name of stability. Political pluralism and political stability are thus juxtaposed as opposing forces. Whereas stability is equated with a healthy and harmonious polity, pluralism is framed as a serious threat to both.

[17] Answering these additional questions is an important next step. In a follow-up study, we will compare Kazakhstan with its smaller and more pluralistic neighbor, the Kyrgyz Republic. In contrast to Kazakhstan, youth in Kyrgyzstan have grown up under a political system that exhibits greater contestation—including leadership turnover involving both uprisings and elections. Does this institutional difference carry over to differences in young people's economic and political attitudes? Armed with original survey data from 2007 and 2012 in both countries, our research design allows us to compare cross-nationally and temporally to discover whether there are statistically significant differences in youth attitudes at the country level.

Methodological Appendix: Selection of Respondents

To select respondents, we used a sample of households, rather than a sample of individuals, as is normally used. This is because existing lists of residents, such as voter lists and address books, are outdated and incomplete. Because there no comprehensive list of households exists, we followed the most widely used method for obtaining nationally representative data in Kazakhstan—a multistage stratified probability sample of households.

The first stage involved selection of cities, towns, and villages from the existing list of settlements available from the State Statistical Agency (*Goskomstat*). To make the selection, all settlements were first classified into groups (strata) defined by region and population size. Kazakhstan is typically divided into five geographic regions: north, west, south, east, and central. Within each region, all settlements are classified into large urban (*oblast* capitals), other urban (other towns), and rural. This means that each of the five regions is further divided into three sub-strata. Within each region, a number of settlements from each sub-stratum were randomly selected. And within each settlement, the total number of interviews required was determined by the settlement's population size.

Following the selection of settlements and the determination of the number of interviews to be conducted, households were chosen using the random route sample method. Using this method, postal codes were first randomly chosen; similarly, streets within postal code areas were randomly selected. Finally, actual households from each street were randomly selected. After a household was identified, respondents were chosen using the most recent/next birthday method. All adults aged 18 and older were eligible for participation.

References

Almond, Gabriel, and Sidney Verba. 1963. *The Civic Culture*. Princeton, NJ: Princeton University Press.

Alwin, Duane F., and Jon A. Krosnick. 1991. Aging, Cohorts, and the Stability of Sociopolitical Orientations over the Life Span. *American Journal of Sociology* 97 (1): 169–195.

Beck, Paul Allen, and M. Kent Jennings. 1991. Family Traditions, Political Periods, and the Development of Partisan Orientations. *Journal of Politics* 53 (3): 742–763.

Braungart, Richard G., and Margaret M. Braungart. 1986. Life-Course and Generational Politics. *Annual Review of Sociology* 12: 205–231.

Brill Olcott, Martha. 2010. *Kazakhstan: Unfulfilled Promise*. Washington, DC: Carnegie Endowment for International Peace.
Carmines, Edward T., and James A. Stimson. 1989. *Issue Evolution*. Princeton, NJ: Princeton University Press.
Colton, Timothy J. 2000. *Transitional Citizens: Voters and What Influences Them in the New Russia*. Cambridge, MA: Harvard University Press.
Corning, Amy, and Howard Schuman. 2015. *Generations and Collective Memory*. Chicago: Chicago University Press.
Daly, John C. K. 2008. Kazakhstan's Emerging Middle Class. *Silk Road Paper*, March. Washington, DC: Central Asia-Caucasus Institute & Silk Road Studies Program. Accessed 19 September 2016. http://www.silkroadstudies.org/resources/pdf/SilkRoadPapers/2008_03_SRP_Daly_Kazakhstan-Middle-Class.pdf.
Dinas, Elias. 2013. Opening "Openness to Change": Political Events and the Increased Sensitivity of Young Adults. *Political Research Quarterly* 66 (4): 868–882.
Erickson, Robert S., and Laura Stoker. 2011. Caught in the Draft: The Effects of Vietnam Draft Lottery Status on Political Attitudes. *American Political Science Review* 105 (2): 221–237.
Erikson, Robert S., Michael B. MacKuen, and James A. Stimson. 2002. *The Macro Polity*. New York: Cambridge University Press.
Fendrich, James Max, and Robert W. Turner. 1989. The Transition from Student to Adult Politics. *Social Forces* 67 (4): 1049–1057.
Franklin, Charles H. 1984. Issue Preferences, Socialization, and the Evolution of Party Identification. *American Journal of Political Science* 28 (3): 459–478.
Funk, Carolyn L., Kevin B. Smith, John R. Alford, Matthew V. Hibbing, Nicholas R. Eaton, Robert F. Krueger, Lindon J. Eaves, and John R. Hibbing. 2013. Genetic and Environmental Transmission of Political Orientations. *Political Psychology* 34 (6, December): 805–819.
Geddes, Barbara. 1999. What Do We Know about Democratization After Twenty Years? *Annual Review of Political Science* 2: 115–144.
Glazer, Myron. 1966. The Professional and Political Attitudes of Chilean University Students. *Comparative Education Review* 10 (2): 282–295.
Grosjean, Pauline, Frantisek Ricka, and Claudia Senik. 2013. Learning, Political Attitudes and Crises: Lessons from Transition Countries. *Journal of Comparative Economics* 41: 490–505.
Hacker, Jacob S., and Paul Pierson. 2010. *How Washington Made the Rich Richer—and Turned Its Back on the Middle Class*. New York: Simon and Schuster.
Hahn, Jeffrey W., and Igor Logvinenko. 2008. Generational Differences in Russian Attitudes Towards Democracy and the Economy. *Europe-Asia Studies* 60 (8): 1345–1369.
Hale, Henry. 2015. *Patronal Politics: Eurasian Regime Dynamics in Comparative Perspective*. New York: Cambridge University Press.

Harmel, Robert, and Yao-Yuan Yeh. 2015. China's Age Cohorts: Differences in Political Attitudes and Behavior. *Social Science Quarterly* 96 (1): 214–234.

Highton, Benjamin, and Cindy D. Kam. 2011. The Long-Term Dynamics of Partisanship and Issue Orientations. *The Journal of Politics* 73 (1): 202–215.

Hooghe, Marc, and Britt Wilkenfeld. 2008. The Stability of Political Attitudes and Behaviors across Adolescence and Early Adulthood: A Comparison of Survey Data on Adolescents and Young Adults in Eight Countries. *Journal of Youth Adolescence* 37: 155–167.

Howell, Llewellyn. 1986. Looking East, Looking West: The International Political Attitudes of Malaysia's Successor Generation, 1971–81. *Journal of Southeast Asian Studies* 17 (1): 137–155.

Inglehart, Ronald. 2000. Culture and Democracy. In *Culture Matters: How Values Shape Human Progress*, ed. Lawrence E. Harrison and Samuel Huntington. New York: Basic Books.

Inglehart, Ronald, and Christian Welzel. 2005. *Modernization, Cultural Change, and Democracy: The Human Development Sequence*. New York: Cambridge University Press.

Iyengar, Shanto. 1979. Childhood Political Learning in a New Nation: The Impact of Partisanship. *Comparative Politics* 11 (2): 205–223.

Jennings, M. Kent. 1996. Political Knowledge Over Time and Across Generations. *The Public Opinion Quarterly* 60 (2): 228–252.

Junisbai, Barbara, and Azamat Junisbai. 2005. The Democratic Choice of Kazakhstan: A Case Study in Economic Liberalization, Intra-elite Cleavage, and Political Opposition. *Demokratizatsiya: The Journal of Post-Soviet Democratization* 13 (2): 373–392.

Kedem, Peri, and Mordechai Bar-Lev. 1989. Does Political Socialization in Adolescence Have a Lasting Influence? The Enduring Effect of Israeli Youth Movements on the Political Ideology and Behavior of Their Graduates. *Political Psychology* 10 (3): 391–416.

Kwong, Julia. 1994. Ideological Crisis among China's Youths: Values and Official Ideology. *The British Journal of Sociology* 45 (2): 247–264.

Levintova, Ekaterina, and Jim Butterfield. 2010. History Education and Historical Remembrance in Contemporary Russia: Sources of Political Attitudes of Pro-Kremlin Youth. *Communist and Post-Communist Studies* 43: 139–166.

Lipset, Seymour Martin. 1959. Some Social Requisites of Democracy: Economic Development and Political Legitimacy. *American Political Science Review* 53 (1): 69–105.

Mainwaring, Scott. 1999. Democratic Survivability in Latin America. In *Democracy and Its Limits: Lessons from Asia, Latin America and the Middle East*, ed. Howard Handelman and Mark Tessler. Notre Dame: University of Notre Dame Press.

Mannheim, Karl. 1952. The Problem of Generations. In *Essays on the Sociology of Knowledge*, ed. Paul Kecskemeti, 276–320. London: Routledge & Kegan Paul.

Markus, George B. 1986. Stability and Change in Political Attitudes Observed, Recalled, and Explained. *Political Behavior* 8 (1): 21–44.

Marwell, Gerald, Michael T. Aiken, and N.J. Demerath III. 1987. The Persistence of Political Attitudes Among 1960s Civil Rights Activists. *The Public Opinion Quarterly* 51 (3): 359–375.

McGlinchey, Eric. 2011. *Chaos, Violence, Dynasty: Politics and Islam in Central Asia*. Pittsburgh, PA: The University of Pittsburgh Press.

Mendelson, Sarah, and Theodore Gerber. 2006. Failing the Stalin Test: Russians and Their Dictator. *Foreign Affairs* 85: 2–8.

Niemi, Richard G., and J.D. Klingler. 2012. The Development of Political Attitudes and Behaviour among Young Adults. *Australian Journal of Political Science* 47: 31–54.

Niemi, Richard G., R. Danforth Ross, and Joseph Alexander. 1978. The Similarity of Political Values of Parents and College-Age Youths. *The Public Opinion Quarterly* 42 (4): 503–520.

Nikolayenko, Olena. 2008. Life Cycle, Generational and Period Effects on Protest Potential in Yeltsin's Russia. *Canadian Journal of Political Science* 41 (2): 437–460.

O'Kane, James M. 1970. Economic and Noneconomic Liberalism, Upward Mobility Potential, and Catholic Working-Class Youth. *Social Forces* 48 (4): 499–506.

Osborne, Danny, David O. Sears, and Nicholas A. Valentino. 2011. The End of the Solidly Democratic South: The Impressionable-Years Hypothesis. *International Society of Political Psychology* 32 (1): 81–107.

Pacheco, Julianna Sandell. 2008. Political Socialization in Context: The Effect of Political Competition on Youth Voter Turnout. *Political Behavior* 30 (4): 415–436.

Page, Benjamin I., Larry M. Bartels, and Jason Seawright. 2013. Democracy and the Policy Preferences of Wealthy Americans. *Perspectives on Politics* 11 (1): 51–73.

Pateman, Carole. 1970. *Participation and Democratic Theory*. Cambridge: Cambridge University Press.

Rekker, Roderik, Loes Keijsers, Susan Branje, and Wim Meeus. 2015. Political Attitudes in Adolescence and Emerging Adulthood: Developmental Changes in Mean Level, Polarization, Rank-Order, Stability, and Correlates. *Journal of Adolescence* 41: 136–147.

Rintala, Martin. 1963. A Generation in Politics. *The Review of Politics* 25 (4): 509–522.

Rose, Richard, and Ellen Carnaghan. 1994. *Generational Effects on Attitudes to Communist Regimes: A Comparative Analysis*. Glasgow, UK: Centre for the Study of Public Policy, University of Strathclyde.

Rose, Richard, and William Mishler. 1996. Testing the Churchill Hypothesis: Popular Support for Democracy and Its Alternatives. *Journal of Public Policy* 16 (1): 29–58.

Sears, David O., and Carolyn L. Funk. 1999. Evidence of the Long-term Persistence of Adults' Political Predispositions. *The Journal of Politics* 61 (3): 3–17.

Sen, Amartya. 1999. Democracy as a Universal Value. *Journal of Democracy* 10 (3): 3–17.

Shanahan, Michael J. 2000. Pathways to Adulthood in Changing Societies: Variability and Mechanisms in Life Course Perspective. *Annual Review of Sociology* 26: 667–692.

Svolik, Milan. 2012. *The Politics of Authoritarian Rule*. New York: Cambridge University Press.

Tessler, Mark. 2002. Do Islamic Orientations Influence Attitudes toward Democracy in the Arab World? *International Journal of Comparative Sociology* 43 (3–5): 229–249.

Tessler, Mark, Carrie Konold, and Megan Reif. 2004. Political Generations in Developing Countries: Evidence and Insights from Algeria. *Public Opinion Quarterly* 68 (2): 184–216.

Tezcür, Güneş Murat, Taghi Azadarmaki, Mehri Bahar, and Hooshang Nayebi. 2012. Support for Democracy in Iran. *Political Research Quarterly* 65 (2): 235–247.

Tilly, Charles. 2002. *Stories, Identities, and Political Change*. New York: Rowman & Littlefield.

Verba, Sidney. 1965. Germany: The Remaking of Political Culture. In *Political Culture and Political Development*, ed. Lucian W. Pye and Sidney Verba. Princeton, NJ: University of Princeton Press.

Whitefield, Stephen. 2005. Culture, Experience, and State Identity: A Survey Based Analysis of Russians, 1995–2003. In *Leading Russia: Putin in Perspective*, ed. S. Whitefield. New York: Palgrave Macmillan.

CHAPTER 7

Youth Organizations and State–Society Relations in Kazakhstan: The Durability of the Leninist Legacy

Dina Sharipova

Introduction

In his book "The World Disorder: The Leninist Extinction" written in 1992, Kenneth Jowitt predicted that the Leninist legacy would be a long-lasting phenomenon across all post-Soviet countries (Jowitt 1992). He said, "The Leninist legacy is currently shaping, and will continue to shape, developmental efforts and outcomes in Eastern Europe" (Jowitt 1992: 304). Almost 30 years later, this is still very much true for ex Soviet republics, including Kazakhstan. Despite landmark transformations in economic and political life, the Soviet heritage is still present in varying degrees in this country's political and social institutions as well as in its collective consciousness. Recent heated public discussion on the celebration of the centenary of the Komsomol organization in Kazakhstan have highlighted that memories, attitudes, and norms created in the Soviet period are still alive three decades after the collapse of the USSR. This continuity can be traced to the on-going blurred state–society relations, a highly centralized bureaucracy, and passive political culture, which were also salient features of the

D. Sharipova (✉)
KIMEP University, Almaty, Kazakhstan
e-mail: dina.sharipova@kimep.kz

J.-F. Caron (ed.), *Kazakhstan and the Soviet Legacy*,
https://doi.org/10.1007/978-981-13-6693-2_7

Soviet system. In this chapter, I will focus on state–society relations and state-created youth organizations in Kazakhstan through the lenses of the ideological recycling concept, showing that there is much of continuity with the past Soviet experience rather than rupture.

The Leninist/Soviet Legacy Paradigm

After the demise of the Soviet Union, a spate of works emerged focusing on the Leninist heritage across ex-communist countries. The research centered not only on structures and institutions but also on behaviors, norms, and ideas among elites and citizens (LaPorte and Lussier 2011). But, what should we count as a legacy? Should we adopt Jason Wittenberg's perspective that differentiates between institutions, structures, and norms that are "replicated" years or decades after the disappearance of those they are copying and those that "survived" a regime change (2010)? According to him, only those structures and institutions that "survived" can be considered as legacies. Although this distinction is useful, I believe that it is too strict. The youth organizations found in post-independence Kazakhstan, did not survive the collapse of the Soviet Union. However, the way they were organized at the turn of the millennium strongly replicates those existed in the USSR showing a continuity with the Soviet past.

When it comes to Central Asia, a number of works have analyzed the continuity of the Soviet socialist legacy both at the material and the ideological levels. Scholars have focused on informal institutions such as kinship ties and networks (Sharipova 2015, 2018; Bekus 2017, Schatz 2004; Atai 2012), ethnic identities and language policies (Kudaibergenova 2013; Burkhanov and Sharipova 2014), cultural legacies, and many other aspects of political, cultural, and social life. One of the recent works has examined capital cities as a space for the promotion of the ideologies of the nation-state. According to Nelly Bekus, the leadership of Kazakhstan has used the Soviet instrumental logic for symbolic politics to build states and nations (Bekus 2017). Another work, an edited volume by Sevket Akyildiz and Richard Carlson, contains a collection of essays on the Soviet legacy in Central Asia in which the authors have analyzed various aspects of this heritage, including education, culture, literature, and other (Akyildiz and Carlson 2013). Despite a growing number of important scholarly works on Soviet legacy, little has been written on youth organizations and institutions in Kazakhstan.

For the purpose of this study, I will be using the concept of *ideological recycling* introduced by Kendall and Koster (2007). This concept implies that certain ideas and strategies are re-appropriated from the past and introduced in the present post-communist societies by the contemporary ruling elites in their nation-building strategies (Bekus 2017). This concept is in line with the definition of Jan Kubik on legacies as ideas or patterns of behavior which are transmitted from the past and enacted in the present (Kubik 2003). As I will show, the structure, symbols, and administration of the state-created youth organizations in Kazakhstan are very much similar to those that existed in the Soviet Union. Despite the fact that the Soviet youth organizations—Komsomol and the Pioneers—have not survived the collapse of the Soviet Union in Kazakhstan (they were dissolved in 1991), these organizations have served as models or concepts for the post-independence *Zhas Kyran*, *Zhas Ulan*, and *Zhas Otan* organizations. The latter were not established right after the demise of the USSR, rather they emerged almost 20 years later on the initiative of the president of Kazakhstan. The ruling elites of the Soviet era have replicated the Leninist ideas and models to the post-independence context. The *Zhas* organizations are good examples of "recycling of socialist legacy both at the level of declared values and in the actual practice of state-building" (Bekus 2017: 795). It is important to note that the creation of youth state organizations can only be understood in light of the existing model of state–society relations that is also inherited from the Soviet period.

Indeed, the creation of the mass organizations by the state demonstrates the continuity of state–society relations that existed in the Soviet Union. The Soviet leadership purposefully blurred the boundary between state and society both in policy and its rhetoric (Jowitt 1992). This model of blurred state–society relations is different from the one that exists in the West where the state is portrayed as autonomous and independent from societal actors. In the case of the USSR (and in contemporary Kazakhstan), the state did not leave any room for autonomous actors to organize independently (Grzymala and Jones Luong 2002). Most public organizations, including mass youth organizations—the Komsomol and the Pioneer organization—were created from above by the party leaders who wanted to use them as a way to foster people's support for the regime. The state interfered into citizens' negative freedom by imposing its control over many social activities. Joel Migdal in his book problematized the Western approach toward the state as a unitary and independent actor suggesting a "state in society" approach. He investigated social boundaries between the state defined in terms of public actors and agencies, on the one hand, and societal actors, who are subject to the state's rules, on the other. The difference of this approach from the Western classical model is that state and society are strongly interconnected with one another (Migdal 2001).

Nowadays, we can still observe blurred social boundaries between the state and society in Kazakhstan. The former interferes into what the civil society does through a firm control thanks to the presence of multiple state organizations or quasi-state institutions and national companies. This "statist" model implies that state and society are interdependent rather than autonomous entities. In this model, "non-state society is seen as completing the state rather than diminishing or challenging it" (Gilbert 2016: 1574). As a result, the state plays a primary role in the creation and activities of civil society organizations (Hale 2002; Domrin 2003). Under this model, the state encourages those organizations that implement "useful" activities by providing funding, grants, or other support, while restricting those organizations that might challenge the state's priorities or its leaders.

The creation of the youth organizations—*Zhas Otan, Zhas Ulan, and Zhas Kyran*—is a good example of this statist model in Kazakhstan as they are aiming at promoting patriotism and, most importantly, providing support to the policies of the country's president. In the following section, I will discuss the Soviet youth organizations and those created during the post-independence period and show that the latter follow the model of the Soviet youth organizations albeit with some minor differences.

State-Created Youth Organizations: *Zhas Otan, Zhas Ulan*, and *Zhas Kyran*

The Soviet experience in the creation of mass state organizations was one of the most successful endeavors of the Soviet system. Youth organizations such as the Komsomol, the Pioneers, and the Octobrists were able to include all children and young people of all Union Republics and to develop their true love for the Marxist ideology. Since those organizations were created from above by the Communist party leaders, they were able to inculcate the ideology of communism and raise the generation of would-be communists transforming them into genuine "*homo sovetkus*".

All Soviet children and young people had to go through those youth organizations starting as early as eight years old when they first joined the Octobrists (Oktyabryata). From the age of ten until 14 years old, children became members of the Pioneer organization. This organization prepared them to join the Komsomol organization, which was the main recruiting base for the Soviet Communist party. The membership in those organizations was a must for every Soviet child. Expulsion from the organizations was, however, possible and served as an effective tool to influence children's public and private behavior. Through the membership (or exclusion from it) the *Vozhaty* (leader or coordinator) and teachers were able to discipline young children and adolescents in order to bring them up in the spirit of Soviet people. It is therefore not surprising that some Soviet children did not hesitate to denounce their parents for their alleged anticommunist behaviors: the example of Pavel Morozov being of course the most famous.

These organizations allowed young people to be involved in various social activities, such as tourist trips, song competitions, sport competitions, and others. In addition, every organization had their own symbols and traditions. The Oktyabryata had to wear badges with the image of Lenin in his young age, while pioneers had to put on red scarves and wear red hats on special occasions. For their part, the Komsomol members wore badges with the image of Lenin (in his adulthood). Moreover, all members of the organizations had to give an oath of faith to the principles of Leninism and the Communist party. In the next section, I am going to focus more specifically on each organization and compare them to the post-independence youth organizations in Kazakhstan in order to highlight the striking similarities between them.

From the Komsomol to *Zhas Otan*

The Komsomol—The Communist Union of the Youth—was created on 29 October 1918, at the First All-Russian congress of working and peasant youths. The organization was established under the aegis of the Communist Party. The program adopted at the congress declared that "The goal of the Union is the spread of the communist ideas and the involvement of working and peasant youth in the active construction of Soviet Russia". Later the Union was renamed after Lenin and was called as the Russian Lenin Communist Union of the Youth. In March 1922 it was renamed again as the "All-Union Communist Union of Youth" (VLKSM).

According to the Charter of the Communist Youth Union, young people at the age 14–28 could be accepted to the organization. The age of membership however changed over time.

The structure of the Komsomol was highly centralized and hierarchical following the model of the Communist party of the Soviet Union. The lowest primary organizations (caucuses) of the VLKSM could be created in various places where young people worked or studied—*kolkhoz, sovhoz*, industrial enterprises, universities, schools, army, or fleet. Those primary organizations were united in district, city or other higher-level units based on territorial principle. The highest administrative body was the Congress of the VLKSM that was called every five years. In between congresses, the Central Committee elected the Secretariat and the Bureau and was responsible for the work of all Komsomol organizations as well as the All-Union Pioneer organizations.

In Kazakhstan, the Komsomol organization was created at the first Komsomol conference in July 1921. There were about 21,960 members in the organization in 1921. By 1981, the number of members increased up to 2,270,501, spread across 24,986 primary organizations.[1] From the moment of its creation until its dissolution, 200 millions of young people were members of this organization during some part of their lives. This of course allowed the Communist party to mobilize the young people through the VLKSM for various big soviet projects—the construction of cities in Siberia and big industrial projects, the cultivation of virgin lands, and many others. The Komsomol members were the vanguard of the Communist party in the implementation of the directives of the Politburo.

Today, the legacy of the Soviet Komsomol is still very much alive in Kazakhstan not only through the creation of the youth *Zhas Otan* organization but also in people's collective memory. Recent celebration of the centenary of the VLKSM on 20 October 2018, organized by the former Komsomol members in Kazakhstan stirred heated debates in the public space on whether such a commemoration was needed. It was nonetheless allowed since many representatives of the political and economic elites of Kazakhstan are former secretaries or members of the VLKSM, including the country's President Nursultan Nazarbayev, the

[1] Leninskii Komsomol Kazakhstana v faktah i tsifrah, 1921–1981, [The Lenin Komsomol of Kazakhstan in Facts and Numbers], Alma-Ata: Kazakhstan, 1981, p. 105, accessed 15 November 2018, available at http://meeting.nlrk.kz/result/ebook_387/index.html#ps, internet.

former Vice Prime Minister and current Ambassador to the Russian Federation, Imangali Tasmagambetov, the Chairman of the Lower Chamber of the Parliament, Nurlan Nigmatulin and many others. The attachment of the current apparatchiks for this Soviet organization is obvious. For instance, in one of his interviews, Tasmagambetov said that the VLKSM was a "phenomenal, unique in its dynamics, mobility and management" organization (Adilov 2018). For many of those who served in the government and parliament of Kazakhstan, the Komsomol organization provided a good career opportunity and mobility up the social ladder. It is therefore easy to understand why the veterans of the Komsomol were awarded with medals during the jubilee.

The debates showed that the Kazakhstani society is divided between those who support and positively evaluate the Soviet legacy and those who are very negative about it. One of the accusations of the VLKSM in Kazakhstan by the opponents of the 100 Jubilee was the participation of the Komsomol activists in the prosecution of the 1986 riot participants in Almaty against Moscow's control on the Soviet Kazakh Republic and, as such, these celebrations were seen as unpatriotic. Others believed that a highly negative reaction against the celebration of jubilee was an attempt to destabilize the internal situation of the country and divide the elites and the Kazakhstani society (Isabaeyva 2018). However, despite these criticisms, the fact that the jubilee was openly celebrated by the current political elites of Kazakhstan and some part of the population shows that, as one of the journalists noted, "[the Kazakhstani people] are still mentally living in the Soviet Union" (Alimov 2018). Indeed, the ideological recycling of Soviet models, ideas, structures, and institutions is still happening in Kazakhstan. *Zhas Otan*, the youth wing of the Nur Otan political party, to some degree resembles the Komsomol organization. In the next section, I will show how the two organizations are different or similar to each other.

Zhas Otan

Zhas Otan is a "youth branch" of the Nur Otan political party—the dominant party in Kazakhstan. Today there are more than 150,000 members in the organization (Spotkai 2018) and is by far the biggest one in Kazakhstan. In terms of membership, the organization is not as big as the Komsomol was. The President Nazarbayev played a direct role in the creation of the organization which was officially established in May 2008 at the Congress of Youth held in Astana. It is clear that its purpose shows how this organization is a quintessential example of the Soviet state–society paradigm. At the congress, President Nazarbayev said, "Zhas Otan is a movement that unites thousands of active educated patriots, who support all my initiatives, strategic plans and are the conductors of my policies". In the strategy of the organization, it is declared that "Zhas Otan" is a "leading mass youth organizations of the country and the goal of which is the defense of the interests of each young Kazakhstani".[2] The *Zhas Otan* program aimed at the "development of social capital, quality education and professional development…"[3] One of the important goals is spiritual and moral development of the young people, respect toward traditional values and support of interethnic peace and communication. The strategic program "Zhastar—Otanga", which can be translated as "The Youth to the Fatherland", states that one of the tasks of the organization is the consolidation of the youth in support of the strategic policies of the president. This sounds similar to the principles and agenda of the Komsomol organization, that provided support in implementation of policies of the Communist party. Another important strategic goal of the *Zhas Otan* is the expansion of the social basis of the Nur Otan party through the involvement of young people in the activities of *Zhas Otan*.[4] The mechanisms have been developed to increase the number of members of the party among the young people. The Soviet Komsomol also served as a stepping-stone for the future members of the party.[5] In this sense, we can also expect that *Zhas Otan* members will more likely become members of Nur Otan political party.[6] Alongside its supportive role for the political elites and their policies, the organization also has its own symbols such as a flag, anthem, logo, and badge.

[2] Strategy "Zhastar Otanga", accessed 20 November 2018, available at https://www.do.ektu.kz/studentlifenew/StudLife/UserFiles/Files/The_strategy_MK_Zhas_Otan_Project.pdf.

[3] Strategy "Zhastar Otanga", accessed 20 November 2018, available at https://www.do.ektu.kz/studentlifenew/StudLife/UserFiles/Files/The_strategy_MK_Zhas_Otan_Project.pdf.

[4] Strategy "Zhastar Otanga", accessed 20 November 2018, available at https://www.do.ektu.kz/studentlifenew/StudLife/UserFiles/Files/The_strategy_MK_Zhas_Otan_Project.pdf.

[5] This is why most communist members and leaders were recruited from the Komsomol organization.

[6] The Charter of the organization states, "A Member of *Zhas Otan* can become a Member of the Nur Otan Party at the Age of 18 Years Old".

The structure of the organization also bears similarities with the Komsomol. As it was the case with the latter, *Zhas Otan* primary organizations are created on a territorial basis. The organization has its branches in all oblasts and three major cities of Kazakhstan as well as the district and city levels. The primary organizations can be established in different organizations except for civil service and organs of self-governance. Currently, there are 230 primary caucuses in Kazakhstan (Spotkai 2018). The caucus consists of minimum three people and is established by the decision of the district or city council. According to the Charter of the *Zhas Otan*, primary originations can be established by the district (or city) council of *Zhas Otan*. The decision on the creation of the regional, as well as Astana and Almaty, city, and district branches is made by the Executive Secretariat of *Zhas Otan*. The branches of the organization should follow the decisions of the higher-level bodies.

Similarly to the Komsomol, the highest governing body of *Zhas Otan* is the Congress that is called by the decision of the Central Council no less than one time every four years. The leading organ is the Central Council, which is responsible for the activities and governance of the regional branches in between the congresses. The Central Council consists of the representatives from regional branches, those of Astana and Almaty cities, activists and leaders of other youth organizations. It also includes members of the Majilis, Maslikhats (local governance bodies), leaders of youth NGOS, and other. The highest governing organs of regional and city branches are conferences called by the Council. Conferences are called by the council of *Zhas Otan* of the corresponding branch no less than once in two years. *Zhas Otan* also leads *Zhas Ulan* organization, which is similar to the Soviet Pioneer Organization. In the following section, I will discuss the Pioneer organization existed in the Soviet Union and then focus on *Zhas Ulan* organization.

Zhas Ulan: The Pioneers of Independence

The Pioneer Organization of the Soviet Union has its roots in the scout movement which was developed in pre-revolutionary Russia. However, the Bolsheviks used the idea to create their own organization that was "scout in shape and communist in content". In Kazakhstan, the first pioneer organization was created on 19 November 1922, in Petropavlovsk. The first squad of pioneers named "Spartak" consisted of 20 children.

One year later, there were already eight pioneer squads that united 800 children. Other pioneer squads also emerged in such cities as Alma-Ata, Ust-Kamenogorsk, Semipalatinsk, and Chimkent. By 1928, the number of young pioneers increased up to 33,000. Two years later, the first Congress of pioneers took place in August in Alma-Ata; 742 delegates attended the event. In the Soviet Union in 1970 there were 23 million pioneers who were united in more than 118 pioneer squads (Krechetnikov 2012).

The structure of the Pioneer organization was also hierarchical and centralized. The entire school—the squad—was divided into regiments (each class) and each class, in turn, was partitioned into squadrons consisting of 10–15 people. The school squads were subordinate to the district, regional or city pioneer headquarters and the Central Council under the aegis of the Komsomol committees (Charter 1989). The organization had its own Charter, its newspaper *The Pionerskaya Pravda* and anthem.

The communist ideology also penetrated the organization at all levels and was used in various activities. Similarly to the Komsomol, the organization served as a tool to control the minds of the young people of Soviet Union. The indoctrination with communist ideas began with the oath and symbols of the organizations. All newcomers had to solemnly swear and promise "to live, to study and to struggle as great Lenin willed, according to the teaching of the Communist Party". This objective lasted until the final days of Soviet Union. In 1989 the organization still prescribed that "A pioneer [was] a young creator of communism who work[ed] and studie[d] for the benefit of Motherland and prepare[d] to become its defender. A pioneer [was to] look up to communism, prepare[d] to become a Komsomol member, and [willing to] lead the Octobrists".[7] The red scarves, red hats, and the pioneer salute were also important tools used to instill discipline among children.

Similarly to the Komsomol, the organization officially ceased to exist following the break-up of the Soviet Union. However, ex-Soviet countries ether continued to have the pioneers or decided to create new organizations that played a similar role. In the first case, the pioneer organization was preserved in Belarus with only some minor change in its symbols. Instead of Soviet red scarves, the pioneers of Belarus wear scarves of the national flag color. For its part, Kazakhstan has chosen to revive the

[7] Zakony I klyatvy pionerov SSR, accessed 26 November 2018, available at https://ckych-novosti.livejournal.com/916189.html.

Pioneer organization, although differently than in Belarus. In 2011, at the 13th Congress of the Nur Otan political party, President Nazarbayev suggested the creation of a new youth organization "Zhas Ulan" that would unite children of all ages (Fidchenko 2011). The organization was established on 6 of July 2011, under control of Nur Otan political party, the Ministry of Education and Science and leaders of youth organization (Kontseptsia razvitia 2012). Needless to say that this organization's primary role is to serve as a supporting role for the government. This can be highlighted in many ways. For instance, it is stated that the organization's goal is to "create a united organization of a *national scale*, aimed at the formation of civic consciousness among school students..."[8] The goal of *Zhas Ulan* is "the formation of a person with high level of patriotism, Kazakhstani cultural identity, and civic responsibility..."[9] A year after its creation, the number of members in this organization amounted to around 700,000 members. Today, that number has obviously increased. Although membership to this organization remains voluntary, there is a strong implicit social pressure on the part of children to join it in order to avoid being seen as unpatriotic and to maximize one's chances of building the necessary connections that will be helpful later in life.

Moreover, the ideological recycling of the Soviet rituals, structures, and norms are evident through "new" structures and rituals of the post-independence period. As the Soviet pioneers, the *Zhas Ulan* organization has its own symbols: a motto, anthem, banner, scarf, badge, emblem, and pennon.[10] Although these symbols are not communist in content, they are nonetheless similar in terms of concepts, ideas and shape to those of the Soviet pioneers. For instance, members of *Zhas Ulan* wear the badge with the image of the "Golden Man", one of the symbols of independence, and blue-colored scarf denoting the national flag of Kazakhstan. The Soviet rituals such as giving an oath, using drums, and guard of honors were also replicated from the past. For instance, on special occasions, a guard of honor stands nearby the banner of the *Zhas Ulan* organization as pioneers did during the Soviet period.[11]

[8] Kontstepsia razvitiya edinoi detsko-yunosheskoi organizatsii—Zhas Ulan, http://www.zhuldyz.kz/?type=magazine&iid=38&aid=907, *Жасstar", № 4 (34) 2012 г.*

[9] http://www.zhuldyz.kz/?type=magazine&iid=38&aid=907 Kontstepsia razvitiya edinoi detsko-yunosheskoi organizatsii—Zhas Ulan, *Жасstar", № 4 (34) 2012 г.*

[10] Polozhenie o deyatelnosti Respublikanskoi Edinoi Detsko-yunosheskoi organizatsii "Zhas Ulan", accessed 23 November 2018, available at http://zhasulan.kz/public/upload/files/__.pdf.

[11] Polozhenie o deyatelnosti Respublikanskoi Edinoi Detsko-yunosheskoi organizatsii "Zhas Ulan", accessed 23 November 2018, available at http://zhasulan.kz/public/upload/files/__.pdf.

The structure of the organization is also very similar to the one of the pioneers. It consists of primary children's' organizations (associations, clubs, sections, etc.). *The Kuryltai* (congress) is the highest counseling body, while the Republican Council is the highest governing body that controls oblast, district, and city councils. Another replicated element of the Soviet organization is the appointment of coordinators called the *Vozhaty* (leader) which is very similar to that of the *Vozhaty* of pioneers in the Soviet Union. During the Soviet era, each school had the *Vozhaty* of pioneers responsible for coordination of the primary pioneer organizations. The Vozhaty's functions also include support in the development of children's public organizations and associations and their activities; elaboration of a program for organizations; the development of the content and forms of organizational activities; the creation of favorable conditions in schools helping students to realize their interests and demands, and observation of the rights of children, and many other functions.[12]

The picture of state-created youth organizations would be incomplete without taking into account *Zhas Kyran*, which is a subdivision of the *Zhas Ulan* organization. It has a lot to do with the Soviet organization of Octobrists [Oktyabryata] which included children from 7 to 9 years old. Octobrists were under the supervision of a Pioneer *Vozhaty* and Komsomol members. The prime mandate of this organization was to prepare their members to become pioneers. *Zhas Kyran* follows the same pattern. It includes school children from the first through fourth grades. This organization is another example of the ideological recycling since it is similar in terms of structure, symbols, oath, and rituals to those of the Octobrists. The organization also has a list of "duties" that members have to follow similar to those existed for the Octobrists. More precisely, one of the main ideas of the organization is to inculcate patriotic sentiments in the minds of the young people. It is most likely that members of *Zhas Kyran* will become *Zhas Ulans* and then might be members of *Zhas Otan*. The state seeks to create some continuity across three organizations and mobilize them to support the policies and programs of the leading party in Kazakhstan.

[12] Polozhenie o deyatelnosti Respublikanskoi Edinoi Detsko-yunosheskoi organizatsii "Zhas Ulan", accessed 23 November 2018, available at http://zhasulan.kz/public/upload/files/__.pdf, pp. 4–5.

Conclusion

As this chapter shows, the Leninist legacy is still very much alive in Kazakhstan. Almost three decades later, we observe the functioning of similar structures and institutions and application of the same strategies by the ruling elites to build the state and nation. The creation of mass youth organizations such as *Zhas Otan*, *Zhas Ulan*, and *Zhas Kyran* is a good example of the ideological recycling of the Soviet models and ideas. The hierarchical and centralized structures of the youth organizations are copied from those of Soviet youth organizations. Moreover, they have retained the same use of symbols as their Soviet predecessors. In a similar fashion, rituals and ceremonies performed by the youth in the organizations such as giving the oath and guard of honor are "Soviet in shape and Kazakhstani in content". This continuity can be explained by the fact that those who have been ruling Kazakhstan since its independence have been themselves intimately influenced by the structures and methods of the former Soviet Union. These leaders were first-hand witnesses of the effectiveness of the Komsomol and Pioneer organizations in mobilization of young people to fulfill the directives and programs of the Communist party. Since they did not have "any blueprints for their new state and society" in 1991, they simply reproduced the only form of organization they knew (Akyildiz and Carlson 2013). As a corollary, the political elites apply the same methods and models to use young people to implement their projects. The replication of this model is also an effective way at their disposal to maintain power and control over the young people in the age of internet and globalization.

This analysis of youth organizations also highlights more broadly the continuity of the Soviet state–society relations. As it was the case during Soviet Union, social boundaries between the state and society are blurred. The state interferes into society by creating state organizations that would perform "useful" activities. In the Soviet period, this was the case with the Unions of Writers, Artists, Musicians, and Societies of Gardeners, and many other organizations that were founded mostly by and under control of the omnipresent state and the Communist Party. Today, the state also interferes and violates the boundaries of society by creating youth organizations from above.

In this perspective, is the prophecy of Ken Jowitt fulfilled? Three decades later, we can answer the question positively. Nobody can predict for how long the Leninist legacy will survive and exert an influence on the lives of new generations. However, it is highly probable that those structures, institutions, and forms that have been copied from the Soviet experience will most likely be projected in the future as well as members of the "Nazarbayev Generation" will tend to reproduce the same model when they will replace their elders currently in power: a trend that seems very likely in light of what Azamat and Barbara Junisbai are discussing in another chapter of this book. It is therefore very hard to tell when this model of state–society relations will be broken by one that is not associated with the Soviet legacy.

References

Adilov, S. 2018. Chto dala Kazakhstanksoi elite shkola VLKSM. Accessed 12 November 2018. https://camonitor.kz/26012-chto-dala-kazahstanskoy-elite-shkola-vlksm.html.

Akyildiz, S., and R. Carlson. 2013. *Social and Cultural Change in Central Asia: The Soviet Legacy*. New York: Routledge.

Alimov, M. 2018. Strasti vokrug yubileya VLKSM—svidetelstvo polnogo razdraya v kazakhstanskom obshchestve. Accessed 25 November 2018. https://camonitor.kz/31845-strasti-vokrug-yubileya-vlksm-svidetelstvo-polnogo-razdraya-v-kazahstanskom-obschestve.html; Internet.

Atai, F. 2012. Soviet Cultural Legacy in Tajikistan. *Iranian Studies* 45 (1): 81–95.

Bekus, N. 2017. Ideological Recycling of the Socialist Legacy. Reading Townscapes of Minsk and Astana. *Europe-Asia Studies* 69 (5): 794–818.

Burkhanov, A., and D. Sharipova. 2014. *Kazakhstan's Civic-National Identity. Nationalism and Identity Construction in Central Asia: Dimensions, Dynamics, and Directions*. Lanham, MD: Little and Rowan.

Charter. 1989. Accessed 26 November 2018. http://nksmrf.ru/page/51.

Domrin, A. 2003. Ten Years Later: Society, Civil Society, and the Russian State. *The Russian Review* 62: 93–211.

Fidchenko, A. 2011. V Kazakhstane poyavatya' pionery. Accessed 17 November 2018. http://www.azbyka.kz/v-kazahstane-poyavyatsya-pionery; Internet.

Gilbert, L. 2016. Crowding Out Civil Society: State Management of Social Organizations in Putin's Russia. *Europe-Asia Studies* 68 (9): 1553–1578.

Grzymala, B.A., and P. Jones Luong. 2002. Reconceptualizing the State: Lessons from Post-Communism. *Politics and Society* 30 (4): 529–554.

Hale, H. 2002. Civil Society from Above? Statist and Liberal Models of State-Building in Russia. *Demokratizatsiya* 10 (3): 306–321.

Isabaeyva, S. 2018. Antikomsomolskaya isteria: Komu i zachem eto nuzhno bylo. Accessed 26 November 2018. https://camonitor.kz/31906-antikomsomolskaya-isteriya-komu-i-zachem-eto-bylo-nuzhno.html; Internet.

Jowitt, K. 1992. *New World Disorder: The Leninist Extinction*. Berkeley, CA: University of California Press.

Kendall, T., and K. Koster. 2007. Critical Approaches to Cultural Recycling: Introduction. *Other Voices* 3 (1). Accessed 26 November 2018. http://www.othervoices.org/3.1/guesteditors/index.php; Internet.

Kontstepsia razvitiya edinoi detsko-yunosheskoi organizatsii—Zhas Ulan. 2012. *Zhastar* 4 (34). Accessed 2 November 2018. http://www.zhuldyz.kz/?type=magazine&iid=38&aid=907; Internet.

Krechetnikov, A. 2012. Yubilei pioner: ot skautizma do nashih dnei. Accessed 25 November 2018. https://www.bbc.com/russian/russia/2012/05/120518_pioneers_jubilee; Internet.

Kubik, J. 2003. Cultural Legacies of State Socialism: History Making and Cultural-Political Entrepreneurship in Post-Communist Poland and Russia. In *Capitalism and Democracy in Central and Eastern Europe: Assessing the Legacy of Communist Rule*, ed. G. Ekiert and S. Hanson. Cambridge: Cambridge University Press.

Kudaibergenova, D. 2013. National Identity Formation in Post-Soviet Central Asia: The Soviet Legacy, Primordialism, and Patterns of Ideological Development Since 1991. In *Social and Cultural Change in Central Asia*, ed. S. Akyildiz and R. Carlson. London and New York: Routledge.

LaPorte, J., and D. Lussier. 2011. What Is the Leninist Legacy? Assessing Twenty Years of Scholarship. *Slavic Review* 70 (3): 637–654.

Leninskii Komsomol Kazakhstana v faktah i tsifrah, 1921–1981, [The Lenin Komsomol of Kazakhstan in Facts and Numbers], Alma-Ata: Kazakhstan, 1981, p. 105. Accessed 15 November 2018. http://meeting.nlrk.kz/result/ebook_387/index.html#ps; Internet.

Migdal, Joel S. 2001. *State in Society: Studying How States and Societies Transform and Constitute One Another*. Cambridge University Press.

Polozhenie o deyatelnosti Respublikanskoi Edinoi Detsko-yunosheskoi organizatsii. Zhas Ulan. 2011. Accessed 23 November 2018. http://zhasulan.kz/public/upload/files/__.pdf.

Schatz, E. 2004. *Modern Clan Politics: The Power of "Blood" in Kazakhstan and Beyond*. Seattle, WA: University of Washington Press.

Sharipova, D. 2015. State Retrenchment and Informal Institutions in Kazakhstan: People's Perceptions of Informal Reciprocity in the Healthcare Sector. *Central Asian Survey* 34 (3): 310–329.

Sharipova, D. 2018. *State-Building in Kazakhstan: Continuity and Transformation of Informal Institutions*. Lanham, MD: Rowman & Littlefield.

Spotkai, M. 2018. Zhas Otan: Otrkytost, Kreativ, Innovatsii. Accessed on 20 November 2018. https://liter.kz/ru/articles/show/42285%2D%2Dzhas_otan_otkrytost_kreativ_innovacii; Internet.

Wittenberg, J. 2010. What Is a Historical Legacy? Paper, American Political Science Association, Washington, DC. Accessed 12 November 2018. http://www.jasonwittenberg.org/wp-content/uploads/2013/05/Witty-Legacy-APSA-2013.pdf; Internet.

CHAPTER 8

The Art of Managing Religion in a Post-Soviet Soft Authoritarian State

Hélène Thibault

This chapter aims at presenting a religious topography of contemporary Kazakhstan by focusing on the moderate Islamic religious revival following independence and the subsequent attempts made by the state to control it. With a remaining Russian population of approximately 25%, Kazakhstan is considered to be one of the most Russified and secularized countries of Central Asia. Since its independence in 1991, the Kazakhstani authorities have implemented policies aimed at promoting national traditions, and in particular, the Kazakh language. In parallel, we observe a renewed interest for Islam among the population. However, the society remains strongly influenced by 70 years of atheism imposed by force and this interest translates into a moderate increase of religious practice. Despite this moderate Islamization, the authorities fear a politicization and radicalization of Islam and attempt to channel religious feelings toward an Islam that is considered patriotic, in line with national values and shielded from external influences. The state has reinforced its control over religious organizations and practices, through the Spiritual Direction of Muslims in Kazakhstan, an institution inherited from Soviet times which acts as an

H. Thibault (✉)
Nazarbayev University, Astana, Kazakhstan
e-mail: helene.thibault@nu.edu.kz

J.-F. Caron (ed.), *Kazakhstan and the Soviet Legacy*,
https://doi.org/10.1007/978-981-13-6693-2_8

official clergy. This control is exercised in a context of moderate authoritarianism, which generates tensions in the country. This chapter opens with a historical account of religious dynamics to illustrate how state-religion relations in Kazakhstan possess a unique character due to the legacy of Marxist atheism. The second part paints a portrait of the religious diversity in the country and the tensions inherent to this cohabitation. It will reveal that the most dramatic tensions are not inter-confessional but concern the different interpretations of Islam.

Religious Practice in Historical Perspective

Before the conversion to Islam in the ninth century, the nomadic peoples of Central Asia practiced a variant of paganism, locally known as Tengri (Tengri means sky in many Turkic languages) and strongly connected to natural elements and the souls of ancestors. The shaman was a central figure of the religious life which consisted in "ways of understanding and manipulating the world in order to maintain the central sacred value of (communal) life and (communal) well-being" (DeWeese 2010: 37). Islamization in Central Asia took place progressively from the ninth century with the Arab conquest. At that time, the territory of Kazakhstan was under the authority of different Turkic tribes, united in a confederation. Despite the military character of the conquest, conversions were not necessarily forced and on the contrary, conversion came with some advantages that locals were interested in such as tax exemption and access to circles of power since Islam was the religion of power, literature, and science at that time. The progressive Islamization of the Golden Horde starting from the eleventh century gave an impulse to the implementation of Islam on the territory of Central Asia. However, we must wait until the fourteenth century before Islam becomes the official religion of the khans' court. Despite its official status, the practice of Islam remained strongly influenced by ancient rituals and traditions such as the worship of ancestors and saints (DeWeese 2010). History teaching in Kazakhstan, which is strongly influenced by Soviet tradition, tends to underline the superficial conversion to Islam and undermine its historical significance for peoples of Kazakhstan (Morrison 2014).

In the nineteenth century, the Russian imperial expansion reorganized the socio-religious environment. The Russian military campaign in Central Asia started with the subjugation of the Kazakh territory in 1837 and ended when Russia defeated the Turkmens in 1881 (Fourniau 1994: 56).

Already at the time, religious communities were regulated by a state authority in Russia, the Orenburg Muslim Spiritual Assembly, established under Catherine the Great in 1788. This Assembly oversaw religious services and the registration of religious personnel and communities. However, in 1868, the Russian authorities decided to exempt Kazakhs because they feared that they could fall under the influence of Tatar Muslims and potentially form an alliance (Werth 2013). At the beginning of the twentieth century, a movement of Kazakh intellectuals, which ideas intersect with Islam, nationalism, and secularism, gained momentum. Inspired by Jadidism, a group of reforming Muslim intellectuals active in the Russian Empire, Kazakh intellectuals urged the masses to fight oppression, reject their colonized status and open up to the world. Their emphasis was mostly on Kazakh language but they also moderately encouraged Islam, seen as an integral part of the national identity (Uyama 2013).

At the height of the revolutionary frenzy, Muslims of the Russian empire mobilized and organized in May 1917, the Congress of all Muslims of Russia in Moscow. The Congress gathered almost 1000 participants, among which, were 200 women. Participants denounced Russian imperialism and claimed more autonomy for Muslims. Other demands were very progressive and included, for instance, an eight-hour working day, right to vote for women and the abolishment of polygamy. Even if the Muslim identity was defended, it was understood that Islam did not provide sufficient cohesion to form a nation and discussions reaffirmed the importance of socialism in national construction (Daulet 1989). The Bolsheviks did not keep their promises and their rule dismantled ethno-religious communities since religion and nationalism were considered utterly counter-revolutionary.

Religion in Soviet Times

Marxism-Leninism is an ideology openly hostile to religions as evidenced by Marx's famous formula of "Religion is the opium of the people". Marxism-Leninism denounces religion as an instrument used by ruling classes to keep the working class and peasants in servitude and ignorance. The Soviet transformative project had the objective to eliminate religion in order to create a society free from the clergy's yoke, free from conservative traditions and beliefs obstructing scientific advancement. From the first years of formation of the USSR, during and after the civil war, the clergy was rapidly sidelined, arrested, or outright eliminated. Shrines were destroyed or converted and religious worship was strongly discouraged (Keller 2001). The denigration of religion also involved the emancipation of women, who were considered doubly oppressed by the patriarchal society and by Islam (Massell 2015). However, the Soviet period was not characterized by the complete suppression of religious life but rather by a strict control of religious practices, coupled with an omnipresent anti-religious state propaganda which denigrated all religions. The Soviet management of religion also varied depending on the time period, regions, and the leaders' attitudes toward faith. The international conjuncture too influenced the authorities' stance toward religion (Tasar 2017). After an initial period of intense repression, the Soviets toned down their anti-religious campaigns and tolerated a certain form of religious practice, which was strictly regulated by different religious administrations across the USSR. There were two types of institutions, one administrative, the other, spiritual, which were governed by the Law on Freedom of Conscience and Religious Associations, adopted in 1929. In Central Asia, the Spiritual Direction of Muslims of Central Asia (known as SADUM in Russian), was created in 1943. The Direction was headed by a Mufti, based in Tashkent, Uzbekistan. Not long after its creation, regional representations called Qaziyats, were set up in all the other Central Asian republics. They possessed the authority to nominate the religious personnel in their respective republics. Overall, the SADUM was responsible to rule over issues of religious dogma and transmit their positions to the greater public in the form of fatwas. The SADUM issued recommendations on mullahs' obligations and carried out compliance checks and dismissed personnel if necessary. Finally, it was responsible for approving the importation of religious literature as well as printing and distribution (Sadur 1989: 437). Paradoxically, religious beliefs and rituals were constantly delegitimized and ridiculed by the regime which used propaganda and education campaigns, mobilizations of all kinds to convey an anti-religious message. Those focused on the backwardness of religious beliefs and how religions were an obstacle to socio-economic development. In that regard, Islam was not targeted more than the other confessions since for the Soviet authorities, all religions were equally pernicious.

Another important institution served as a link between the government and religious institutions. Created in 1918, the Committee for Religious Affairs, which had branches in all republics and regions, was responsible for authorizing the registration and establishment of places of worship and inform the government on the religious situation. The

Committee was also regularly answering to the KGB. The control of religious communities was more or less strict depending on the decade and before 1965, the Committee was rather cooperative and tolerant. However, in 1965, the Khrushchev administration implemented a series of repressive measures such as the closing of places of worship and the arrest of religious figures as well as renewed anti-religious propaganda efforts (Tasar 2017). Though some of the directives coming from Moscow were not always strictly implemented and local authorities had some latitude. Many rituals such as Islamic funerals and circumcisions were tolerated and party officials also took part in them without fear of getting in trouble (Ro'i 2000: 694). For that reason, many scholars talk about a "parallel" religious life in the USSR. In the 1980s, there were around 200 official (state-sanctioned) mosques in Central Asia (Abdulgani 1989: 405) but scholars estimate that this represented only 1% of the actual number of mosques. Others were underground mosques that local unofficial mullahs opened for local parishioners and operated more or less secretly (Ro'i 2000: 288).

The imposition of a brutal and accelerated modernization process in the USSR led to profound socio-political transformations. Religious practice was considerably reduced but did not disappear completely. Above all, the political and economic autarchy that prevailed in the Soviet Union resulted in religious isolation and Soviet Muslims remained disconnected from the rest of the Muslim world for decades. Beyond repression, what is important to remember from the Soviet era is the idea of a rigorous supervision of religious practices and discourses and a delegitimization of the place of religion in the society.

As the USSR collapsed, the significance of religion was part of the discussions concerning the future of the newly independent republics. Some observers predicted a strong religious resurgence but what we saw was a moderate Islamic revival, especially in Kazakhstan. Religion was marginally instrumentalized by elites in the process of state consolidation and legitimation. Religion was used as a common identity marker but the respective Constitutions of the new states confirmed their secular character and the perpetuation of state control over religion. In Kazakhstan, in addition to guaranteeing the exclusion of religion from the public sphere, the constitution formalizes the prohibition to establish political parties on a religious basis. On the one hand, this legal provision is tributary of the Soviet legacy and on the other hand of the multiethnic character of the Kazakhstani society.

Diversity and Religious Practice

Kazakhstanis rarely miss an occasion to recall that Kazakhstan hosts more than 128 ethnic minorities, which have linguistic rights and access to education in their native language for some. The peaceful cohabitation and this message of tolerance is a common theme in the discourses praising the legacy of the current (and sole) president, Nursultan Nazarbayev, who managed to maintain social peace in such a diverse country. In 2003, Astana hosted the Congress of the leaders of world and traditional religions. From this meeting came the idea of building a Palace of Peace and Reconciliation in Astana, an impressive futuristic pyramid which was completed in 2009. Interestingly, the propensity to celebrate religious cohabitation through the organization of international events was also used diplomatically by the Soviet authorities (Walters 2005, 26). According to the President: “The four sides of our Palace are oriented to the four sides of the world. In some sense this construction embodies independent Kazakhstan that friendly embraces all people of all nations and practicing different religions”.[1] However, the social fabric underwent many changes since independence. The proportion of ethnic Russians has dramatically decreased from 40% in 1991 to 24% today. Their emigration is sustained year after year and even increased slightly in 2016 (Pannier 2016). Those migration movements are transforming the religious landscape of Kazakhstan. There are currently 63% Kazakhs, 24% Russians, 3% Uzbeks, 2% Ukrainians, 1.5% Uighurs, 1.3% Tatars, 1% Germans, and 4.5% others. We thus find 70% of Muslims, 26% of Christians (mostly Orthodox), 2% of atheists, and 2% belonging to other religions (CIA 2018).

Like its other Soviet counterparts, the number of places of worship has exploded in Kazakhstan in the last few years. The number of mosques went to 63 in 1991 to 2570 in 2017 and the number of Churches is now of 333 (Danilin 2017). Religious education is not part of the school curriculum but religious education is dispensed in sixteen medresses and one Islamic University—Nur Mubarak in the former capital, Almaty. Religious practice has increased but remains moderate. Despite popular beliefs, recent statistics from the Pew Center (2018) show that younger generations are not necessarily more religious. On the contrary, the older people get, the more religious they become. Among the 95% of Kazakhstanis who declare to believe in God, only 15% of adults who are below 40 years old

[1] http://astana-piramida.kz/en/

pray regularly and 26% of adults who are older than 40 pray daily (Pew 2018: 66).[2] Because Kazakhstan is a large and diverse country, we need to distinguish between regions. Indeed, people in the Southern cities of Almaty and Taraz, as well as Aktobe in the West, are more religious. Interestingly, it is also in these regions which have been the theater of terrorist attacks that people reported feeling more religious instability (Nadirova et al. 2014). Another indicator of moderate religious practice is the number of pilgrims to Mecca. Kazakhstan barely reaches the number of Kazakhstani pilgrims allowed to Mecca. The current quota set by Saudi Arabia is currently 4000 but could be higher, according to the size of Kazakhstan's population. President Nazarbayev only performed his pilgrimage in 2004. The discrepancy between the number of mosques and the moderate practice of Islam can be explained by the fact that Islam is seen more as an important cultural marker than as a strict dogma that should regulate social life. For instance, many newly married couples who normally do not attend religious services go to the mosque to perform the religious marriage *Nikah*. As such, it can be said that the Soviet secularization project has achieved its goals of creating secular subjects and that this effect has long-lasting consequences.

This moderate religious revival comes along a moderate promotion of Islam at the state level which contributes to the promotion and normalization of this religious identity. After the Soviet ideology was dismissed, elites sought new identity markers and turned their attention to religion, culture, and ethnic identities. Typically, Central Asian elites underline the cultural Islamic heritage while also performing state control of religion through Soviet-style institutions and condemning foreign interpretations of Islam (Khalid 2006; Roy 2010; Thibault 2018). In Kazakhstan, the valorization of Islam has been moderate given that a significant portion of the population is not Muslim and that the society is very secular.

The country's Muslim identity also serves in diplomacy. Kazakhstan joined the Organization of Islamic Cooperation in 1995 and even chaired it in 2011. In the first years of independence, Kazakhstan opened its frontiers to various Arab missionary groups but their presence has been less and less tolerated over the years for fear of religious "contamination". Indeed, Islam as practiced in Arab countries is generally considered as foreign to Kazakhstanis, whose practice of Islam is more moderate and

[2] In comparison, in Tajikistan, respectively 40 and 59% of adults younger and older than 40 years old pray daily (Pew 2018: 67).

intertwined with local traditions. The state promotion of a Muslim identity is aligned with an idealized conception of the secular nation. Finally, promotion is also done via the construction of mosques, partly or entirely sponsored by the state, as well as the restoration of one of the most visited mausoleums in Central Asia, that of Ahmad Yasawi, in the city of Turkestan in southern Kazakhstan. The Islamic finance sector is also supported by the state since the 2000s. In 2011, Nursultan Nazarbayev declared that the global economic crisis had shown that the Islamic economic and financial model was stable and viable (Botoeva 2018: 248). More recently, the government has reconverted the site of the universal exhibition that Kazakhstan hosted in 2017 into a global financial center. Modeled on the centers of Singapore and Dubai that have English as the main language, it allows exemptions from visas and taxes and lets financial players experiment with new products or cryptocurrencies or use the center as a place of international mediation. One of these ambitions is to boost the development of Islamic finance in Kazakhstan. On that matter, Achilov mentions that in the long run, Islamic institutions can become important social actors in Kazakhstan, through the development of the financial sector, in which believers can elaborate business strategies consistent with their faith (Achilov 2015).

Beyond the state promotion of religion, Islam appears to provide a common identity, a social capital which regulates interactions within certain communities. The cult of saints and mausoleums lead to meetings and exchanges and their activities are at the heart of regional political and economic dynamics. Bigozhin shows us in particular how the wardens of traditional mausoleums, who are often descendants from sacred lineages (qozha) seek the patronage of political and economic elites to build, maintain and develop their mausoleum (Bigozhin 2018). Certain religious institutions and groups provide a cohesive ensemble of shared values for believers who reject secular lifestyles. In fact, more and more halal shops and services are being developed in Kazakhstan, including restaurants, shops, and service providers. Data from the agriculture and food processing industry show that the halal food market is estimated to more than $ 3 billion, which represents about 13% of food and beverage expenditures in Kazakhstan (World Food 2017).

A similar dynamic is unfolding in the neighboring countries. In Tajikistan, faith enables the formation of social connections and the creation of solidarity circles. Economic uncertainty and the decline of the welfare system after independence leave the field open for the creation of new solidarities around religious communities. Also, in a context characterized by heavy corruption, the display of one's faith, and by association, one's virtue, is a way to prove oneself socially (Thibault 2018). However, rigorist interpretations of Islam, manifested for instance, by an assiduous practice, different praying methods, as well as exterior signs such as long beards, short trousers, and hijabs, are perceived negatively by a great portion of the population. These are often interpreted as signs of radicalism. This negative perception resonates in the circles of power.

Non-traditional Islam and Radicalization

The communal character of certain religious groups generates strong connections and reinforces a sense of solidarity between members but similar solidarity networks can be developed among Islamic radical groups. Recent research has shown that contrary to previous understanding, radicalization does not necessarily only happen online on social media (Tucker 2016) but via real-life social networks (Tucker 2018) in which individuals are drawn by people they already know. In a number of villages in Kazakhstan, Kyrgyzstan, and Tajikistan, entire families, sometimes up to 40 people, left for Syria or Iraq. A Kazakh family became famous for the wrong reasons in 2014 when the Islamic State (ISIS) published a video showing several Kazakh children receiving both theological and military training. Another particularly disturbing video released in 2015 showed a Kazakh child of about 12 years old shooting two Russian hostages at close range. According to official figures, between 250 and 400 Kazakhstani citizens have joined the Islamic State in Syria and Iraq (Tucker 2016: 2) of which one-third are women (Bondal 2017). However, other sources estimate that 500–1000 individuals from Kazakhstan left the country to fight alongside ISIS. If this number appears to be high, we should recall that a similar number of Tajikistanis (Lemon 2015: 68) and Belgians (van San 2018: 39) also joined ISIS. With respectively 8 and 11 million inhabitants, these smaller countries have disproportionally contributed to the jihadist movement in comparison to Kazakhstan. Despite that, with the expected military defeat of ISIS in the Middle East, the authorities fear the return of militants who could influence and mobilize individuals vulnerable to radical ideas.

Kazakhstan has been the target of few radical individuals in the last decade. Since 2008, 18 deadly attacks have claimed 134 lives in Central Asia. Of these, nine occurred in various regions of Kazakhstan, but mainly in Aktobe and in the country's former capital, Almaty (Lemon 2018). The most tragic incidents occurred in 2011 and 2016 in the city of Aktobe, a city of 400,000 inhabitants located in the oil-producing region. On 17 May 2011, an individual linked to extremist networks committed a suicide bombing inside the state security's offices. Later in June, two policemen were murdered, and a police operation to arrest the suspects turned into a shooting incident causing several deaths. Shortly afterward, a police officer stalking a suspect in Aktobe was shot dead inside a house, in which a man then blew himself up. These incidents resulted in the death of 19 people, including five members of security forces and two bystanders (Lillis 2011). In 2016, even more dramatic events unfolded in Aktobe again. On June 5, a group of 25 men raided two gun shops before attacking a local military unit. As a result of this attack and the following police response, eight civilians, three policemen, and 18 suspects were killed. President Nazarbayev described the suspects as followers of a radical pseudo-religious movement (Orazgaliyeva 2016). On July 18 in Almaty, Ruslan Kulikbayev, an ex-convict, killed ten persons (eight policemen and two civilians) in a police station in Almaty. The killer admitted that this attack was a retaliation against the mistreatment of Muslims in Kazakhstan (Toleukhanova 2016). Following these events, President Nazarbayev ordered the adoption of stronger national security legislation and proposed the creation of a new ministry of religion.

Those threats have pushed the government to invest considerable resources in the fight against extremism. In 2013–2017, the budget of the national program to fight against religious extremism and terrorism was of almost one billion dollars and the current plan (2018–2022) has a similar budget (Syundyukova 2018). The state policy in the fight against violent terrorism focuses on the correct understanding of "good" and "authentic" Islam versus a "fake" versus "foreign" one. The problem is said to be in the poor religious knowledge of Kazakhstanis who cannot distinguish between the two (Beissembayev 2016). However, scholars argue that radicalism has little to do with religious sentiments and for some, it appears when "old values are abandoned and new ones have taken shape yet", which is the case in Kazakhstan since the collapse of the USSR (Sanseeva 2017). Others argue that for both men and women, fraternity and group solidarity seem very determinant in the motivations of socially or economically marginalized individuals who are drawn to extremist ideas and groups (Orazabayeva 2015; Tucker 2018). Finally, Beissembayev's research (2016) which is based on interviews with individuals convicted for terrorism reveals an important connection between their petty criminal past and their implication within extremist circles. Similar research has also shown the prevalence of criminal antecedents among European jihadists (Basra and Neumann 2016). This explanation matches the profile of Ruslan Kulikbayev, the 2016 Almaty shooter, who had been to prison twice for theft and possession of illegal arms.

The authorities are also concerned with ISIS even this group does not have a physical presence in Kazakhstan, nor anywhere in post-Soviet Central Asia. Its active presence in the region is limited to Afghanistan and to some extent in Pakistan (Giustozzi 2018). Other radical groups such as Hizb ut-Tahrir and Jamaat Tablighi have been operating in the region since the late 1990s. Founded in East-Jerusalem in 1953 and exiled in Great Britain since the 1980s, the Hizb ut-Tahrir (Party of Freedom) aims at establishing a world caliphate. They propose to achieve this through peaceful methods and reject the use of violence. The refusal to participate in electoral politics and their approach can be considered fundamentalist in the sense that it focuses on a bottom-up social transformation aiming at the creation of a world caliphate governed by Sharia. However, the party is considered as a threat in many countries given that it does not recognize the legitimacy of nation-states and the current political order. Its presence in Central Asia is evident but discreet since the party is on the list of extremist organizations in all the Republics. In 2006, Karagiannis estimated the number of Kazakhstani sympathizers to 1000 (Karagiannis 2007: 302). Its presence appeared to be stronger in the South, the most densely populated region where the majority of the population is below 30 years old. According to Karagiannis, the party was particularly attractive to Uzbek refugees who have fled the political and religious repression in their country in the 1990s. Widespread poverty in the region also contributed to the popularity of the party. In 2004, 23% of the population of South Kazakhstan lived under the poverty line (Karagiannis 2007: 306). While Hizb ut-Tahrir often made the news in the years 2000 but it is no longer the case in the 2010s. It is unclear if this is due to its decline or because its members have gone underground because of repression. Over the past 10 years, 160 members of this organization have been convicted in Kazakhstan (*Eurasia Daily* 2017). Jamaat Tablighi, a peaceful, yet fundamentalist missionary organization is also considered as an extremist organization and since 2015, 65 people have been imprisoned because of their association with this movement (Corley 2018). In 2018, there were 550 people imprisoned on charges of extremism or terrorism-related offenses in Kazakhstan (Razdykov 2018).

In recent years, public discourses have identified Salafism as the new threat to the established order. The term Salafism comes from the Arabic word *salaf*, which means ancestors, and refers to an ultra-conservative branch of Islam according to which the followers practice a "pure" Islam, like at the time of the prophet. Some underline the inherent violent character of Salafism while others recognize its multiple declinations, from pietism to jihadism (Khalid 2006). In fact, Salafism appears to be the post-Soviet version of Wahhabism, which represented the Islamic threat in the USSR (Knysh 2004). Contrary to Tajikistan, Salafism is not officially banned in Kazakhstan and the state discourses tend to refer to a mixture of Salafism and "non-traditional" or "destructive" religious movements to designate undesirable trends. But defining what is non-traditional brings a lot of challenges. Indeed, who possesses the authority to determine what is acceptable or not? In January 2018, Nurlan Yermekbayev, the then Kazakhstani Minister of Religious Affairs declared:

> Among the external attributes of destructive religious movements, we could include elements that are characteristic of radical movements in Islam. For instance, to preach intolerance, wear clothes that cover the face, some types of beards and short trousers. (Sevostyanova 2018)

These attributes are known to be common among very pious Muslims. This statement echoes the president's speech at the occasion of a meeting with representatives of the Spiritual Direction of Muslims in Kazakhstan few months before. Nazarbayev suggested that these types of clothes were contrary to national Kazakh traditions and even made it a question of national security:

> If young people follow rules that are foreign to our people, what will happen with the state? We will not allow this. Independent Kazakhstan should have a bright future, the nation should be united, the country should be secular and develop furthermore. We will not tolerate those who are opposed to this. These are not only the state's interests but also those of the Kazakhstani people, it's its future. (*Tengrinews* 2017)

Here, religious practice is associated with danger. It is understood that individuals who do not dress according to national traditions do not abide by the Nation's civic values and therefore, represent a threat. This ideological shortcut creates a lot of tensions within the society, and this type of discourse is likely to alienate those who do not follow Hanafi Islam or wear those types of clothes. By identifying the plurality of interpretations of Islam as a problem, Islam becomes a security problem, in other words, the state securitizes religious practice (Omelicheva 2011). However, the state does not only punish, but also defines adequate religious rites and practices. In Kazakhstan, many institutions bear this responsibility. The following section provides an overview of the management of religion and illustrates the absence of state neutrality in matters of religion.

Managing Religion

The Constitution adopted in 1992 recognizes the secular character of the state. However, like its neighbors, the Kazakhstani Constitution goes a step further by forbidding the establishment of political parties based on ethnic or religious grounds. Secularism in Kazakhstan corresponds to the assertive type of secularism as proposed by Kuru, in which the state does not limit itself to being neutral toward all religions but "plays an 'assertive' role as the agent of a social engineering project that confines religion to the private domain" (Kuru 2011: 571). This managerial vision of the religious sphere can be partly explained as a remnant of the Soviet legacy. This management is executed via three institutions: the *Law on religious activities and religious associations*, the Ministry of social development and the Spiritual Direction of Muslims in Kazakhstan (SDMK). The first two are formal state institutions whereas the SDMK has an ambiguous status. Other religions, such as Orthodoxy and Catholicism, also have their own official clergy, and even though they maintain close relations with the authorities, the nomination of their respective head is made in accordance to the rules of their Churches.

Being a secular country, Kazakhstan does not have an official religion and yet, the Spiritual Direction of Muslims in Kazakhstan acts as an official clergy. Inherited from the USSR, this institution bears the same name as its Soviet predecessor.[3] The SDMK is headed by the Grand Mufti Serikbay Satybaldyly Oraz since 2017. He is seconded by two aides called Naib Muftis. The institution is divided into seven administrative departments. The most significant of them is probably the department of fatwas which is responsible for providing recommendations on a wide range of topics concerning the practice of Islam such as the appropriate behavior to adopt

[3] Other countries of the former Soviet Union, including Russia, have similar institutions.

during Ramadan, suitable clothing for women, the dangers of Islamic extremism, and so on.

The responsibilities of the SDMK are the following:

- the promotion and sufficient dissemination of Islam and the sermons of the prophet Muhammad,
- the preservation of the understanding between Muslims of Kazakhstan,
- the preservation of Shari'a canons within religious organizations,
- solving the problems of Muslims,
- the training of specialists to teach the population,
- the establishment of links with religious organizations of foreign countries, associations, educational institutions, and
- the publication of religious literature and textbooks.[4]

The SDMK also nominates its regional representatives as well as the imams in each province and in many of the large cities (18 imams in total). The religious personnel also act as unifying figures, for example, when natural disasters strike, regional imams call on believers to donate money to help. Their positions are rather conservative on a number of topics, including homosexuality, abortion, and the place of women in the family. However, some of these conservative positions are in line with those of the society. From a theological point of view, the SDMK promotes Hanafism, an Islamic school of jurisprudence that is considered traditional in Central Asia. The Spiritual Directorate seeks to extend and standardize this school throughout the territory of Kazakhstan and rejects Salafism as well as Sufism, despite the historical presence of the latter, in the name of a unitarian and rationalist conception of religion (Fathi 2007: 235).

Representatives of the SDMK often express their support of government's initiatives to fight against extremism. In 2015, the Spiritual Direction elaborated a "Concept of the development of religious education until 2020", meant to spread the teaching of Hanafism but also to integrate secular disciplines into the curricula of religious educational institutions. This way, the status of madrassas can be raised to that of colleges and graduates can apply for public service positions. This initiative also aims to reduce the number of Kazakhs pursuing religious studies abroad (Nurseitova 2017).

[4] http://www.muftyat.kz/ru/kmdb.

In 2013, the SDMK adopted a position on the hijab, consistent with that of the authorities:

> In Kazakhstan, women traditionally covered their heads with scarves whereas older women wore kimesheks.[5] The Kazakhs had their own traditional national clothes corresponding to Sharia. Therefore, we need to stick to this. And there is no need for our women to adopt Arab or Pakistani styles, the point is that the aurat[6] must be covered. (*Azan* 2013)

In 2016, the SDMK supported the Ministry of Education's controversial decision to forbid hijabs in schools, which created resentment in some communities. Following this decision, the Direction reminded the public that according to Shari'a, minors do not have the obligation to wear a headscarf, and should only do so after they reach puberty, that is to say, when they reach the majority.[7] The SDMK urged parents to abide by school rules. The fatwa also stated:

> Our Constitution and other laws regulate public relations and give citizens freedom to choose their religion. And Muslims, at the behest of Allah, abide by the law and treat it with respect. Since the laws and regulations of a secular society are the guarantee of equal rights for all and of the direction of the citizens' life. The Spiritual administration asks Allah the Almighty to strengthen the unity and harmony of the people and spare the country from turmoil. (*Tengrinews* 2016b)

Indeed, many of the position adopted by the Spiritual administration are in line with those of the government and we see that this institution's independence is limited. It seems important to recall however that the SDMK operates under the strict framework of the *Law on religious activities and religious associations* inherited from Soviet times.

The first years of independence were characterized by great freedom of religion and attempts to strengthen the law started later in the early 2000s. In 2004 and 2005, the government adopted amendments that introduced

[5] This is a traditional white high-top hat worn with a white shawl that covers the hair and neck.

[6] This is an Arabic word that refers to the private parts of a women's body that must be hidden.

[7] The age of puberty comes earlier than the age of majority, which is 19 in Kazakhstan. It is not clear if SDMK's mistake is intentional or a sign of its misapprehension of women's reality.

mandatory registration of religious organizations and missionaries. Failure to register and an insufficient number of members (less than ten), resulted in the banning of the activities of several organizations. The law also stated that the Committee of Religious Affairs (a sub-division of the Ministry of Justice) was responsible for reviewing the religious material used by organizations for the purpose of excluding destructive sects (Kassenova 2018: 128).

In 2005, the government adopted a new law to fight against extremism which focused heavily on religious extremism defined as "inciting religious hatred or discord, including violence or calls for violence, and any religious practices that pose a threat to security, life, health, morals and rights and citizens' freedoms". As underlined by the Organisation for Security and Cooperation in Europe (OSCE) in its preliminary opinion on proposed amendments, the legal definition of extremism was ambiguous and gave the courts too much latitude when interpreting the law. The OSCE also recommended that only violent extremism be criminalized (OSCE/ODIHR 2016).

Terrorist attacks in Aktobe in 2011 led the government to strengthen the law on religion. In October 2011, the *Law on religious activities and religious associations* replaced the 1992 *Law on freedom of conscience and religious associations*. The new law underlined the importance of Hanafi Islam and Orthodoxy in the "development of culture and spiritual life of the people of Kazakhstan". Legally, this does not imply that other religions are undesirable but certainly accentuate the congruence of those two faiths and the national identity. Other minority movements such as Jehovah's Witnesses and Hare Krishna often face repression as their members are often brought to justice on charges of proselyting, but also harassed on the basis of administrative offenses (Corley 2017).

The law canceled the registration of all religious organizations and forced them to register again according to the new requirements. The minimum number of members has been established at 50 at the local level, 500 at the provincial level and 5000 at the national level. By law, it is forbidden to perform collective prayers outside designated areas and to distribute religious literature outside the offices and buildings of a given organization, even if the literature has been approved by the local authorities, a control which has been made mandatory. Those amendments have made proselytizing very complicated and penalize small and minority religious movements. Finally, the law prevents religious associations to participate in the activities of political parties as well as to support them financially.[8]

The Ministry of religious affairs and civil society of Kazakhstan has been founded in September 2016 as a reaction of the Almaty and Aktobe attacks in 2016. The government judged that the situation required the creation of an institution entirely dedicated to religious issues and the Ministry has been mandated to update the law on religion. The responsibilities of the Ministry were previously under the authority of the Committee for Religious Affairs of the Ministry of Culture and Sport. However, in April 2018, it has been renamed the Ministry of Social Development and the religious element has been removed from the name.

At the moment of its creation, Nurlan Yermekbayev was the Minister but he was nominated Minister of Defence in April 2018 and replaced by Darkhan Kaletayev. The Ministry has the responsibility of elaborating and implementing policies concerning non-governmental and non-commercial sectors but also to maintain and reinforce secular principles in the country. Another important task is to sustain the interactions with religious associations to promote a new interfaith agreement in the country. Notable changes include the interdiction of public display of symbols associated with destructive religious movements. That includes certain clothes, but the law is not very precise as to what these clothes are, except that it specifies clothes that hide a person's face. The new law introduced conditions for pursuing religious instruction abroad, criminalizes desecration of the feelings and dignity of believers and non-believers, and prohibits state officials from openly demonstrating their religious beliefs. Changes also include the "humanization of administrative sanctions" which results in providing warnings to offenders prior to the imposition of fines and the suspension of activities for violations. The law proposes a new coordination with local and/or foreign religious associations to prevent minors from participating in religious activities without their parents' consent. Finally, the law simplifies registration of religious associations but raises the minimum membership threshold to 250 (Nurseitova 2018b). Some of those proposals are problematic because they do not provide a specific definition of what constitutes a destructive religious symbol or what qualifies as an act of desecration. These legislative changes were passed by the Kazakhstani Majilis (Parliament) in May 2018 but not approved by the Senate in September 2018 because of their

[8] http://online.zakon.kz/Document/?doc_id=31067690#pos=3;-274.

controversial nature. The senators returned the draft to the Majilis and requested amendments in order to remove two clauses. The first concerns the use of "advertisement" to promote destructive religious movements, including external attributes and garments that demonstrate their belonging to destructive religious movements. It was rejected on the basis that its implementation by law-enforcement institutions was too problematic. The second one concerns the provision according to which the citizens of Kazakhstan can receive religious education abroad only after receiving a religious education in the Republic of Kazakhstan (Kazakhstan Today 2018). These proposed amendments demonstrate a certain understanding that legal uncertainty can eventually lead to abuses, and the authorities are worried of their reputation and potential backlash even if the Chairman of the Committee of Religious Affairs of the Ministry, Yerkin Ongarbayev, insisted that 80% of these changes came from recommendations made by the public and are therefore representative of a social consensus (Nurseitova 2018a).

Conclusion

Despite numerous religious restrictions, Kazakhstan has a moderate attitude in comparison to some of its neighbors, except for Kyrgyzstan which is the most liberal country in Central Asia. In Kazakhstan, condemnations are usually milder, ranging from warnings and administrative fines to a few years of imprisonment (usually a maximum of eight), whereas in Tajikistan, condemnations for extremism can go up to 25 years (Thibault 2018). Kazakhstani lawmakers are also more moderate concerning religious practice. In Tajikistan, Salafism has been added to the list of terrorist organizations even if it is not an organized movement such as Al-Qaeda or ISIS for instance. Because of the diffuse aspect of Salafism, which is more a way of life than a political project, it is difficult to detect it and even more problematic to prosecute people because of their beliefs. The former Minister of religious affairs of Kazakhstan said the following about Salafism:

> Salafism is not an organization, it is a religious movement, a belief system. In some countries based on Sharia, religious movements close to Salafism exist as traditional movements. For what concerns us, contemporary national theologians agree that Salafism has a destructive potential in Kazakhstan. (*Tengrinews* 2016a)

Despite this dubious interpretation of Salafism, changes of wordings in the judicial terminology represent an encouraging sign of political receptiveness. The identification of non-Hanafi religious currents from "non-traditional" to "destructive" gives a certain freedom to peaceful believers who do not necessarily adhere to Hanafism, which is considered to be the traditional Islamic school of thought in Kazakhstan and which is strongly promoted by the state. In Kazakhstan, even if the state-religion relations are strongly influenced by the securitization of Islam, they are also characterized, like in Soviet times, by the cooperation of religious personnel who have complementary interests, rather than authoritarian control (Achilov 2015; Bissenova 2016).

However, in 2017, the United States Commission on International Religious Freedom (IRFA) put Kazakhstan on the list of Tier-2 countries for having tolerated "particularly severe violations of religious freedom" meaning systematic, ongoing, and egregious violations of religious freedom (Freedom 2018). Interdictions and restrictions used as a way to prevent extremism are not very effective. On the contrary, they are often counterproductive and foster more resentment among people who feel that their religious beliefs are under attack and that the society or the government considers them as deviants. The decision of forbidding girls to wear hijabs in schools has created a lot of resentment in particular. Some parents and children have even defied the decision of the ministry of education but ended up being fined. As a result of the implementation of this new rule, many girls have dropped of school, especially in Aktobe and Southern Kazakhstan (Zhursin 2018). In some regions marked by poor economic performance and few perspectives, discontent can grow even stronger. Also, this religious control takes place in a broader authoritarian context and the anti-terrorist efforts can easily be used to justify authoritarianism. Central Asian governments have the tendency to associate all dissident movements with radical Islam in order to justify their repressive policies and methods. Freedom of expression and press have been decreasing year after year in Kazakhstan, a decline that has been coupled with a stronger censorship of the Internet.[9] In 2017, the Ministry of Religious Affairs and civil society alone has analyzed the content of 10,174 Internet resources. Among them, 3555 sources containing illegal material were identified (Khabar 2018). In most cases, the content of the website is subsequently made unavailable to Kazakhstani residents.

[9] Kazakhstan is ranked 157th (out of 180) in the 2017 World Press Freedom Index.

Kazakhstan faces challenges similar to other countries which fight against radicalization and try to maintain a balance between the respect of individual liberties and the responsibility to protect. Abusive electronic surveillance and arrests conducted without mandates are symptoms of the erosion of democratic principles in many western democracies as well. The systematic surveillance and monitoring of the Internet can lead to excesses and makes it possible to censure not only extremist and destructive ideas but also opposition groups that criticize the government. It is the case with certain parties such as the Democratic choice for Kazakhstan, which leader is in exile and which website is blocked in the country. Access to social media such as Facebook and VKontakte is also frequently constrained (Baidildayeva 2018).

Religion, especially Islam, continues to be perceived as a social phenomenon which bears a threatening potential. Kazakhstan has been the target of a few radicals but the actions of these individuals do not indicate an extended network of radical Islamists connected to global jihad. Domestic issues such as unemployment, poverty, and feelings of injustice are likely to explain those manifestations of violence. In this context of democratic limitations, the government does not respect the plurality of religious interpretations which might foster the alienation of citizens who already feel marginalized. The anticipated return of ISIS fighters who are radicalized, well-trained and accustomed to violence is a legitimate concern as their presence in the country can be destabilizing. However, because the society is largely secular, the support for violent militancy is extremely limited and the Kazakhstani society is unlikely to be vulnerable to ISIS' radical ideas. Overall, balancing religious freedom and the responsibility to protect is a delicate act, especially in a soft authoritarian state which seeks legitimacy both domestically and internationally.

References

Abdulgani, A. 1989. Musul'mane v uslovyax glastnosti, perestroika i novovo mishelnya (Muslims in the Conditions of Glasnost, Perestroika and New Thoughts). In *Perestroika: Glastnost, Democratiya, Socialism. Na puti k svobode sovesti (Perestroika: Glastnost, Democracy, Socialism. On the Road to Freedom of Conscience)*, ed. D.E. Furman. Moscow: Progress.

Achilov, D. 2015. Islamic Revival and Civil Society in Kazakhstan. In *Civil Society and Politics in Central Asia*, ed. C.E. Ziegler. Lexington, KY: University Press of Kentucky.

Azan. 2013. Fetva DUMK v otnoshenii musul'manskogo platka (Fatwa de la SAMK au sujet du foulard musulman). *Azan*, 23 March. https://azan.kz/ahbar/read/fetva-dumk-v-otnoshenii-musulmanskogo-platka-2419.

Baidildayeva, D. 2018. Internet Censorship in Kazakhstan: More Pervasive Than You May Think. *Open Democracy*, 26 March. https://www.opendemocracy.net/od-russia/dina-baidildayeva/internet-censorship-in-kazakhstan.

Basra, R., and P.R. Neumann. 2016. Criminal Pasts, Terrorist Futures: European Jihadists and the New Crime-Terror Nexus. *Perspectives on Terrorism* 10 (6): 25–40.

Beissembayev, S. 2016. Religious Extremism in Kazakhstan: From Criminal Networks to Jihad. *The Central Asia Fellowships Papers* (15).

Bigozhin, U. 2018. Local Politics and Patronage of Sacred Lineage Shrine in Kazakhstan. *Central Asian Affairs* 5 (3): 232–251.

Bissenova, A. 2016. Building a Muslim Nation. The Role of the Central Mosque of Astana. In *Kazakhstan in the Making: Legitimacy, Symbols, and Social Changes*, ed. M. Laruelle, 211–228. Lanham, MD: Lexington Books.

Bondal, K. 2017. Kazakhstan boretsya s radikalizatsiyey zhenshchin (Le Kazakhstan lutte contre la radicalisation des femmes). *Karavansarai*, 1 November. http://central.asia-news.com/ru/articles/cnmi_ca/features/2017/01/11/feature-01.

Botoeva, A. 2018. Islam and the Spirits of Capitalism: Competing Articulations of the Islamic Economy. *Politics & Society* 46 (2): 235–264.

CIA, Central Intelligence Agency. 2018. The World Factbook.

Corley, F. 2017. Kazakhstan: Worship Banned. *Forum 18*, 6 September.

———. 2018. Kazakhstan: 40 Months, 65 Criminal Convictions. *Forum 18*, 22 May. http://www.forum18.org/archive.php?article_id=2379.

Danilin, N. 2017. V kakikh regionakh Kazakhstana mechetey i tserkvey bol'she, chem bol'nits—Infografika (Dans quelles régions du Kazakhstan y'a-t'il plus de mosquées et d'églises que d'hôpitaux—Infographie). *Caravan*, 29 April. https://www.caravan.kz/news/v-kakikh-regionakh-kazakhstana-mechetejj-i-cerkvejj-bolshe-chem-bolnic-infografika-400543/.

Daulet, S. 1989. The First All Muslim Congress of Russia Moscow, 1–11 May 1917. *Central Asian Survey* 8 (1): 21–47.

DeWeese, D. 2010. *Islamization and Native Religion in the Golden Horde: Baba TŸkles and Conversion to Islam in Historical and Epic Tradition*. University Park, PA: Pennsylvania State University Press.

Eurasia Daily. 2017. Kazakhstan Squeezes Hizb ut-Tahrir. *Eurasia Daily*, 2 March. https://eadaily.com/en/news/2017/03/02/v-kazahstane-dozhimayut-hizb-ut-tahrir.

Fathi, Habiba. 2007. Les réseaux mystiques au Kazakhstan: entre dhikr et militantisme? *Cahiers d'Asie centrale* 15/16: 223–261.

Fourniau, V. 1994. *Histoire de l'Asie centrale*. Paris: Presses Universitaires de France.

Freedom, U.S. Commission on International Religious. 2018. *USCIRF Annual Report*. Washington, DC: U.S. Commission on International Religious Freedom.

Giustozzi, A. 2018. *The Islamic State in Khorasan: Afghanistan, Pakistan and the New Central Asia*. London: Hurst & Co.

Karagiannis, E. 2007. The Rise of Political Islam in Kazakhstan: Hizb Ut-Tahrir Al Islami. *Nationalism and Ethnic Politics* 13 (2): 297–322.

Kassenova, N. 2018. Kazakhstan: Islamic Revival and Trajectories of State-Society Relations. In *Religion, Conflict, and Stability in the Former Soviet Union*, ed. Katya Migacheva and Bryan Frederick, 115–138. Santa Monica, CA: Rand Corporation.

Kazakhstan Today. 2018. Senat vernul v mazhilis zakonoproyekt o religioznoy deyatelnosti (The Senate Returned the Bill on Religious Activities to the Majilis). *Kazakhstan Today*, 27 September. https://www.kt.kz/rus/state/senat_vernul_v_mazhilis_zakonoproekt_o_religioznoj_dejateljnosti_1153663125.html.

Keller, S. 2001. *To Moscow, Not Mecca: The Soviet Campaign Against Islam in Central Asia, 1917–1941*. Westport, CT: Praeger.

Khabar. 2018. 35% proverennykh saytov v RK soderzhali protivopravnyy kontent (35% des sites contrôlés dans la République du Kazakhstan possédaient des contenus illégaux). *Khabar 24*, 26 January. http://24.kz/ru/news/social/item/217935-35-proverennykh-sajtov-v-rk-soderzhali-protivopravnyj-kontent.

Khalid, A. 2006. L'Islam et l'État post-soviétique en Asie centrale. In *Éclats d'empires: Asie centrale, Caucase, Afghanistan*, ed. M. Laruelle and S. Peyrouse. Paris: Fayard.

Knysh, A. 2004. A Clear and Present Danger: "Wahhabism" as a Rhetorical Foil. *Die Welt des Islams* 44 (1): 3–26.

Kuru, A.T. 2011. Passive and Assertive Secularism: Historical Conditions, Ideological Struggles, and State Policies toward Religion. *World Politics* 59 (4): 568–594.

Lemon, E.J. 2015. Daesh and Tajikistan: The Regime's (In)Security Policy. *The RUSI Journal* 160 (5): 68–76.

Lemon, E. J. 2018. Assessing the Terrorist Threat In and From Central Asia. *Voices on Central Asia*, 18 October. http://voicesoncentralasia.org/assessing-the-terrorist-threat-in-and-from-central-asia/.

Lillis, J. 2011. Kazakhstan: Astana Confronts Extremist Threat. *Eurasianet*, 6 September. https://eurasianet.org/node/64133.

Massell, G.J. 2015. *The Surrogate Proletariat: Moslem Women and Revolutionary Strategies in Soviet Central Asia, 1919–1929*. Princeton, NJ: Princeton University Press.

Morrison, A. 2014. Teaching the Islamic History of the Qazaqs in Kazakhstan. In *Islamovedenie v Kazakhstane: sostoyanie, problemy, perspektivy Astana*, ed. Yu. V. Shapoval, A.S. Kabylova, and N. Robinson. Astana: ENU.

Nadirova, G., et al. 2014. *Religioznaya situatsiya v Kazakhstane i protsessy aktivizatsii religioznogo soznaniya molodezhi (La situation religieuse au Kazakhstan et les processus d'activation de la conscience religieuse de la jeunesse)*. Almaty: Al-Farabi University.

Nurseitova, T. 2017. Verkhovnyy muftiy RK: My protiv, chtoby kazakhstantsy postupali v somnitelnyye zarubezhnyye vuzy (Mufti suprême de la RK: Nous sommes contre le fait que des Kazakhstanais soint entrés dans les universités étrangères discutables). *Zakon.kz*, 20 February. https://www.zakon.kz/4844971-verkhovnyjj-muftijj-rk-my-protiv-chtoby.html.

———. 2018a. V Kazakhstane zapretyat provodit' «nikakh» vne mecheti (In Kazakhstan It is Forbidden to Conduct "Nikah" Outside the Mosque). *Zakon.kz*.

———. 2018b. Vosem samykh znachimykh popravok, kotoryye budut vneseny v zakon o religii RK (Les huit amendements les plus importants à introduire dans la loi sur la religion de la République du Kazakhstan). *Zakon.kz*, 6 February. https://www.zakon.kz/4902447-vosem-samyh-znachimyh-popravok-kotorye.html.

Omelicheva, M.Y. 2011. Islam in Kazakhstan: A Survey of Contemporary Trends and Sources of Securitization. *Central Asian Survey* 30 (2): 243–256.

Orazabayeva, G. 2015. Zhenskiy zhamagat: problemy i resheniya (Female Jamagaat: Problems and Solutions). *Akmolinskaya Pravda*, 26 August. http://apgazeta.kz/2015/08/26/zhenskij-zhamagat-problemy-i-resheniya/.

Orazgaliyeva, M. 2016. Kazakh President Declares June 9 as National Day of Mourning. *Astana Times*, 9 June. https://astanatimes.com/2016/06/kazakh-president-declares-june-9-as-national-day-of-mourning/.

OSCE/ODIHR. 2016. Opinion on the Draft Amendments to the Legal Framework on Countering Extremism and Terrorism in the Republic of Kazakhstan. Organization for Security and Cooperation in Europe.

Pannier, B. 2016. A New Wave of Ethnic Russians Leaving Kazakhstan. *Radio Free Europe/Radio Liberty*.

Pew Research Center. 2018. The Age Gap in Religion Around the World.

Razdykov, G. M. 2018. Salafizm predstavlyayet ugrozu dlya natsional'noy bezopasnosti Kazakhstana—RIRG (Salafism is a Threat to the National Security of Kazakhstan—RIRG). *New Time*, 21 November. https://newtimes.kz/obshchestvo/81882-salafizm-predstavlyaet-ugrozu-dlya-natsionalnoj-bezopasnosti-kazakhstana-rigg.

Ro'i, Yacoov. 2000. *Islam in the Soviet Union: From the Second World War to Gorbachev*. London: Hurst.

Roy, O. 2010. *L'Asie centrale contemporaine*. Paris: Presses Universitaires de France.

Sadur, V.G. 1989. Musulmane v SSSR: istorya i sovremennost (Musulmans en Union Soviétique: Histoire et Modernité). In *Perestroika: Glastnost,*

Demokratiya, Socialism. Na puti k svobode sovesti (Perestroika: glastnost, democracy, socialisme. Sur la voie d ela liberté de conscience), ed. D.E. Furman. Moscow: Progress.

Sanseeva, D. 2017. Ogranicheniya mogut porodit' novyye problemy («Les restrictions peuvent engendrer de nouveaux problèmes»). *Radio Azattyq*. https://rus.azattyq.org/a/kazakhstan-religija-ogranichenija/28733652.html.

Sevostyanova, I. 2018. Politsii predlagayetsya dat' polnomochiya vyyavlyat' priznaki posledovateley destruktivnykh religioznykh techeniy (La police est invitée à autoriser l'identification des adeptes de mouvements religieux destructeurs). *Atameken*, 29 January.

Syundyukova, N. 2018. About 287 Billion Tenge to Spend on Fighting Religious Extremism. *The Qazaq Times*, 30 January. https://qazaqtimes.com/en/article/32755.

Tasar, E. 2017. *Soviet and Muslim: The Institutionalization of Islam in Central Asia*. Oxford: Oxford University Press.

Tengrinews. 2016a. Ministr: Salafizm ne yavlyayetsya priemlemyim dlya Kazakhstana (Ministre: Le salafisme n'est pas acceptable pour le Kazakhstan). *Tengri News*, 14 October. https://tengrinews.kz/kazakhstan_news/ministr-salafizm-ne-yavlyaetsya-priemlemyim-dlya-kazahstana-304119/.

———. 2016b. V DUMK vyskazalis' o noshenii khidzhaba v shkolakh (La DSMK s'est exprimé sur le port du hijab dans les écoles). *Tengri News*, 24 October. https://tengrinews.kz/kazakhstan_news/v-dumk-vyiskazalis-o-noshenii-hidjaba-v-shkolah-304742/.

———. 2017. Nazarbayev vyskazalsya o kazakhstankakh v chernykh odeyaniyakh (Nazarbayev s'est exprimé sur les Kazakhs en habits noirs). *Tengri News*, 19 April. https://tengrinews.kz/kazakhstan_news/nazarbaev-vyiskazalsya-o-kazahstankah-v-chernyih-odeyaniyah-316434/.

Thibault, H. 2018. *Transforming Tajikistan: State-building and Islam in post-Soviet Central Asia*. London: I.B. Tauris.

Toleukhanova, A. 2016. Kazakhstan: Almaty Shooting Spree Trial Comes to a Close. *Eurasianet*, 28 October. https://eurasianet.org/s/kazakhstan-almaty-shooting-spree-trial-comes-to-a-close.

Tucker, N. 2016. Public and State Responses to ISIS Messaging: Kazakhstan. *CERIA Brief*, 13.

———. 2018. What Happens When Your Town Becomes an ISIS Recruiting Ground? Central Asia Program Papers, 209.

Uyama, T. 2013. The Changing Religious Orientation of Qazaq Intellectuals in the Tsarist Period: Sharia, Secularism, and Ethics. In *Islam, Society and States Across the Qazaq Steppe (18th-Early 20th Centuries)*, ed. Paolo Sartori and Niccolo Paciola. Vienna: Austrian Academy of Sciences Press.

Van San, M. 2018. Belgian and Dutch Young Men and Women Who Joined ISIS: Ethnographic Research among the Families They Left Behind. *Studies in Conflict & Terrorism* 41 (1): 39–58.

Walters, Philip. 2005. A Survey of Soviet Religious Policy. In *Religious Policy in the Soviet Union*, ed. Sabrina Petra Ramet, 3–30. Cambridge University Press.

Werth, P. 2013. The Kazakh Steppe and Islamic Administrative Exceptionalism: A Comparison with Buddhism among Buriats. In *Islam, Society and States Across the Qazaq Steppe (18th-Early 20th Centuries)*, ed. Niccolò Pianciola and Paolo Sartori. Vienna: Austrian Academy of Sciences Press.

World Food, Kazakhstan. 2017. Kazakhstan's $3 Billion Halal Food Sector. *World Food Kazakhstan*, 19 April.

Zhursin, Zhanagul. 2018. Khidzhab ili ucheba. Pochemu roditeli v Kazakhstane zabirayut devochek iz shkol (Hijab or Study. Why Parents in Kazakhstan Take Girls from School). *Current Times*, 10 August. https://www.currenttime.tv/a/29422529.html.

CHAPTER 9

The Contemporary Politics of Kazakhisation: The Case of Astana's Urbanism

Jean-François Caron

Introduction

In contrast to many other former republics of the Soviet Union, Kazakhstan occupies a special place with regard to the question of ethnocultural diversity. It has not only been able to maintain peace, order and good governance despite the presence of more than 100 different minority groups and various religious faiths, but it has also managed to ensure the peaceful coexistence of its two main national groups, Kazakhs and Russians, since the collapse of the Soviet Union. While it is not unique in the former USSR, Kazakhstan can be perceived as a multicultural success story, and it constitutes the other side of the coin of many other states that have failed to create unity in diversity. In this regard, examples include Ukraine, which has been—and still is—torn apart by rivalries between its Ukrainian and Russian populations; Kyrgyzstan, which has seen violent ethnic clashes between the Kyrgyz people and the ethnic Uzbeks; and Tajikistan, which experienced a violent ethnic and religious civil war in the 1990s.

To a certain extent, the interethnic cohabitation of Kazakhstan is rather surprising, especially in light of the historical relationship between Kazakhs

J.-F. Caron (✉)
Nazarbayev University, Astana, Kazakhstan
e-mail: jean-francois.caron@nu.edu.kz

J.-F. Caron (ed.), *Kazakhstan and the Soviet Legacy*,
https://doi.org/10.1007/978-981-13-6693-2_9

and the Russian-speaking population. Based upon the historic treatment of the Kazakhs, many people would not have been astonished had Kazakhs taken advantage of their independence in December 1991 to implement discriminatory nationalist policies against their fellow Russian citizens (Schatz 2000: 71). After all, historians have documented various injustices perpetrated by the Russian imperial and Soviet regimes against Kazakhs.

In contrast, following Kazakhstan's independence, the Kazakhstani authorities rather favoured an official discourse of openness and tolerance towards all ethnic groups and religious minorities in the newly formed country. A system of linguistic dualism between Kazakh and Russian was even established (and remains in place today), allowing every Kazakhstani citizen to communicate with the authorities in one of the two languages without suffering discrimination. This idea has been reiterated numerous times by Kazakhstan's first (and, until today, only) president, Nursultan Nazarbayev, who has made the cultivation of harmonious relations between the numerous ethnic communities of his country and the fight against ethnic discrimination core elements of his tenure as head of state since 1991.

In fact, the official patriotic discourse advocated by President Nazarbayev is not based on ethnic exclusiveness or on the main traditions, myths and folklore of the ethnic Kazakhs. Rather, it is culturally neutral because it clearly refers to civic political values deemed to be shared by all citizens of the country. As he has stated, the following common values unite all Kazakhstanis:

> The independence of Kazakhstan and Astana; national unity, peace and accord in our society; secular society and high spirituality; economic growth based on industrialisation and innovation; the society of universal labour; the commonality of history, culture and language; national security and global participation of our country in addressing global and regional problems. These constituent, national values are the ideological basis of the new Kazakhstan patriotism. (*News-4-u* 2015)

However, this official rhetoric hides an unofficial process of what many authors have called 'Kazakhisation', which refers to the desire to implement gradually and in a subtle manner 'the dominance of ethnic Kazakhs in the economic, cultural, educational and political spheres of independent Kazakhstan' (Sarsembayev 1999: 331; see also Karin and Chebotarev 2002). Such a policy can be observed through various initiatives, such as the renaming of streets in major cities, the rewriting of history with a special emphasis on Kazakh cultural heritage, a policy of changing the demographic balance of the country to marginalise Russian speakers and the suppression of Russian nationalist organisations. This is what the present chapter will analyse. Although it will highlight the presence and strength of this unofficial policy in many aspects of people's live in Kazakhstan, the reader should be aware that this chapter should not be interpreted as a criticism of this trend, nor will it evaluate its moral relevance in a context of deep ethnocultural diversity. As an outsider to the debate and a nonaligned observer, it will nonetheless offer an objective analysis of its possible flaws for the future of the country.

This policy of Kazakhisation will be analysed through what has been labelled as its 'most conspicuous example' (Lancaster 2012), namely, the urbanism of its capital, Astana. Up until the end of the 1990s, this city lost in the middle of the steppe was only inhabited by 300,000 people, who were mostly of Russian origin. However, in a contested decision, President Nazarbayev decided in 1998 to transfer the capital from Almaty to this small town. Since then, Astana has become a contemporary example of a planned city with a clear Kazakhisation intent. Through the case of Astana, this chapter will show how urban imagery, which has historically been used by authoritarian or totalitarian regimes to legitimate their power, produce social consensus or to demonstrate their strength, can also be a constitutive element of how imagined communities are built as a way to promote a certain conception of national identities (Anderson 1983): a nation-building process that often favours the dominant ethnocultural group (Gagnon et al. 2011). Before discussing the role of Astana in this nation-building process, this chapter will first present the official nationalist discourse of Kazakhstan followed by a thorough presentation of the various manners in which Kazakhisation has been implemented in the country.

The Official Conception of the Kazakhstani 'We'

As previously stated, the policies implemented after Kazakhstan's independence in 1991 were rather surprising, considering the historical relationship the ethnic Kazakhs had with Russia, whether under the tsarist or the Communist periods. As mentioned by Henry E. Hale:

> During the late tsarist period, not only did large numbers of Russian settlers move into the land on which the traditionally nomadic Kazakhs lived and disrupted their local economies, but the Russian government successively

> imposed a regressive system of taxation, claimed state ownership of the land the herdsmen used, selectively expropriated some of it to give to incoming Russians, and, during the First World War, systematically slaughtered tens of thousands of Kazakhs after an effort to mobilize them militarily met with armed resistance. (Hale 2009: 4)

He goes on to discuss the Soviet period, during which the level of suffering went well beyond what they experienced under the tsarist regime. He adds:

> The best known of the grievances that the Kazakhs of 1990 could be plausibly pointed to as crimes committed by a Moscow-based power against ethnic Kazakhs, however, centered on the grain requisition, [...] collectivization and sedentarization campaigns that all took place sometime between 1928 and 1934. By the most reliable estimates, some 1.5 million Kazakhs (over a third of the nation at the time) perished during this period [known as the Holodomor], and another half million fled to places such as Mongolia and China as the Soviet authorities employed extreme violence to irreversibly restructure traditional Kazakh society and economy. (Hale 2009: 4–5)

Because these policies were not sufficient, later policies (implemented mainly by Nikita Khrushchev) had the effect of marginalising the Kazakhs in their homeland. More precisely, at the beginning of the 1960s, the Soviet authorities decided to resettle hundreds of thousands of Slavs in Kazakhstan to cultivate its 'virgin lands'. As a result, the proportion of Kazakhs reached a historical low of 29% (Khazanov 1995), which of course facilitated the Russification process in the region. Russian became the *lingua franca* in the areas of administration, politics and economy, thus transforming Kazakh into a marginalised language. As a consequence, ethnic Russians became overrepresented in highly skilled, well-paid jobs, while Kazakhs experienced difficulties accessing quality education and high standards of living. The message was clear: being able to enjoy a successful life in Kazakhstan under the Communist regime was only possible by learning Russian. This incentive was reinforced by no fewer than 700 Kazakh schools being closed following the implementation of the Virgin Lands Policy (Khazanov 1995: 159). Ainur Kulzhanova sums up the situation:

> Russian became the 'high culture,' the urban, the modern, the one that everyone aspired to be part of, while Kazakh became the kitchen language, preserved in rural areas where, because of a lack of quality education, people

remained poor and could hope only for low-paid and low-skill jobs. Urban Kazakhs, 26.5% of [the] whole urban population of the country in 1989, were predominantly Russophone. (Kulzhanova 2012: 8)

Moreover, this policy also had the effect of destroying the last parts of the Kazakhs' traditional way of life because it resulted in the destruction of their pasturelands and the displacement of their livestock. The policy also resulted in the repression of the members of the Kazakh national intelligentsia who opposed it. These purges left a void within the republic and left the Kazakhs beheaded as a nation.

Therefore, it would not have been surprising to see ethnic Kazakhs use these terrible historical experiences as the basis of an exclusive and revanchist nationalist agenda at the expense of Russians at the time of their independence. Moreover, such a possibility could have been expected, considering the previous grievances against the interference of Moscow during the self-determination of Kazakhstan in the penultimate years of the USSR. The culmination is generally considered to be the December events of 1986 (*Zheltoksan* in Kazakh), when the Communist First Secretary of the Kazakh Soviet Socialist Republic Dinmukhamed Kunayev, an ethnic Kazakh, was replaced by the central government of Moscow with the ethnic Russian Gennady Kolbin. The student uprising in the contemporary capital Almaty, with 60,000 participants, demanded local autonomy regarding power and the end of the Soviet dictatorship. Kazakhs demonstrated to express their dissatisfaction with Soviet governance and demanded recognition of their national identity. Although the clear motives of *Zheltoksan* were not well defined, there is the opinion that ethnic tensions did play a role. Apart from Kolbin being an ethnic Russian, the majority of Russians remained outside of the conflict, and some accused Kazakhs of anti-Russianism (Sarsembayev 1999: 325).

However, Kazakhstan's independence did not lead to the official implementation of an exclusive Kazakh nationalist policy. Rather, the authorities quickly made it clear that their objective was to create a new 'Kazakhstani' identity that would fully recognise the multiethnic nature of the republic. As a result, numerous minority ethnic groups were accommodated and coexisted peacefully in the nation, and the promotion of the country's diversity and the peaceful cohabitation of various ethnic groups was officially recognised through the Assembly of the People of Kazakhstan, an institution created in 1995 with the goal of preserving the diverse ethnocultural heritage of Kazakhstan while promoting unity and peace among various demographic groups.

The creation of official bilingualism in Kazakhstan is also a good example in this regard. Although Kazakh is formally the official language of the country, Russian is used equally in documentation, media and both formal and vernacular communications. President Nazarbayev has also declared publicly on many occasions (most recently in February, 2016) that Russian speakers should not be discriminated against on a governmental level and that these citizens should be able to communicate in their language with governmental agencies and institutions.

Of course, geopolitical reasons might explain this magnanimity of the Kazakhs towards Russian speakers living in the country. It is important to recall that, at the time of Kazakhstan's independence, Kazakhs only constituted 39.7% of the population of the country, while Russians and other nationalities represented 37.8 and 22.5%, respectively. Most importantly, there was an ethnic divide between the northern and the southern parts of the country: the former was 49.8% Russian and only 29.6% Kazakh, while the latter had 67.8% Kazakhs and only 8.2% Russians. Consequently, there was a fear that half of the country might follow the call made by Aleksandr Solzhenitsyn (1990) to secede from the newly formed republic and demand a political union with Russia. This danger was strengthened by demonstrations that occurred in 1992 in northern and eastern Kazakhstan, where people demanded that the Russian language be treated on an equal footing with Kazakh. For President Nazarbayev, the survival of Kazakhstan's territorial integrity made it mandatory for him to adopt a tolerant policy towards Russian speakers and led to the development of an official discourse of civic nationalism. This policy was rather successful because, as noted by Edward Schatz, by the end of the 1990s, 'the view that Kazakhstan would experience ethnic strife had virtually disappeared', and during that period, 'the ugliest forms of coercive ethnicisation had never become manifest, and effective institutions for accommodating and channeling ethnic grievances had not emerged' (Schatz 2000: 71–72).

However, it would be a mistake to conclude, based solely on this official nationalist rhetoric, that the country is a multiethnic success story or a model that should be copied elsewhere. In contrast, it has been challenged since 1991 by an unofficial policy called Kazakhisation, which contradicts the philosophical core and objectives of the Kazakhstani civic conception of the nation.

Kazakhisation: The Unofficial Form of Exclusive Nationalism

Although many public officials would strongly deny the existence of this policy, it remains a well-known empirical reality among the people of Kazakhstan, as well as an observable notion at many levels. As stated previously, Kazakhisation refers to the desire of ethnic Kazakhs to dominate all social spheres of the country and to redefine the collective ethnosymbolism around their particular culture and history. Therefore, such an aspiration has been identified by many as a form of exclusive nationalism that exposes the spiritual life of other ethnic groups to a lack of recognition (Karin and Chebotarev 2002: 2), which might eventually result in ethnic grievances on their part. This process can be observed in many regards, such as various state policies that seem to favour ethnic Kazakhs in a manner that is detrimental, especially to Russian speakers who 'have been redefined from "elder-brothers" to colonizers and removed from the public sector, business, banking, and law' (Kuzio 2002: 257).

First, as mentioned by Michele E. Commercio, the Kazakhstani government 'has implemented a series of political and demographic change policies that seek to promote the political hegemony and demographic preponderance of Kazakhs within Kazakhstan' (Commercio 2004: 97). From this perspective, many ethnic Russians have been ousted from key political positions in local and regional governments in the northern part of the country (Bremmer 1994). This desire to marginalise Russians in the regions where they are massively concentrated is twofold. It was made possible by the incorporation of various regions (*oblasts*) together. As a result, compared with 1989, the proportion of ethnic Kazakhs increased from 27.2 to 48.5% in east Kazakhstan, from 17.1 to 27.5% in Karagandy and from 18.6 to 29.6% in northern Kazakhstan (Masanov 2002: 56). Second, according to Commercio, the government has also encouraged ethnic Kazakhs to resettle in the northern part of the country through numerous incentives, such as 'subsidized housing, guaranteed jobs and placements in Kazakh-language schools' (Commercio 2004: 98).

The Kazakhisation process can also be observed through the replacement of street names using Russian historical figures with Kazakh figures. Almaty is probably the prime example in this regard because the main boulevards (with only one exception, Gogol Street) have all been

'Kazakhified' since 1991. For instance, Tole Bi Street (which refers to a famous Kazakh horde leader) was previously known as Komsomolskaya (in reference to the Young Communist Leagues in the USSR); Mir Street was renamed Zheltoksan Street in reference to the aforementioned events that occurred in the city in 1986. Kommunist Prospekt was renamed Abylai Khan (for a famous Kazakh ruler), and Soviet Street was renamed Kazybek Bi Street (after a Kazakh sage). This renaming policy also affected various city names. In post-Soviet Kazakhstan, many locality names had Russian linguistic origins. A nationwide campaign to rename these cities in a Kazakh manner was intended to erase the legacy of the Russian presence. For example, Guryev was named Atyrau in 1991, Semipalatinsk was renamed Semey in 2007 and Ust'-Kamenogorsk was renamed Oskemen.

Replacing monuments dedicated to historical figures of Russian origin is another manifestation of Kazakhisation. Such demolished monuments include the memorial 'To the Patrons of the Virgin Land' in Astana, a monument to Nikolay Przhevalsky in Zaisan and one dedicated to Yermak Timofeyev in Aksu (formerly called Yermak). These figures were not ethnic Kazakhs and had no common pre-Soviet history with Kazakhstan. Their removal tends to show the willingness on the part of the government to replace the remembrance of the Soviet past with a celebration of Kazakh history. The demolition of monuments has resulted in a disapproving reaction from the ethnic Russian population. For example, when the city administration of Pavlodar ordered the demolition of a monument to Cossack ataman Yermak Timofeevich, who started the Russian conquest of Siberia during the reign of Tsar Ivan the Terrible, it resulted in strong criticisms from the local Russian population.

The primary and high school curricula also provide good examples of Kazakhisation because, as shown by Olga Mun (2014, 2015), they are mainly oriented around Kazakh ethnicity and do not pay equal attention to the history and culture of the other ethnocultural minority groups of the country. On the contrary, the mandatory textbooks used in schools tend to portray the expected manner of behaving and addressing other people exclusively according to traditional Kazakh usage. (Children are taught to address a woman as a *hanym*, a man as a *myrza* and an unmarried woman as a *bikesh*.)

Finally, the state-sponsored film industry should not be neglected when discussing Kazakhisation because 'it is often portrayed as an agent of culture and identity formation, which can aid the establishment of a common sense of national identity by revising myths, historical struggles and symbols' (Isaacs 2015: 403). From this perspective, it is not surprising that the Kazakhstani government has not hesitated to fund Kazakh films as a means of shaping a sense of Kazakh nationhood, organised mainly around common traditions and historical struggles. Although the share of state-sponsored movies in the country is rather marginal (i.e., in 2012, they corresponded only to 5% of all box office revenues), the Kazakhstani cinema industry is on the rise and might have an important impact on the psyche of its audience in the future. Considering that the main narrative trend of these movies focuses on particular heroes and characteristics of Kazakh national identity (Isaacs 2015: 404), the film industry might eventually play a major role in the process of Kazakhisation.

All of the elements discussed in this section have clearly shown what the Kazakhisation process is all about. Despite being an unofficial policy, it is effective by virtue of its being a form of banal nationalism, which exposes citizens on a repetitive, daily basis to an implicit conception of the nation (Billing 1995). For the 860,000 individuals currently living in Astana, the state capital, this subliminal conception of the nation is also associated with the city's urbanism. Although the official reasons for moving the capital from Almaty to Astana are in themselves culturally neutral,[1] we cannot ignore that President Nazarbayev said in an interview in the same year that this decision was 'solely a Kazakh policy pursued for the benefit of the Kazakhs' (Nazarbayev 1997). Indeed, considering the location of Astana and the initial choice envisaged by President Nazarbayev, it is obvious that the transfer of the capital was animated by ethnic considerations. At first, the location of Ulytau was considered because it was at this location that the Kazakh tribes used to gather and was seen by the head of the

[1] Indeed, 'the starting point of Nazarbayev's brainstorming was the realisation that Almaty had insurmountable disadvantage as the capital of an independent nation state. Emotionally and personally the President was attached to the city. He loved its beauty, its cosmopolitan culture, its vibrant life style and its jewel-like setting on the edge of the Alatau Mountains. But those mountains were a barrier to the expansion of Almaty. Already an overcrowded city of more than 1.5 million inhabitants, it had no space for future growth. Its horrendous traffic congestion made the conurbation a notorious smog trap whose air pollution problem was the worst in Central Asia. The airport was too close to the centre and too often fog-bound. Perhaps there could have been upward expansion as in Manhattan or Hong Kong, but because of the region's record of earthquakes, building skyscrapers in Almaty would have involved prohibitively expensive construction costs. In any event, the shortage of land available for development meant that there was little or no room for the new public edifices Nazarbayev envisaged' (Aitken 2009: 224–225).

Kazakhstani state as the place where 'the Kazakh nation became cemented' (Aitken 2009: 225). Even though Astana did not have the same historical significance for the Kazakhs as Ulytau, it nonetheless played a significant role over the last 20 years in the Kazakhisation process, mainly through its urban planning.

Urban planning is not something that can be considered neutral. On the contrary, it is either connected with religious elements—as it was the case with traditional Islamic urban planning (AlSayyad 1987, 1996)—or is a political tool that political leaders have used for various purposes. For instance, it has been a way for totalitarian regimes to perpetuate its presence and strength and to credit the idea that the ideals supporting it would last forever. Berlin, Rome, Moscow and Pyongyang offer great examples of this desire to express power and eternity through architecture. Urbanism is also a way for authoritarian leaders to create a cult of personality as a way to provide a sense of legitimacy for their rule. Central Asian countries have used this method, which is by no means a novelty in the region, since Lenin and Stalin were celebrated in the main cities of the 'five Stans'.[2] This was especially the case in Turkmenistan from 1991 until 2006, when former President Saparmurat Niyazov, who renamed himself 'Turkmenbashi' (meaning 'Head of the Turkmens'), constructed the environment of the country around his person. The capital, Ashgabat, is certainly contemporary evidence of such megalomaniacal architecture.[3] For instance, Turkmenbashi's cult of personality included the display of his portrait everywhere in the capital as well as on statues, but this display also extended to his family that was decimated during the 1948 earthquake. Specific monuments were erected and placed in a park dedicated to their memory, and avenues of Ashgabat were given the name of his father and mother (Fauve and Gintrac 2009).

Although Kazakhstan cannot be considered a prime example of democracy and the rule of President Nazarbayev has many similarities with that of Turkmenbashi, the constructed environment of Astana is not aimed at building a cult of personality. It is true that President Nazarbayev's person is celebrated in Astana, mainly through a university that bears his name (Nazarbayev University), on a bas relief of the Kazakh Eli monument located on Independence Square as a way to commemorate him as the first

[2] Namely, Kazakhstan, Kyrgyzstan, Tajikistan, Turkmenistan and Uzbekistan.

[3] For an explicit discussion of the connection between the architecture of Ashgabat and Niyazov, see Šír (2008) and Polese and Horak (2015).

Fig. 9.1 Kazakh Eli monument

president of the country (see Fig. 9.1) and on another one on the Triumphal Arch. But this is the extent of his cult of personality (if it can even be defined as such). It is important to note that the Kazakhstani parliament has asked President Nazarbayev on various occasions to rename Astana after himself (the latest request being in November, 2016). He has nonetheless always rejected these requests. In fact, the urban planning of Astana clearly serves another main purpose, as an instrument of Kazakhisation, which illustrates how architecture and nationalist policies can often be interwoven.

Astana's Urbanism and Kazakhisation

Those who have had the opportunity to visit the city have noticed that there are few places comparable to it in Central Asia. The gigantic urban ensembles can only find comparisons with the cities of Baku in Azerbaijan or Ashgabat in Turkmenistan. Nevertheless, the shrewd observer realises that the government has created a capital that strongly emphasises the cultural and historical references of ethnic Kazakhs and ignores those of their ethnic Russians compatriots, which is a rather odd feature for a self-defined multicultural country. This connection between ethnicity and urbanism is first perceived in the landmarks and buildings that reflect the major cultural features and traditions of the Kazakhs, such as Khan Shatyr and Baiterek.

This Kazakhisation process through urbanism was, however, a difficult challenge for the government because, considering the people's nomadic traditions, Kazakh history and culture were never linked to any specific urban architectural design (Köppen 2013: 598). However, with the help of numerous internationally recognised architects (such as Norman Foster and Kisho Kurokawa), the authorities found a way to manage what seemed to be an impossible task. This was the case with Khan Shatyr (see Fig. 9.2), which is an enormous multifloor shopping and entertainment centre located in downtown Astana. Its shape, which is a tent (*shatyr* in Kazakh), remains closely connected to traditional Kazakh culture, as it recalls the Kazakh nomadic tradition. In fact, when asked about the significance of this building, Astana's head architect, Amanzhol Chikanayev, said that it 'was a symbol of the steppe' and of the ancient way of life of Kazakhs (Kucera 2011).

Another building, known as Baiterek, is another example that reflects an ethnic Kazakh mythology at the very heart of the capital (see Fig. 9.3). Baiterek was one of the first construction projects in the city after it became the country's capital and President Nazarbayev played a role in its design. According to a Kazakh legend, a bird named Samruk came every year to lay a golden egg in a tree called Baiterek. However, a dragon named Ajdahar came to destroy the egg and, symbolically, future generations of Kazakhs. Fortunately, Samruk and his egg were saved by a brave warrior (*batyr*) named Jertostyk. In the same vein, the shape of the new arena of the local hockey team (Astana Barys) inaugurated in 2015 clearly follows the same shape as the traditional Kazakh yurt: a typical architectural design in Astana[4] (see Fig. 9.4).

It has to be mentioned that the interconnection between these buildings and monuments of the country's capital with the government—especially President Nazarbayev himself—is explicit. In fact, as reported by former British MP and Cabinet minister Jonathan Aitken, who wrote a

[4] For instance, the domestic terminal of Astana Airport is also shaped like a yurt.

Fig. 9.2 Khan Shatyr

biography of President Nazarbayev, Astana was designed by 'one dominant decision-maker who instructed the planners and architects, selected the colour schemes, sketched his own drawings for many of the important buildings and conceptualised the entire city. This decision-maker was Nazarbayev' (Aitken 2012: 105). Indeed, he sketched out himself the

Fig. 9.3 Baiterek

plans of Baiterek on a napkin (Aitken 2012: 105; Lancaster 2012; Dalton 2013; Fauve and Gintrac 2009) and played a major role in the design of other buildings.[5] As reported by Rowan Moore:

> Khan Shatyr's [opening] (…) coincided with the 70th birthday of President Nursultan Nazarbayev, who is the beginning and end of everything that

[5] Barys Arena was commissioned by the Astana Presidential Sports Club, whose honorary president is Nursultan Nazarbayev.

Fig. 9.4 Astana Barys arena

happens in Astana. The building is there 'because the idea came from the president', says its German-born manager: that there were four other malls within a square kilometre 'didn't matter for him'. The gold orb on the white steel tower, which signifies the egg laid annually on the tree of life by the mythical bird Samruk, was designed by Nazarbayev himself. When Nazarbayev commissioned [Norman] Foster to design his Palace of Peace and Reconciliation, he told them he wanted it pyramid-shaped, which may be the first and only time a client has told the mighty Foster what a building should look like, and been obeyed.[6]

[6]As was said by David Nelson, a member of Foster & Partners who worked for the Kazakhstani President, 'He had thought about the building. That's what's impressive'. Moreover, according to the city's head architect, Amanzhol Chikanayev, 'There's no project he doesn't participate in. The President's head works very hard, and he asks about very small details' (Kucera 2011). Mr. Chikanayev has also stated that the president 'dominates the country's decision-making, right down to which architectural bid should win next in Astana. [He] has such a mind for architecture that it's sometimes very difficult for us professionals to contradict him' (Dalton 2013). In fact, the extreme micromanagement of Astana by President Nazarbayev finds its full expression in the fact that his minutiae of city planning goes as far as the choice of flowers that are laid out in the capital (Lancaster 2012).

These buildings and monuments are skilfully located in the restricted area of downtown Astana. This localisation is by no mean a coincidence and is on par with the traditional logic of the structural virtue of the centre, where all the roads converge on the trophies of the state, which inspire a feeling of respect and pride. As it has been shown by Pierre Gentelle (1974) or Violette Rey (1975), former Soviet states all focused on transforming their city centres into the quintessential representation of Communism and of its strength as the most powerful ideology. In this sense, Astana clearly follows this pattern but has changed the focus from ideology to a nationalist conception of the country's collective identity.

Similar to the case in Almaty, all major roads in the capital refer to Kazakh traditions or historical figures. In the government district, this is precisely the case for boulevards such as Kabanbay Batyr (referring to a famous Kazakh warrior from the 18th century) and Dinmukhamed Kunayev (who, as previously mentioned, was the incarnation of the contemporary resistance of Kazakhs to Moscow's interference). Moreover, it is difficult to ignore the desire on the part of the government to commemorate individuals who have fought against Russian or Soviet policies throughout history by naming streets after them. This is the case with Zhumabek Tashenov, a former chairman of the Council of Ministers of the Kazakh Soviet Republic, who actively opposed Khrushchev's Virgin Lands Campaign in the 1960s, leading to his dismissal.

In addition, statues representing Kazakhstan's historical figures[7] spread all over the city are almost exclusively connected with ethnic Kazakhs. The only exceptions are statues of Pushkin, Charles de Gaulle and Mustafa Kemal, a thorough research of the inventory of all monuments of this type in Astana shows. They either solely commemorate ethnic Kazakhs connected with arts and culture (such as Abay Kunanbaev; Saken Seifullin, a poet and writer who fought for greater independence for Kazakhs and was executed in 1939; and Kurmangazy Sagyrbayuly, a composer and folk artist) or important Kazakh historical political figures (such as the two founders of Kazakh statehood [Janybek Khan and Kerei Khan] located on a statue in front of the Museum of the First President of Kazakhstan; Kenesary Khan, who was the last ruler of the Kazakh state before the kingdom was conquered by the Russians; or Tole Bi, Kazybek Bi and Aiteke Bi, the respected, wise Kazakh judges who contributed to the unification

[7] This chapter considers only statues representing historical figures, which is why artistic statues have been omitted from this list.

of the Kazakh tribes threatened by foreign invaders, found on the Justice Monument).

Moreover, it is worth noting that some of these immortalised individuals are either famous for their resistance against Russian or Soviet imperialism or were neglected by the Russian-dominated USSR. This is especially the case with the statue of Baurzhan Momyshuly,[8] which commemorates the famous Kazakh soldier who bravely fought during the Second World War and whose recommendations for a promotion and awarding of the title of Hero of the Soviet Union[9] were rejected because of his Kazakh patriotism and his refusal to Russify his surname.[10] This is also the case for the statue of Rakhymzhan Koshkarbaev, who was the first man to hoist the red banner over the Reichstag in April 1945 alongside his comrade Gregory Bolatov. However, since his feat angered Marshall Zhukov, who famously said, 'Why did some Asians do that? Tomorrow, Georgians and Russians must raise the colours' (*Kazinform* 2009), his name was omitted from the official history. Similar to Momyshuly, even though he was recommended for the title of Hero of the Soviet Union by his unit commander, this honour was denied and rather given to the two soldiers (one Russian and the other one Georgian) who hoisted the flag one day after. These two examples show that the Kazakhstani authorities are attentive to honour individuals of Kazakh ancestry who have been denied their deserved recognition during Soviet times simply because of their ethnic background or their pride in their ancestral heritage. By doing so, the government is implicitly awakening through these monuments the strained relationship and the feeling of past injustice between Russians and Kazakhs.

The same can be said with Astana's Triumphal Arch, which officially opened in 2011 to commemorate the 20th anniversary of the country's independence (which is why the arch is 20 metres high). However, a closer look reveals that most of its symbols are exclusively linked to the history of the Kazakh culture (Taikazan). For instance, we can find on this monument a sculpture of an Aqsaqal (the traditional elder and leader of Central Asian villages prior to Soviet domination) and another of a nomadic Kazakh warrior. The side walls are, for their part,

[8] Momyshuly also has a statue in Almaty where he can be found wearing what is an odd sword for a former Soviet officer. But when analysed within a context of Kazakhisation, the shape of this weapon finds an explanation: he is wearing a curved blade sword with a handle that recalls a traditional Kazakh *narkesken*.

[9] He was awarded this title only in 1990, eight years after his death.

[10] In Kazakh, the patronym '-uly' is very typical and refers to 'the son of'.

Fig. 9.5 Astana's Triumphal Arch

decorated with traditional Kazakh ornaments, while the inside of the arch doorway represents the different periods that led to the establishment of Kazakh statehood in 1465 (see Fig. 9.5). From this perspective, one can only wonder if the mention of 'Mangilik El' on the monument (which means 'Eternal Nation' in Kazakh) does not refer to the Kazakh nation rather than the Kazakhstani one.

These examples, which emphasise the struggle of the Kazakh people against foreign domination (mainly Russian domination), can be perceived as alienating symbols for ethnic Russians living in Astana because they either celebrate individuals who showed a spirit of resistance against their ancestors or recall the terrible struggles against Moscow that the Kazakhs endured. Moreover, this sense of being strangers in their homeland is fostered by the architecture surrounding them being entirely related to Kazakh traditions and culture. This feeling can also be reinforced by the almost total absence of statues or monuments of historical Russian figures in the country's capital, despite the close historical connections of Kazakhstan with Russia and the USSR. Furthermore, this feeling can be supported by the fact that most of the 400 street names that originally had Russian or Soviet cultural and historical references were renamed for famous ethnic Kazakhs, ancient cities associated with the famous Silk Road or ethnic Kazakh historical figures who were at risk of being lost to history.

This discussion shows how powerful urbanism can be on the collective psyche. As previously mentioned, it serves, in some cases, the purpose of a personality cult (such as the late President Saparmurat Niyazov and Ashgabat) or a support for a state's ideology (like Pyongyang in North Korea or any of other major cities in the former USSR, where the proletarian Marxist–Leninist cult was central).

However, Astana is rather different. Even though it serves as a traditional way[11] to legitimise President Nazarbayev's autocratic rule and to preserve his future legacy for the upcoming generations of Kazakhstanis, it is also a means for the State to show the modernisation of the country and the positive prospects for its future development (Fauve and Gintrac 2009), Astana's urbanism is also an essential and central tool of Kazakhisation and of a desire to break away from the country's Soviet and Russian legacy. By exposing its citizens on a daily basis to buildings, statues, monuments and street names that focus solely on Kazakh history and culture, the Kazakhstani state is proposing to its citizens a form of banal nationalism that clearly contradicts its official discourse regarding the country's policy regarding ethnocultural diversity.

This shows a dichotomy between 'hot nationalism', for example, the explicit rhetoric of Kazakhstani statesmen who are imposing a top-down vision of what its national identity ought to refer to, and its banal form, which silently reproduces a contradictory idea of the nation through mundane and unnoticed ways (Billig 1995). For Michael Billig, this latter form of nationalism is usually implicitly noticeable through the way in which the

[11] It is traditional in the sense that 200 years ago, the prevailing idea of the city was a conception of urbanity as a work of art, with the goal to impress its viewers and to legitimise in their eyes the rule of the sovereign (Boyer 1994).

news is usually divided between 'us' and 'everybody else' (through the division in newspapers or bulletins on TV between national news and international news, or simply through focusing on the country's weather, which has the impact of reminding people the centrality of their nation in their lives), or through references to the country's currency (with its representations of historical figures, a motto or national symbols) (Billing 1995: 188–189).

In this case, it has to be noted that the national meaning of Astana's urban design is reinforced with the help of this latter form of banal nationalism. This is especially the case when Kazakhstani people are paying their goods with *tenge* (the national currency), which incorporates many of the aforementioned buildings and monuments of Astana. For instance, the Baiterek monument can be found on all notes (200, 500, 1000, 2000, 5000 and 10,000 *tenge*) issued in 2006 by the National Bank. Just like a subliminal message, Kazakhstanis living in Astana are reminded on a daily basis the centrality of Kazakh cultural symbols on their way to work or when looking at the city landscape while sitting on a terrace during summer, a view that clashes with the official state's rhetoric heard during every national celebration. This form of banal nationalism fosters among Kazakhs the idea that their peculiar ethnosymbolism should be at the core of the state's national identity. This case shows the intimate link between national identity and its capital in such a manner that we can discuss the urban territorialisation of national sentiment (Fauve and Gintrac 2009). In the case of Astana, the connection between urbanism and the proposed version of Kazakhstan's national identity brings as a consequence the danger that the country's collective psyche can be perceived as rather exclusive of those not ethnically Kazakh.[12]

Conclusion

As this chapter has suggested, the construction of a common national identity in Kazakhstan obviously suffers from the tension between the official rhetoric of the government and an official policy called Kazakhisation.

[12] It has to be noted that urban planning can also play an opposite role, for example, erasing the historical ethnosymbolism of a peculiar group. For instance, after the occupation of Warsaw by the Germans in 1939, they carefully identified all the historically significant buildings of the city (Tung 2001: 74). Their objective was to obliterate them from the collective memory of the Poles, a people destined to serve as slaves of the Germans according to Hitler's philosophy. On the other hand, the Polish resistance spent a great deal of time to document these buildings for the sake of postwar reconstruction.

While the former advocates a form of civic nationalism, the latter is associated with the exclusion of ethnocultural minorities living in the country. In many ways, Kazakhisation has much in common with the way national identity was considered in the past (Kymlicka 2009: 3). The process of Kazakhisation is clearly the antithesis of this contemporary norm because it seeks to marginalise politically, as much as possible, the influence of ethnic Russians in the country and to erase symbolically their history and culture from the collective psyche. Although this process is not as extreme as other forms of cultural negation, it nonetheless sends the message that the publicly advertised notion of Kazakhstan as a multicultural and tolerant society is a misleading rhetorical façade hiding, in reality, an anachronistic strategy of cultural assimilation. As has been shown, the constructed environment of Astana is a central piece of this policy. The urbanism of the state's capital must also be connected with the rhetoric used when certain monuments are unveiled, which tends to show a redefinition of the nation's collective 'we'. For instance, when the Holodomor monument, which commemorated the terrible fate the Kazakh people had to endure because of Russian-based authorities, was unveiled in 2012, President Nazarbayev used an exclusive conception of the nation, by equating its people solely with ethnic Kazakhs. He stated:

> The starvation and its terrible consequences became the largest humanitarian disaster of the Soviet period. Our people have suffered enormous sacrifices: starvation killed over a half million people, [and] more than 600,000 Kazakhs fleeing hunger and repression left their historical homeland. It is an enduring, unforgettable pain of our people (emphasized added). (*Trend News Agency* 2012)

This choice of wording was highly significant and deserves closer attention. In his previous years in office, on Constitution Day or Independence Day, President Nazarbayev was always careful in his conception of the country's 'we'. More precisely, 'we' always referred explicitly to the Kazakhstani people as a whole. In fact, this inclusive nationalist rhetoric was always a constitutive element of speeches by the head of state. For instance, in his inauguration speech on 11 January 2006, after his re-election as head of state, he stated:

> Assuming this post, I'm proud of the fact that I was supported and would be accompanied by Kazakhstani people—honest, patriotic, loyal citizens. Therefore, achievements of the highest goals are feasible. We are strong in our diversity—the diversity of our nationalities and confessions. Our strength

> lies in unity—unity of the values and aspiration to progress and the prosperity of our homeland. We should achieve these lofty goals courageously and consistently, with a strong will for the welfare of our nation. (Embassy of the Republic of Kazakhstan 2006)

The unveiling of the Holodomor monument was the first time when he connected the nation's 'we' solely with the dominant ethnocultural group. This commemoration can be seen as a triggering moment in the evolution of a new conception of the nation, which was also clearly visible in the summer of 2015 when the country celebrated the 550th anniversary of the first Kazakh state. These celebrations were a response to Vladimir Putin's statement that Kazakhs had never had their own statehood before Russian colonisation. The Kazakh Khanate celebration was a means for the government to commemorate the foundation of Kazakh statehood by Janybek Khan and Kerey Khan in 1465, which was followed by numerous battles against foreign tribes for the control of the Kazakh steppe until its disappearance, when the Kazakhs were conquered in the mid-19th century by tsarist Russia. Very clearly, the celebration was a way to recall for many Kazakhs the strained historical relationships between them and those who conquered them.

In fact, in contrast to his numerous previous speeches on Constitution Day or Independence Day, President Nazarbayev once again referred explicitly to the Kazakhstani 'we' in an exclusive manner. For instance, at the opening ceremony for a monument dedicated to the Khanate in the city of Taraz, he said, 'The celebration of the Kazakh Khanate's 550th anniversary is to make our descendants understand history and promote our culture' (*Global Times* 2015). He also stated during a speech at the Palace of Independence on 11 September 2015, that 'celebrating the 550th anniversary of the Kazakh Khanate is a tribute to the glorious past of our nation and a reminder of history for the new generation' and that 'the new generation of the independent Kazakhstan has enhanced the prestige of the country, having fulfilled the dream of their ancestors' (emphasis added) (Embassy of the Republic of Kazakhstan 2015).

This rhetoric marks an explicit shift in the conceptualisation of the country's collective 'we'. However, this transformation did not come out of nowhere. Rather, it was the result of a long and implicit process of Kazakhisation that has taken many forms in the past. The choice of the architectural design of the capital is a clear example in this regard. From this perspective, we can wonder if Kazakhisation has now moved from an unofficial policy to an official one. Whatever the answer is, Kazakhisation—with Astana's urbanism being the tip of the iceberg—is one of the very few aspects of Kazakhstan moving away from its Soviet and Russian legacy. Only time will tell what impacts this rupture from the past may have on its stability.

References

Aitken, J. 2009. *Nazarbayev and the Making of Kazakhstan*. London and New York: Continuum.

———. 2012. *Kazakhstan: Surprises and Stereotypes After 20 years of Independence*. London and New York: Continuum.

AlSayyad, N. 1987. Space in an Islamic City: Some Urban Design Patterns. *Journal of Architectural and Planning Research* 4 (2): 108–119.

———. 1996. The Study of Islamic Urbanism: An Historiographic Essay. *Built Environment* 22 (2): 91–97.

Anderson, B. 1983. *Imagines Communities: Reflections on the Origin and Spread of Nationalism*. London: Verso.

Billing, M. 1995. *Banal Nationalism*. London: Sage Publications.

Boyer, C. 1994. *The City of Collective Memory: Its Historical Imagery and Architectural Entertainments*. Cambridge, MA and London: MIT Press.

Bremmer, I. 1994. Nazarbayev and the North: State-Building and Ethnic Relations in Kazakhstan. *Ethnic and Racial Studies* 17 (4): 619–635.

Commercio, M.E. 2004. The 'Pugachev Rebellion' in the Context of Post-Soviet Kazakh Nationalism. *Nationalities Papers* 32 (1): 87–113.

Dalton, B. 2013. Astana: A City Built for Giants. *International Reporting Project*, August 28.

Fauve, A., and C. Gintrac 2009. Production de l'espace urbain et mise en scène du pouvoir dans deux capitales 'présidentielles' d'Asie Centrale. *L'Espace Politique* 8 (2). http://espacepolitique.revues.org/1376.

Gagnon, A-G., Lecours, A. Nootens G. 2011. *Contemporary Majority Nationalism*, Montreal and Kingston: McGill-Queen's University Press.

Gentelle, P. 1974. Les villes en Chine: une stratégie 'différente. *L'Espace géographique* 3 (4): 255–265.

Hale, H.E. 2009. Cause without a Rebel: Kazakhstan's Unionist Nationalism in the USSR and CIS. *Nationalities Papers* 37 (1): 1–32.

In Passports of Citizens of Kazakhstan to Raise Patriotism will Enter Nazarbayev's Words. 2015. *News-4-u*. http://en.news-4-u.ru/in-passports-of-citizens-of-kazakhstan-to-raise-patriotism-will-enter-nazarbayevs-words.html.

Isaacs, R. 2015. Nomads, Warriors and Bureaucrats: Nation-Building and Film in Post-Soviet Kazakhstan. *Nationalities Papers* 43 (3): 399–416.

Karin, E., and A. Chebotarev. 2002. The Policy of Kazakhization in State and Government Institutions in Kazakhstan. In *The Nationalities Question in Post-Soviet Kazakhstan*, M.E.S. Series No. 51. Chiba: IDE-Jetro.
Rakhymzhan Koshkarbaev's Feat Recognized after 62 Years. 2009. *Kazinform*, 30 September.
Khazanov, A.M. 1995. *After the USSR: Ethnicity, Nationalism, and Policies in the Commonwealth of Independent States.* Madison, WI: University of Wisconsin Press.
Köppen, B. 2013. The Production of a New Eurasian Capital on the Kazakh Steppe: Architecture, Urban Design, and Identity in Astana. *Nationalities Papers* 41 (4): 590–605.
Kucera, J. 2011. Kazakhstan Rising. http://www.joshuakucera.net/2011/08/kazakhstan-rising.html.
Kulzhanova, A. 2012. Language Policy of Kazakhstan: An Analysis. M.A. Thesis in Public Policy, Central European University.
Kuzio, T. 2002. History, Memory and Nation Building in the Post-Soviet Colonial Space. *Nationalities Papers* 30 (2): 241–264.
Kymlicka, W. 2009. *Multicultural Odyssey: Navigating the New International Politics of Diversity.* Oxford: Oxford University Press.
Lancaster, John. 2012. Tomorrowland. *National Geographic*, February.
Masanov, N. 2002. Perceptions of Ethnic and All-National Identity in Kazakhstan. In *The Nationalities Question in Post-Soviet Kazakhstan*, ed. N. Oka et al. Chiba: Institute of Developing Economies.
Monument to Holodomor Victims Opens in Astana. 2012. *Trend News Agency.* http://en.trend.az/casia/kazakhstan/2032744.html.
Mun, O. 2014. Re-imagining National Identity through Early Literacy Textbooks in Kazakhstan. M.A. Thesis, Lehigh University.
———. 2015. (Re)constructing Citizens through Citizenship Education in Kazakhstan. M.A. Thesis in Nationalism Studies, Central European University.
Nazarbayev, N. 1997. *Ana Tili*, 4 December.
Polese, A., and S. Horak. 2015. A Tale of Two Presidents: Personality Cult and Symbolic Nation-Building in Turkmenistan. *Nationalities Papers* 43 (3): 457–478.
President of Kazakhstan Nursultan Nazarbayev Attends the Solemn Meeting to Celebrate the 550th Anniversary of the Kazakh Khanate. 2015. Embassy of the Republic of Kazakhstan to the United Kingdom of Great Britain and Northern Ireland. http://www.kazembassy.org.uk/en/articles/article/71.
President Nazarbayev Marks Kazakh Kanate's 550th Anniversary in Taraz. 2015. *Global Times.* http://www.globaltimes.cn/content/946131.shtml.
Rey, Violette. 1975. *La Roumanie, essai d'analyse régionale.* Paris: SEDES-CDU.
Sarsembayev, A. 1999. Imagined communities: Kazak nationalism and Kazakhification in the 1990s. *Central Asia Survey* 18 (3): 319–346.

Schatz, E.A.D. 2000. Framing Strategies and Non-Conflict in Multi-Ethnic Kazakhstan. *Nationalism & Ethnic Politics* 6 (2): 71–94.

Šír, J. 2008. Cult of Personality in Monumental Art and Architecture: The Case of Post-Soviet Turkmenistan. *Acta Slavica Iaponica* 25: 203–220.

Solzhenitsyn, A. 1990. Kak nam obustroit' Rossiu? *Literaturnaia gazeta*, 18 September.

Speech of the President of the Republic of Kazakhstan N. Nazarbayev at Inauguration Ceremony. 2006. Embassy of the Republic of Kazakhstan in the Kingdom of Saudi Arabia and The Arabian Gulf Countries. http://www.kazembgulf.net/pr1.html.

Tung, A.M. 2001. *Preserving the World's Great Cities: The Destruction and Renewal of the Historic Metropolis*. New York: Three Rivers Press.

Index[1]

A

B

C

D

[1] Note: Page numbers followed by 'n' refer to notes.

J.-F. Caron (ed.), *Kazakhstan and the Soviet Legacy*,
https://doi.org/10.1007/978-981-13-6693-2

The manufacturer's authorised representative in the EU is Springer Nature Customer Service Centre GmbH, Europaplatz 3, 69115 Heidelberg, Germany. If you have any concerns regarding our products, please contact ProductSafety@springernature.com

Printed and bound by CPI Group (UK) Ltd, Croydon, CR0 4YY

30/09/2026

02225442-0005